REMEMBERING ANNE BEACH

REMEMBERING ANNE BEACH

Love, Scandal, and Sickness in
Eighteenth-Century Britain

CAROLYN A. DAY

UNIVERSITY OF TORONTO PRESS
Toronto Buffalo London

ISBN 978-1-4875-9390-2 (paper)   ISBN 978-1-4875-9392-6 (EPUB)
                                   ISBN 978-1-4875-9393-3 (PDF)

Library and Archives Canada Cataloguing in Publication

Title: Remembering Anne Beach : love, scandal, and sickness in eighteenth-century Britain / Carolyn A. Day.
Names: Day, Carolyn A., author
Description: Includes bibliographical references and index.
Identifiers: Canadiana (print) 20240513428 | Canadiana (ebook) 20240513525 | ISBN 9781487593902 (paper) | ISBN 9781487593926 (EPUB) | ISBN 9781487593933 (PDF)
Subjects: LCSH: Beach, Anne, 1749–1771 – Health. | LCSH: Beach, Anne, 1749–1771 – Marriage. | LCSH: Women – Great Britain – Biography. | LCSH: Married people – Great Britain – Biography. | LCSH: Scandals – Great Britain. | LCGFT: Biographies.
Classification: LCC DA483.B43 D39 2025 | DDC 941.07092 – dc23

Cover design: Louise OFarrell
Cover image: Carolyn A. Day

We welcome comments and suggestions regarding any aspect of our publications – please feel free to contact us at news@utorontopress.com or visit us at utorontopress.com.

Every effort has been made to contact copyright holders; in the event of an error or omission, please notify the publisher.

We wish to acknowledge the land on which the University of Toronto Press operates. This land is the traditional territory of the Wendat, the Anishnaabeg, the Haudenosaunee, the Métis, and the Mississaugas of the Credit First Nation.

University of Toronto Press acknowledges the financial support of the Government of Canada and the Ontario Arts Council, an agency of the Government of Ontario, for its publishing activities.

CONTENTS

CONCLUSION
Fortune-Hunting Rake or Loving Husband?
Making Sense of the Accusations
141

FIGURES

✠

ACKNOWLEDGMENTS

Acknowledgments are always strange, as there is no way I can adequately thank everyone who played a role in making this book possible in both tangible and intangible ways. Just as the book is the product of innumerable hours of labor, it also rests on the shoulders of my family, friends, colleagues, and students, who all played crucial roles in getting this across the finish line. This entire project was only possible because of the hard work and invaluable assistance of numerous archivists and librarians, most importantly the amazing staff at the Gloucestershire Archives, the Wiltshire and Swindon History Centre, the Bath Record Office, the Hampshire Archives and Local Studies, and the Somersetshire Archives and Local Studies. I am especially indebted to the kindness and generosity of Flavia Vernon, Rosemary Green, and Bryan Berrett, without whom I would never have been able to walk the spaces in which this story occurred. Special thanks as well to Baron Timothy Campbell-Methuen and Joanna Martin for their assistance and kindness in uncovering and making available crucial documents that allowed me to break through some of the archival silences. Thanks as well to my former students Collins Warren and Maddee DePree, whose undergraduate research with me was essential in moving the project forward. To my countless friends and colleagues who listened to me throughout this project, thank you for helping me, not just with your cheerleading but also for allowing me to talk through the challenges I faced, for listening, and for reading parts of the book as it developed. Thank you, Alexandra Churchill, for your humor, pep talks, company in archives, coffee shops, and in online writing dates and especially for helping me see my work in new and interesting ways. Thank you to Dr. Chris Mounsey and Dr. Wendy Turner for your constant support and intellectual exchange, I cherish your friendship and our conversations, and I am a better scholar for working alongside you both. To Dr. Amelia Rauser, thanks for being my scholarly partner in crime and always encouraging me to chase my ideas. To Dr. MaryAlice Kirkpatrick, thank you for the constant support and advice as I mulled over this manuscript. To Dr. Savita Nair, thank you for always being my champion and my institutional rock. Dr. Victoria Turgeon, words are insufficient to encapsulate all the ways you have supported me. Thank you for your amazing friendship and always being there for me in every way, and thanks for throwing a manuscript draft-reading dinner party that allowed me to gauge audience reaction. To my parents (Donal and Lorraine), my brother (Benjamin), and to my amazing niece and nephew (Avalyn and Brennan), I am so thankful we are a family. Finally, to my amazing husband, Dr. Matthew Cathey, you are the best! Thank you for your unwavering support and love. Thank you for always being so excited about my work, the countless hours you spent photographing things with me in the archives, listening to my frustrations and my drafts. I adore you and appreciate all of the ways in which you constantly lift me up in every way, personally and professionally.

FAMILY TREE

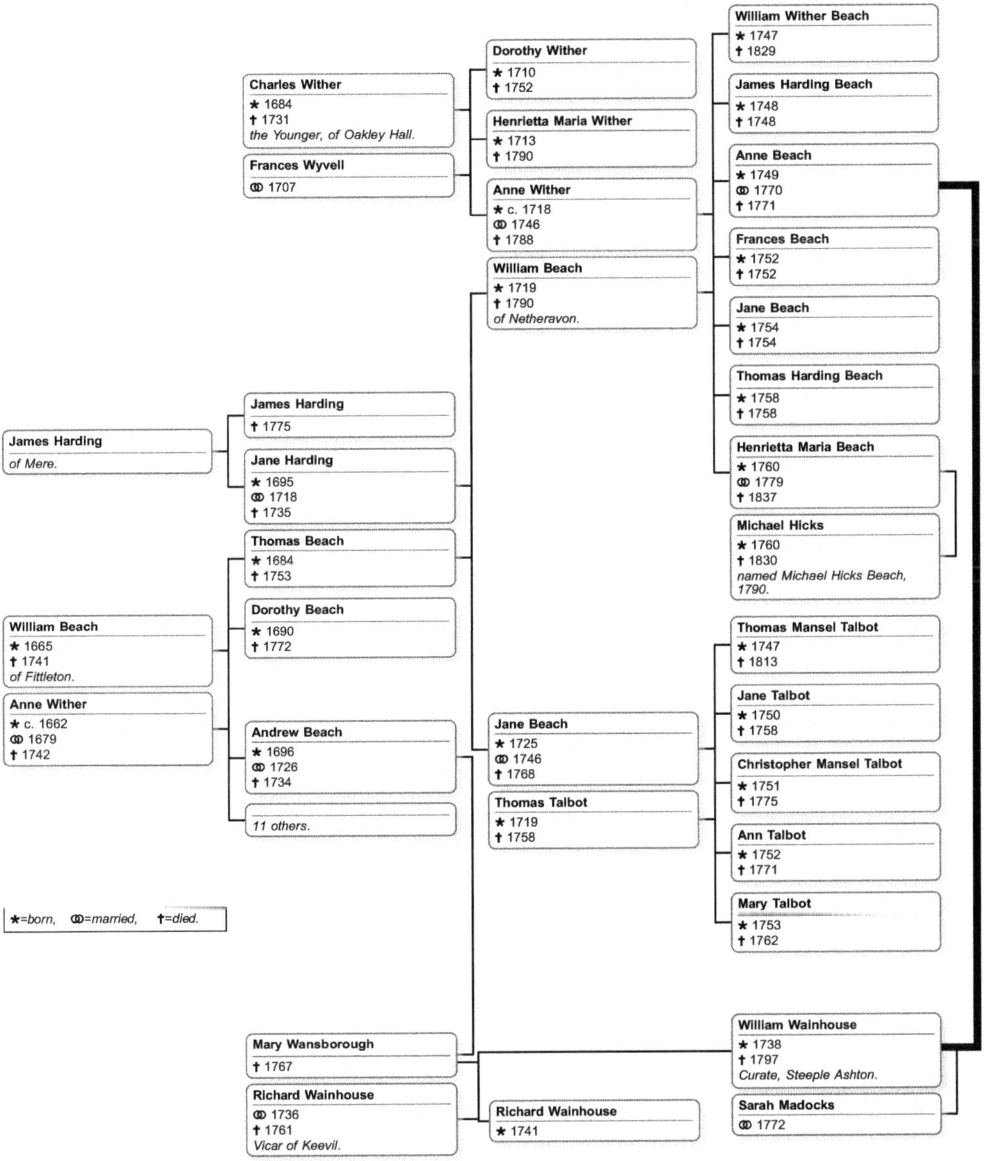

Charles Wither
★ 1684
✝ 1731
the Younger, of Oakley Hall.

Frances Wyvell
⚭ 1707

James Harding
of Mere.

William Beach
★ 1665
✝ 1741
of Fittleton.

Anne Wither
★ c. 1662
⚭ 1679
✝ 1742

James Harding
✝ 1775

Jane Harding
★ 1695
⚭ 1718
✝ 1735

Thomas Beach
★ 1684
✝ 1753

Dorothy Beach
★ 1690
✝ 1772

Andrew Beach
★ 1696
⚭ 1726
✝ 1734

11 others.

Dorothy Wither
★ 1710
✝ 1752

Henrietta Maria Wither
★ 1713
✝ 1790

Anne Wither
★ c. 1718
⚭ 1746
✝ 1788

William Beach
★ 1719
✝ 1790
of Netheravon.

Jane Beach
★ 1725
⚭ 1746
✝ 1768

Thomas Talbot
★ 1719
✝ 1758

William Wither Beach
★ 1747
✝ 1829

James Harding Beach
★ 1748
✝ 1748

Anne Beach
★ 1749
⚭ 1770
✝ 1771

Frances Beach
★ 1752
✝ 1752

Jane Beach
★ 1754
✝ 1754

Thomas Harding Beach
★ 1758
✝ 1758

Henrietta Maria Beach
★ 1760
⚭ 1779
✝ 1837

Michael Hicks
★ 1760
✝ 1830
named Michael Hicks Beach, 1790.

Thomas Mansel Talbot
★ 1747
✝ 1813

Jane Talbot
★ 1750
✝ 1758

Christopher Mansel Talbot
★ 1751
✝ 1775

Ann Talbot
★ 1752
✝ 1771

Mary Talbot
★ 1753
✝ 1762

Mary Wansborough
✝ 1767

Richard Wainhouse
⚭ 1736
✝ 1761
Vicar of Keevil.

Richard Wainhouse
★ 1741

William Wainhouse
★ 1738
✝ 1797
Curate, Steeple Ashton.

Sarah Madocks
⚭ 1772

CAST OF MAIN CHARACTERS

✠

William Beach of Fittleton (1665–1741)	He married Anne Wither (c. 1662–1742) in October 1679 and they had fourteen children, including Thomas Beach (1684–1753), Dorothy Beach (1690–1772), Andrew Beach (1696–1734), Joan Beach (1700–1765), and Sophia Beach (1705–1787).
Anne Wither Beach (c. 1662–1742)	Daughter of Rev. Gilbert Wither of Hall Place in Hampshire, married William Beach of Fittleton in October 1679 and had fourteen children, including Thomas Beach (1684–1753), Dorothy Beach (1690–1772), Andrew Beach (1696–1734), Joan Beach (1700–1765), and Sophia Beach (1705–1787).
Andrew Beach (1696–1734)	Barber-surgeon in London who married Mary Wansborough in 1726. They had no children that survived to adulthood.
Mary Beach/Wainhouse (neé Wansborough) (d. 1767)	Wife of Andrew Beach, then after his death was remarried to Richard Wainhouse, the vicar of Keevil, in 1736 and was mother to William Wainhouse and Richard Wainhouse.
Reverend Richard Wainhouse (d. 1761)	Vicar of Keevil and husband of Mary Beach, they married in 1736. They had two sons, William Wainhouse and Richard Wainhouse.
Dorothy Beach (1690–1772)	Daughter of William Beach of Fittleton and Anne Wither Beach, sister of Thomas and Andrew, and aunt of William Beach of Netheravon.
Joan Beach (1700–1765)	Daughter of William Beach of Fittleton and Anne Wither Beach, sister of Thomas and Andrew, and aunt of William Beach of Netheravon.
Sophia Beach (1705–1787)	Daughter of William Beach of Fittleton and Anne Wither Beach, sister of Thomas and Andrew, and aunt of William Beach of Netheravon.

Thomas Beach, Esq. (1684–1753) — Son of William Beach of Fittleton and Anne Wither Beach. He married Jane Harding (1695–1735), daughter of James Harding of Mere, in 1718 and they had several children, including William Beach of Netheravon (1719–1790) and Jane Beach (1725–1768).

Jane Beach (neé Harding) (1695–1735) — Daughter of James Harding of Mere. She married Thomas Beach in 1718, and they had several children, including William Beach of Netheravon (1719–1790) and Jane Beach (1725–1768).

Jane Talbot (neé Beach) (1725–1768) — Daughter of Thomas Beach and Jane Harding Beach. She married the Rev. Thomas Talbot (1719–1758) in 1746, and they had five children – Thomas Mansel Talbot (1747–1813), Jane Talbot (1750–1758), Christopher Mansel Talbot (1751–1775), Ann Talbot (1752–1771), and Mary Talbot (1753–1762).

Charles Wither, "the younger" of Oakley Hall (1684–1731) — He married Frances Wyvell in 1707 and they had three daughters – Dorothy (1710–1752), who died unmarried; Henrietta Maria (1713–1790), who first married Mr. Thynne and then Edmund Bramston (1708–1763); and Anne (c. 1718–1788), who married William Beach of Netheravon (1719–1790) in 1746 and had two daughters and one son who survived into adulthood.

Mr. Beach: William Beach of Netheravon (1719–1790) — Son of Thomas Beach and Jane Harding. He married his cousin Anne Wither (c. 1718–1788) in 1746 and they had the following children: William Wither Beach (1747–1829), James Harding Beach (born and died 1748), Anne Beach (1749–1771), Frances Beach (born and died 1752), Jane Beach (born and died 1754), Thomas Harding Beach (born and died 1758), and Henrietta Maria Beach (1760–1837, later Henrietta Maria Hicks-Beach).

Mrs. Beach: Anne Beach (neé Wither) (c. 1718–1788) — She was the daughter of Charles Wither, "the younger" of Oakley Hall (1684–1731) and married her cousin William Beach of Netheravon (1719–1790) in 1746. They had the following children: William Wither Beach (1747–1829), James Harding Beach (born and died 1748), Anne Beach (1749–1771), Frances Beach (born and died 1752), Jane Beach (born and died 1754), Thomas Harding Beach (born and died 1758), and Henrietta Maria Beach (1760–1837, later Henrietta Maria Hicks-Beach).

Billy Beach: William Wither Beach (1747–1829)	Son of William Beach of Netheravon and Anne Wither Beach. He went mad and was eventually disinherited by parliamentary decree in 1790.
Anne Wainhouse (neé Beach) (1749–1771)	Daughter of William Beach of Netheravon and Anne Wither Beach. Sister of William Wither Beach and Henrietta Maria Beach. She married William Wainhouse on November 22, 1770, and died of consumption on February 10, 1771.
Henrietta Maria Beach (1760–1837) [later Henrietta Maria Hicks Beach]	Daughter of William Beach of Netheravon and Anne Wither Beach. Sister of William Wither Beach and Anne Wainhouse. She married Michael Hicks, Esq. (1760–1830), of Beverstone Castle and Williamstrip Park in 1779. In 1790, Michael Hicks took on the additional surname of Beach, after the disinheritance of William Wither Beach.
William Wainhouse (1738–1797)	Curate of Steeple Ashton and husband of Anne Beach. After her death he remarried Sarah Madocks of Denbigh in Wales in 1772 and they had two sons and three daughters who survived to adulthood.

Adventures in the Archives

In the summer of 2013, I began in earnest the research for what I thought would be my second book, an in-depth investigation into the illness and death of the youngest daughter of King George III, Princess Amelia, who had been an invalid for many years before finally succumbing to her illness in 1810. I first stumbled across her while working on my PhD and was thrilled that after my dissertation, I actually had a new topic lined up and ready to go. Amelia had saved me from the dreaded "what next" moment that often accompanies finishing a project. I tackled the concentrated collections in the Royal Archives, National Archives, British Library, and Dorset History Centre and then set myself the daunting task of collecting every letter relating to, or mentioning, her that I could find in far-flung archives all over Great Britain. The easy work was done. Now it was time to spend countless hours on the train, hopping from county record office to county record office. As both money and time were tight, I forewent sleep and fun (okay, I will admit to some fun, and the archival detective work was pretty entertaining), and in a fifteen-day period visited twenty-one separate archives in England and Scotland.

On one of these days, I fell headlong into a trap I should have seen coming. I experienced the perils of the online catalog and the simple differences in terminology that one must be cognizant of as a British historian from America. I found a reference in the catalog of the Greater Manchester Record Office for a diary that mentioned Princess Amelia's illness and the King's insanity. I was giddy with excitement, a diary! Finally, something that could provide the kind of detail I was looking for. I took a train at six in the morning from London to Manchester. Bleary eyed and desperately in need of coffee, I wandered the streets consulting my map printout while trying to find the record office.

After what seemed like ages, I finally located it, marked by a small, unassuming round sign and nestled among the abandoned wreckage of Manchester's industrial past.

I eagerly buzzed the button, stated my business, and was let in. I presented my credentials, double checked the catalog reference, filled out the call slip, handed it to the archivist, and then sat down to wait. Thirty toe-tapping minutes later, the archivist delivered an unassuming book bound in red leather measuring two inches by one inch. Here it was! I carefully opened it and immediately had the "OH DAMN!!!" moment that no historian ever wants. I put my head down in frustration and banged it softly on the table. It was a diary alright, I had simply forgotten that a "diary" in England is not only a diary in the style of a personal record, but it is also the name given to a datebook or calendar. This particular "diary" was *Peacock's Polite Repository or Pocket Companion* and my magnificent piece of evidence had evaporated, condensed into three short phrases:

- *October 27: Got to Windsor – The King quite deranged*

- *Fri Nov 2nd: Princess Amelia Died*

- *Tues Nov 13: Funeral of Princess Amelia*[1]

You can imagine my disappointment. Fortunately, I didn't let it stop me and I spent the rest of the day in two other archives before once again boarding the train for the several-hour ride back to London.

As I continued my jaunts to record offices, some of which I knew only had one or two relevant letters, I decided on a new strategy for maximizing the impact of my short trip. I began looking for other possible documents, in every archive I went to, related to consumption (the eighteenth- and nineteenth-century term for the disease now known as tuberculosis) and the subject of my first book. This strategy of casting a wide net allowed me to stumble upon another book; this one was larger than the diary, measuring maybe five by seven inches. It was sandwiched between two marbled pasteboard covers and was a seemingly unbelievable tale, written in a careful measured hand, that began with an advertisement cut out of a newspaper. It read, "A NARRATIVE, Exemplifying the Cruelty of Mr. and Mrs. B– –CH, of K– – – –l in the County of W– – – –, though actually prepared for the Press, is withheld from Publication for the following Reasons:

---

1 "1810 Records Death & Funeral of Princess Amelia," E4/98/3, *Egerton Family Papers*, Greater Manchester Record Office, UK.

The injur'd Lady's Parents, – who exist in an obscure, unnotic'd State of Affluence, – who cou'd break the Heart and Constitution of the meekest Child by a Series of unkind Usage, from the Cradle to the Grave, – who cou'd deliberately abandon their expiring Offspring; – such Parents, through the Hardness of their Hearts, and the Particularity of their Situation, must needs be impenetrable, and insensible to the Shame and Censure of the World: They cannot, therefore, be expos'd. – The Deceas'd may be vindicated by a proper Circulation of her Story in Manuscript. – A Tale of domestic and uncommon Parental Barbarity is of too horrid, as well as of too private, a Nature, for the general Ear. – Wherefore, the Delinquents are left to Heaven and their own Consciences, from which they cannot be shelter'd by Obscurity, Wealth, or Flattery.[2]

What followed was a love story with a plot that read like a novel, a scandal with a dash of revenge thrown in for good measure, and the subject of this microhistory.

Historian Roy Porter's groundbreaking challenge to historians of medicine – to interrogate the patient's view – crucially changed the physician-centered approach to the experience of illness, and the assertion that "medical events frequently have complex social rituals involving community and family" remains an essential point in unpacking disease narratives.[3] More recent scholarship on the social construction of illness, by scholars like cultural historian Ludmilla Jordanova, and on the role of narrative in medicine, by literary scholars like Rita Charon, has sought to elucidate the sociocultural frameworks still at work in medical narratives.[4] Although any attempt to reconstruct the illness events of historic persons is necessarily constrained by the nature of the textual evidence, these accounts need to be interrogated with an eye to wider cultural and social

---

2 *Wainhouse Narrative*, D2455/F2/5/3/4, Gloucestershire Archives, UK. Hereafter referred to as *Narrative* in the notes.

3 Roy Porter, "The Patient's View: Doing Medical History from Below," *Theory and Society* 14, no. 2 (1985), 175. For more information on the "patient's view," see Lucinda M. Beier, *Sufferers and Healers: The Experience of Illness in Seventeenth-Century England* (Routledge and Kegan Paul, 1987); Roy Porter, ed., *Patients and Practitioners: Lay Perceptions of Medicine in Pre-Industrial Society* (Cambridge University Press, 1985); and Michael MacDonald, *Mystical Bedlam: Madness, Anxiety and Healing in Seventeenth-Century England* (Cambridge University Press, 1981).

4 For more information on narrative medicine, see Franziska Gygax and Miriam A. Locher, *Narrative Matters in Medical Contexts across Disciplines* (John Benjamins Publishing Company, 2015); Rita Charon, *Narrative Medicine: Honoring the Stories of Illness* (Oxford University Press, 2008); and Ludmilla Jordanova, "The Social Construction of Medical Knowledge," *Social History of Medicine* 8, no. 3 (1995): 361–81. Also, for a review of the shifting nature of history of eighteenth-century medicine, see Jonathan Andrews, "History of Medicine: Health, Medicine and Disease in the Eighteenth Century," *Journal for Eighteenth-Century Studies* 34 no. 4 (2011).

trends. This is particularly true of the illness and death of Anne Wainhouse, as there is no surviving evidence from the patient herself; instead, the comprehensive accounting of the onset of her illness, its progression, and termination all come in the form of a narrative written by her husband. Rather than a retelling of the illness and death of a beloved spouse, this unusual production is a carefully crafted piece of rhetoric that not only details the causes and course of her disease, but also serves to restore the reputation of her husband and that of the victim herself. How do we recover a woman who has been intentionally obliterated from the record and whose life after her death was used for a variety of purposes?

There are no letters written by Ann[e][5] in official repositories, and all of my hunting in other places, including private collections, has revealed but a glimpse or two of this elusive lady. The most poignant came in June 2017. It was a bright, sunny day and I could not contain my excitement as we turned off the main road and made our way up the drive towards the house. When the car came to a stop, I grabbed my crutches and gingerly climbed out. Standing on the gravel, I excitedly began to rock back and forth, while internally I was wishing I could jump up and down or do cartwheels. I controlled myself, put on my best professional face, and carefully picked my way through the gravel, all the while trying to avoid yet another ignominious fall like the one that had gotten me into this predicament a week earlier. I had run afoul of some uneven pavement on Baker Street in London, in a spectacularly embarrassing move from vertical to horizontal. One minute I was striding along, talking on the phone to my family, and the next I was sitting on the pavement wondering what had happened. Lying there for a second, while taking quick stock of my predicament, I realized I was still on the phone. I told my worried parents that I would need to call them back because I had somehow managed to hurt myself. Even today I am not sure how I ended up on the ground, but as I sat there mentally castigating myself for being a klutz, I could feel my ankle throbbing. All I could think was: "Seriously! This literally cannot be happening!" I will also admit that a few choice words ran through my brain and may have escaped under my breath. I couldn't believe I had sprained my ankle! It never crossed my mind that it could be anything else. I was just walking – it couldn't be anything worse, right?

Unfortunately, it proved to be a broken tibia and I spent the rest of my weekend resting and trying to figure out how I was going to navigate all the things I had planned to do, as I now faced several weeks in a cast and on crutches as I tromped through libraries, archives, churches, family estates, and even a castle.

---

5 Her name is alternatively spelled with and without an *e* in the documentary evidence. I will use the spelling *Anne*.

Let me tell you, I soon discovered it is really hard to carry your computer in a clear plastic carrier bag on crutches, and picking up the large, leather-bound letter collections at the manuscript desk was completely impossible. In the end it didn't matter, though, because there was absolutely no way I was going to let this stop me. I had spent years tracking down this story. I was happy to navigate cobbles, bat-infested church chapels, and countless sets of stairs in my hunt, as every one of these hurdles had finally brought me to this gravel driveway. All I could think was: "Finally!" After several years of chasing, I was standing in front of the house where it happened.

As I made my way past the stables and hobbled towards the threshold of the lovely country house, I could barely contain my giddiness. I was actually going to see the room! The one that featured so prominently in a fantastical tale of love and revenge, a story that almost seemed to have been ripped from the pages of a novel. Though it had actually been wrested bit by bit from various sites and archives. In that moment, all I could focus on were the scraps from the papers I had read, and the words began to float through my mind:

- *"each Look, expression, every step is Grace."*

- *"Confinement … suffer'd on the account of Love."*

- *"be <u>damn'd</u>, or stay here, & go to the <u>Devil</u>."*

- *"Madam, My dear Wife, your Daughter, is no more."*

- *"A Tale of domestic and uncommon Parental Barbarity."*

I could almost hear the echoes of the words and angry invective as I took in the dark carved paneling and ornate plasterwork.

The current owner of the house, whose family purchased the estate at the turn of the twentieth century, was kind enough to allow me into her home. Despite having no connection to the family I was researching, she answered my questions and then took me upstairs to the front bedroom. Although there had been some material alterations to the house, I was surprised to find that the layout lent credence to the allegations that filled the pages I had carefully collected and transcribed. As I walked (okay, hobbled) into the room I was immediately struck by the opening in the far-left corner. I had no idea that the space I had come to see was attached to a bedroom, rather than being off a hall as I had believed. All of a sudden, certain accusations came into sharp focus and the things I had read finally began to make sense.

I moved through the bedroom, across the wide plank oak floors, and then down three stairs. After years, I was finally standing in the place that featured so prominently in this tragedy, and I was nearly overwhelmed as I tried to take it all in. My eyes darted around, searching for the structural corroboration of the words that had been laid down more than two centuries before. They made a beeline to the window – hoping it was still there. The last photographic evidence of its existence had been taken in the 1980s and anything could have happened to that fragile pane of glass in the time since. Then I saw it: there, etched in the centuries-old glass, were the three words that had animated my search – "Remember Ann Beach."

I had taken that scrawl as a command and had spent years uncovering the story of the woman who had been locked up in this room for the crime of loving the wrong man. Anne, the young woman who had been erased from the narrative of her own life, reduced to a foolish dupe who fell prey to a fortune hunter. The young woman who was removed from the archival record as efficiently as she was cast out of her family. All that remains of Anne Beach is a name scratched in a window, a single lock of hair, a rather childish and unflattering drawing, and two monument stones – but her legacy and the mythology surrounding the death of this seemingly unimportant young woman still resonate in the villages of Steeple Ashton and Keevil.

It is a story that, even today, rouses strong feelings and causes people to take sides. They still whisper about "that horrid man" and state emphatically, "he didn't treat her very well" and "he was only after her money." But was this the case? Was it a love match? Did money and status allow Anne's family to spin the scandal in their favor? They had certainly won the propaganda war in Wiltshire, but there is always more to stories than legends allow, and the evidence seems to suggest something very different about the life and death of Anne Beach.

Unfortunately, all of the existing accounts are through the eyes of others – so what can we learn and how do we work with the perspective of others to uncover the Lady in Red? I had the *Narrative* and a couple of letters from William Wainhouse … now what? Trying to recreate Anne's life from these absences was a challenge, particularly as she, her love, and life remain the subject of a tug of war in the involved villages. Anne's story has been mobilized in a variety of ways, popularized as local lore, and put in print by a descendant of the Beach family (Mrs. Susan Hicks Beach) who published *A Cotswold Family: Hicks and Hicks Beach* in 1909. It is unsurprising that she begins the work by glorifying the great-grandson of Henrietta Maria Beach, who was at that time an important cabinet minister. The book established the significance of the family while dismissing William Wainhouse as "a most ingenious scoundrel."[6] Anne's story has been passed down

---

6 Mrs. William Hicks Beach, *A Cotswold Family: Hicks and Hicks Beach* (William Heinemann, 1909), 297.

FIGURE 1. The remains of Anne Beach. *Top left*: Drawing of a woman, signed "Hall Place Tuesday August 12th 1766 A Beach." The artist is likely Anne Beach. (D2455/F2/5/3/2, Gloucestershire Archives, UK. Image courtesy of Gloucestershire Archives, UK.) *Top right*: *Book of Country Dances*, belonging to Henrietta Maria Bramston the younger, with Mrs. Wainhouse's signature. (D2455/F5/5/11, Gloucestershire Archives, UK. Image courtesy of Gloucestershire Archives, UK.) *Middle right*: "Remember Ann Beach" scratched in a windowpane in Keevil Manor. (Author photograph.) *Bottom right*: Folded paper with writing on the outside that says "Miss Beaches Hair cut off August ye 23d 1768 aged 17." (D2455/F2/5/3/3, Gloucestershire Archives, UK. Image courtesy of Gloucestershire Archives, UK.) *Bottom left*: Lock of Anne Beach's hair. (D2455/F2/5/3/3, Gloucestershire Archives, UK. Image courtesy of Gloucestershire Archives, UK.)

through the words of others, individuals with a specific agenda or interpretation of the events. As historian Antoinette Burton has argued, "archives, that is, traces of the past collected with intentionality or haphazardly as evidence" require a discussion of "provenance, its histories, its effect on its users, and above all, its power to shape all the narratives which are 'found' there."[7] Historians are taught that the basis of our discipline is our sources, and what constitutes these sources has developed as new approaches and methodologies have been employed. For instance, oral history and material culture have provided new ways of accessing the past, but as historians we are ultimately constrained by what survives … or are we? How do we recover the stories and lives in the silences? What do we do when the archives don't exist – do we just ignore that part of the past as too difficult to access? I certainly don't believe that is the right approach. So how do we explain and substantiate, how do we make arguments about the past when the evidence doesn't survive? A great deal of innovative and powerful work has been done on this topic, particularly by gender historians and those scholars working on slavery. For instance, Marissa J. Fuentes, in her book *Dispossessed Lives: Enslaved Women, Violence, and the Archive*, addresses the "difficulties in narrating ephemeral archival presences" – the way in which "the archive conceals, distorts, and silences as much as it reveals," creating "powerful narratives, visual reproductions and archival assumptions."[8] Fuentes builds on the work of scholars like Natalie Zemon Davis, Deborah Gray White, Laura Ann Stoler, and Camilla Townsend, all of whom, she argues, "found ingenious ways to use known biases within particular archives to ask seemingly impossible questions of subjects whose presence, when noted, is systematically distorted."[9] Just as Fuentes examined "archival fragments" to gain "a crucial glimpse into the lives lived under the domination of slavery,"[10] I hope to use these sorts of fragmentary documents to provide a look into eighteenth-century gentry society, Anne Beach's place in it, and the narratives constructed around her. I have sifted through the layers of competing stories to get a picture of a women who died tragically from consumption. In some ways, Anne's story of illness and death is the same as countless others, but it is also an extraordinary one, allowing us to unpack the layers of eighteenth-century gentry society, the challenges, pressures, and concerns of those living at that moment, as well as

---

7 Antoinette Burton, ed., *Archive Stories: Facts, Fictions, and the Writing of History* (Duke University Press, 2005), 3, 6.
8 Marissa J. Fuentes, *Dispossessed Lives: Enslaved Women, Violence, and the Archive* (University of Pennsylvania Press, 2016), 48.
9 Fuentes, *Dispossessed Lives*, 4.
10 Fuentes, *Dispossessed Lives*, 2.

the ways that developments in medicine, law, and society had real and very personal consequences. This story is not just a tale of love and revenge, but a window into the pressures and politics of gender, status, and marriage. It occurs against a backdrop of a changing society in which England's elite classes sought social and material advancement that was grounded in both economics and reputation. It also demonstrates new understandings of illness, the desperate search for health that led to the growth and diversification of the medical marketplace, and the increasing prominence of health retreats and spa towns. More importantly, it allows us to delve into the complexities of the past, particularly the ways in which stories or scandalous local histories memorialize a version of the past that ignores nuance. Storytelling is powerful in making historical memory, but revealing the construction of these narratives and taking a closer look at the productions they produce can help us once again give voice to the erased Anne Beach and remember her, as the windowpane begs, as a person and not just a cliché.

* * * * *

I had been told by someone once – and this is one of the tricky things about any profession – that there are a lot of tricks that you pick up along the way if you are lucky, usually when someone "in the know" clues you in. But it would be so much easier if there was a place to go where you could just find these things out. Why isn't there a big list or a how-to guide? Many people have tried to write these and they are very useful, but because every project is unique and has its own challenges, there is not a one-size-fits-all solution. I have often had students come to me, who are unsure and lacking confidence, who say "but you actually know how to do that!" Here is a secret about historians – we were just as unsure as you are now and were also just left to flounder about and figure it out. I am still running across things I have no idea how to do and am constantly learning. Generally, people only see the final product, not the fits and starts, the labor, the dead ends, or the frustrations that lie beneath the book you are reading. Writing is a process, with layers upon layers; so too are the various stages of the research. I hope you don't mind, but I am going to try to fill you in on a few things I stumbled across as I was trying to work on this project, along with some of the frustrations and problems I encountered on this journey. One of the first challenges was just figuring out what the heck was happening and who these people were. Sounds easy, right? It should have been, but I was faced with the ridiculous task of sorting out a complicated family tree. I started with the catalog entry in the record office. Archivists do amazing work and know their collections far better than those of us off the street. They are the ones who told me about Anne Beach, after all. I started to figure out generally who was who, but then I got into the documents and had a really hard time keeping everyone straight.

Seriously, why were there so many Williams and Annes – couldn't they have been even the littlest bit creative? Give me a Hubert or something. I felt like I needed to create a murder board – you know, the board with pictures and strings that you see in movies and memes. Sadly, all I had was a huge pad of paper, which I used as I sat down to work out all the relationships. While struggling through the documents to find all of the people who played a role in the story, I realized the grandparents had the exact same name as the parents of my Anne!!! I tore up the paper in frustration and there was more under-my-breath cursing (okay, it was actually out-loud cursing in my office with the door shut). I was so annoyed that I actually took a long break from the project, and when I finally got back to it, I spent ages working out who was whom. Just as I thought I had it all sorted, yet another Anne Beach showed up, a niece this time. Seriously??!! Around the same time that I was trying to sort these details, I was also still looking for more documents and had found a scholar who had access to some private family papers that would be useful. While we were talking, she pulled out one of the thickest books I had ever seen (seriously, it was nearly a foot tall). It was John Burke's A Genealogical and Heraldic Dictionary of the Landed Gentry of Great Britain and Ireland *and it had histories for many of the landed families, including the Beaches. Now, I didn't have a copy, and there was no way I could fit one in my suitcase even if I could find a copy, but it was fortunately available on Google Books. Using this book, the archival catalog, letters, and numerous other records, I was finally able to figure out all the players and how they fit together. I have done what I can to make sure you know which Anne and William I am talking about. I call Anne Wainhouse's parents Mr. and Mrs. Beach throughout and refer to their son (also William – grr) as Billy, but please know that I feel your frustration and just wanted to rename them the whole time!*

CHAPTER ONE

Meet the Families

On February 10, 1771, the day his wife Anne lost her battle with consumption, William Wainhouse, in his grief, wrote to his mother-in-law the following notification of her death: "Madam, My dear Wife, your Daughter, is no more." This opening sentence was followed by one of anger, when he stated, "Notwithstanding your implacable Resentment, a Day will come, when you must give an Account for your cruel & unnatural Behavior, that, undoubtedly, contributed to her End."[1] Anne Wainhouse (1749–1771) was the second child of William Beach, Esq., and his wife Anne Wither, members of a wealthy gentry family.[2] What British historian Amanda Vickery termed "the polite or the genteel," made up of professional families or those of gentlemen with smaller landholdings, "they described themselves as 'polite,' 'civil,' 'genteel[,]' 'well-bred[,]' and 'polished.'"[3] By the end of the eighteenth century, more and more individuals were claiming the title of *Esquire*, which had previously been more generally limited to professional men and those with property. It tended to exclude those engaged in business; though upon retirement many of these individuals sought genteel status, using their profits to purchase property or to invest in annuities.[4] The Beaches fell into several of these categories, as landowners, professional men, and investors.

---

1 "William Wainhouse to Mrs. Beach, 10 February 1771," D2455/ F2/5/1/22, Gloucestershire Archives, UK.

2 *Gentry* is a catch-all term that meant landowners who had tenants that farmed their property; however, this definition expanded as the eighteenth century progressed to encompass the growing professions. See Roy Porter, *English Society in the Eighteenth Century*, revised edition (Penguin, 1990), 66.

3 Amanda Vickery, *The Gentleman's Daughter: Women's Lives in Georgian England* (Yale University Press, 1998), 13.

4 Paul Langford, *A Polite and Commercial People: England 1727–1783* (Oxford University Press, 1989), 65.

The Beach Family

The world of William Beach (1719–1790) and Anne Wither (c. 1718–1788) was far different than that of their grandparents, also called William Beach (1665–1741) and Anne Wither (c. 1662–1742).[5] This confusing family tree marked a solidification of land accumulation in the county of Wiltshire, and the eventual expansion into Hampshire and Gloucestershire. Like many families, the Beaches had risen in prominence as country gentry through the judicious acquisition of land and shrewd marital alliances. For the sake of clarity, the elder will be referred to as William Beach of Fittleton (1665–1741), and the younger called William Beach of Netheravon (1719–1790). The Beach family had deep roots in Wiltshire, tracing their ancestry to the Beche's (de la Beche) family of Warminster; however, by the seventeenth century they had acquired land in Fittleton and Keevil, and then in the mid-eighteenth century they purchased a house in Netheravon.[6]

On October 9, 1679, William Beach of Fittleton married Anne Wither, the daughter of Gilbert Wither, Esq., of Hall Place in Hampshire, and the couple seemed to have had a warm relationship.[7] The year after their wedding, William's concerned wife sent him a turkey for his comfort while he was traveling and urged his speedy return, writing "I hope you will bee [sic] as good as your word in making the time as short as you can."[8] They eventually settled into the Beach estate in Fittleton on the opposite bank of the Avon River from the village of Netheravon.[9] The two-story red brick Manor House, acquired by the family in 1665, situated just east of the fourteenth-century Church of All Saints, had five bays of windows and a plain façade enlivened by a geometric design worked in gray flint.[10] The couple had fourteen children, at least half of whom survived to adulthood.[11] Five of the

---

5 Joanna Martin, ed. *The Penrice Letters 1768–1795* (West Glamorgan County Archive Service/South Wales Record Society, 1993), 182.

6 Administrative history, Beach Family of Fittleton, Keevil, and Netheravon, Gloucestershire Archives, UK. For an example of this sort of maneuvering, see R.W. Hoyle, "The Listers of Gisburn: The Fashioning of a Gentry Family in the Early Eighteenth Century," *Northern History* 56, no. 1–2 (2019): 46–77, 46.

7 John Burke, *A Genealogical and Heraldic Dictionary of the Landed Gentry of Great Britain and Ireland*, Vol. 1 (Henry Colburn, 1847), 73.

8 "Mrs. Beach to Mr. William Beach at the Angel and Crown in London, 23 November 1680," D2455/F2/2/1, Gloucestershire Archives, UK.

9 William inherited the estate along with the Manor House in Keevil upon his father's death (William Beach of Brixton Deverill) in 1686.

10 Nickolaus Pevsner, *The Buildings of England: Wiltshire* (Penguin Books, 1974), 245–46; "Fittleton and Hackleston: Notes of Manorial Descent," *Wiltshire Archaeological and Natural History Magazine* 11 (H.F. and E. Bull, 1869), 259.

11 Elizabeth (1680–1710); Ann (date of birth unknown, died 1682, probably an infant); William (1682–1708); Thomas (1684–1753); Mary (1686–1707); Ann (1688–1713); Dorothy (1690–1772); John (1692–1750); Maria (born 1694; her date of death is unknown but she probably died in infancy);

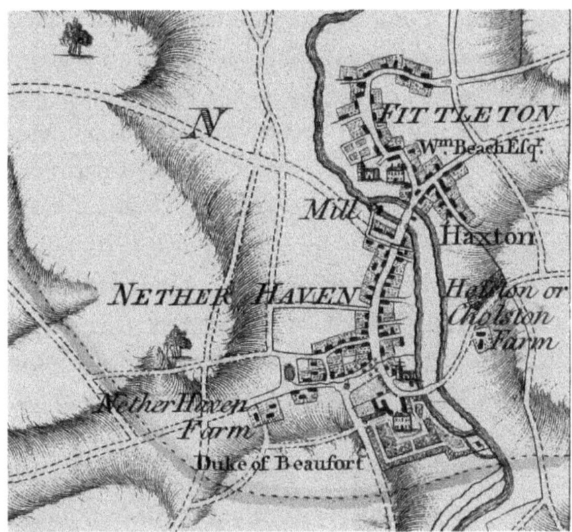

FIGURE 2. Map of Fittleton and Netheravon. ("Fittleton & Netheravon, Plate No. 8, *Andrews'* *and Dury's Map of Wiltshire, 1773: A Reduced Facsimile*, ed. Elizabeth Crittall [1952] [The Wiltshire Record Society, 1952]." Image courtesy of the Wilshire and Swindon History Centre.)

children are of particular interest as they play a role, either directly or indirectly, in the story of Anne Wainhouse. The three unmarried daughters, Dorothy, Joan, and Sophia, were very active in the lives of their brothers, Thomas and Andrew. These women were also close to their nephew, William Beach of Netheravon, and to Andrew's wife, Mary Wansborough.

The educational choices made by the Beaches for their sons reflect the anxieties among gentry families to maintain or enhance their status, secure incomes for their family members, and, if possible, grow the family estate. Economic historians Patrick Wallis and Cliff Webb argue that these choices tended to fall into three broad categories, with gentry sons attending university, gaining training in the law at the Inns of Court, or undertaking an apprenticeship.[12] Andrew Beach (1696–1734), the fourth Beach son, was born at Fittleton on October 3, but at the age of sixteen his parents sent him to London for training. Although he did not go

---

Andrew (1696–1734); Henrietta Maria (1698–1713); Joan (1700–1765); Charles (1703–1705); and Sophia (1705–1787). Administrative history, Beach Family of Fittleton, Keevil and Netheravon, Gloucestershire Archives, UK.

12 Around 90 percent of gentry sons took their apprenticeship with one of the "Great Twelve," those companies at the top of the guild hierarchy that offered the greatest political access and were seen as the top end of the training market. Patrick Wallis and Cliff Webb, "The Education and Training of Gentry Sons in Early Modern England," *Social History* 36, no. 1 (2011), 36, 44.

to one of the Twelve Great Companies, his father paid the princely sum of £180 to apprentice him to the barber-surgeon James Ferne.[13] This high premium indicated the financial potential of this career and was a way of ensuring Andrew's future prospects. As it was for the other companies, historian Celeste Chamberland argues that "the Barber-Surgeons' Company deemed apprenticeship an essential rite of passage that ... ensured they achieved occupational competency, and reinforced social legitimacy and respectability within London's credit-oriented cultural milieu."[14] Although this style of training had existed for centuries, in the eighteenth century it was still against the law to work in a trade unless one had finished an apprenticeship. This training also made one part of a specific community, reinforced through special events and celebrations, political power, social status, and special access to charities and education.[15]

Upon completion, the apprentice could apply for membership in a livery company, which granted citizenship rights in the City of London as well as freeman status – that is, the "freedom to work" in London.[16] Completion of an apprenticeship and reaching the age of twenty-four was the general method for gaining citizenship, and freeman not only gained the right to vote, but the livery companies were responsible for electing the lord mayor and the members of Parliament that represented the City of London. Their political power was extensive, and as such, the completion of an apprenticeship came with benefits beyond the financial, though citizenship also permitted an individual to legitimately pursue their trade and take on apprentices themselves.[17]

13　These were the most prestigious of London guild companies and included the Mercers, Grocers, Drapers, Fishmongers, Goldsmiths, Merchant Taylors, Skinners, Haberdashers, Salters, Ironmongers, Vintners, and Clothworkers. "Christening Record Andrew Beach," Reference Number: 2094/1, *Wiltshire, England, Church of England Baptisms, Marriages and Burials, 1538–1812* [database online], Lehi, UT: Ancestry.com Operations, Inc., 2017; "Andrew Beach Indenture," Reference number: COL/CHD/FR/02/0377–0383, *London, England, Freedom of the City Admission Papers, 1681–1930* [database online], Provo, UT: Ancestry.com Operations, Inc., 2010; *Court Minutes* (1707–1731), folio 67, Worshipful Company of Barbers, UK.

14　Celeste Chamberland, "From Apprentice to Master: Social Disciplining and Surgical Education in Early Modern London, 1570–1640," *History of Education Quarterly* 53, no. 1 (2013), 27.

15　Christopher Brooks, "Apprenticeship, Social Mobility and the Middling Sort, 1550–1800," in *The Middling Sort of People: Culture, Society and Politics in England, 1550–1800*, eds. Jonathan Barry and Christopher Brooks (Macmillan, 1994), 53–4, 60; Joan Lane, "The Role of Apprenticeship in Eighteenth-century Medical Education in England," in *William Hunter and the Eighteenth-Century Medical World*, eds. W.F. Bynum and Roy Porter (Cambridge University Press, 1985), 57, 62.

16　Joseph P. Ward, *Metropolitan Communities: Trade Guilds, Identity, and Change in Early Modern London* (Stanford University Press, 1997), 8–9.

17　Gill Newton, "Clandestine Marriage in Early Modern London: When, Where and Why?" *Continuity and Change* 29, no. 2 (2014), 169; Lane, "The Role of Apprenticeship," 62; Ward, *Metropolitan Communities*, 9.

The formal apprenticeship parameters were laid down in the document of indenture. This spelled out the specifics of training, when a teenager (usually mid- to late teens) moved in with his master to learn a trade with the intention of setting up his own business. In Andrew's case the indenture was set at the standard seven years.[18] The substantial sum paid by William Beach of Fittleton may have also helped ensure Andrew received better treatment than that of boys apprenticed in other, less prestigious, trades like Butchers, Coopers (barrel makers), Wax Chandlers (candle makers), and Sadlers. Legally, the master was allowed to act as a parent, with permission to use physical force to correct behavior, and in some trades this "right" moved to cruelty. However, those apprenticed to surgeons were not normally subjected to the kind of conduct that was serious enough to lead to legal action. Social historian Joan Lane has argued that the cost of apprenticing to a barber-surgeon aided in gaining these boys better treatment because they could have reported abuse to their family members. Additionally, they were working for men who were not plagued by poverty, which could have pushed their masters to overwork them.[19]

There are no surviving letters from Andrew's first two years as an apprentice and those few that do exist for later years speak to his positive relationship to his parents and sisters, as well as his interest in maintaining appearances. His parents complained of his "too seldom writing," though this seems to have been a factor of his letters going awry rather than his inattention to his family.[20] The young apprentice also seemed to be a budding man of fashion, as the majority of his letters request items of clothing made to his specifications by his mother and sisters. Andrew even went so far as to ask his sister Sophia to sacrifice her hair so he could have the new wig he desperately wanted, though he was at least willing to wait until the winter had passed so she would not be cold, writing "wen [sic] ye warm weather begins to come on I hope Sophy will think of cutting her hair off for I want a Perewig [sic] very bad."[21]

There are also a few hints at the relationship between master and apprentice. In 1715, Andrew pleaded with his father to get him permission to come home

18 Brooks, "Apprenticeship, Social Mobility and the Middling Sort," 53; "Andrew Beach Indenture."

19 Lane, "The Role of Apprenticeship," 58–9.

20 "I have writ two letters to you, and two to my mother; but never reciev'd an answer." "Andrew Beach, Esq. to William Beach Esq. at Fittleton, 30 July 1715," D2455/F2/2/8, Gloucestershire Archives, UK.

21 "18 February 1715/6," D2455/F2/2/8, Gloucestershire Archives, UK. For more on wigs, see "Dangerous Excrescences: Wigs, Hair, and Masculinity," in *Hanging the Head: Portraiture and Social Formation in Eighteenth-century England*, ed. Marcia Pointon (Yale University Press, 1993); Margaret K. Powell and Joseph R. Roach, "Big Hair," *Eighteenth-Century Studies* 38, no. 1 (2004): 79–99.

for a visit.[22] In addition to restricting his movements, Andrew's indenture thrust him firmly into London's eighteenth-century medical world, dominated by three organizations. These corporations, in descending order of prestige, were the Royal College of Physicians, the Worshipful Company of Barber-Surgeons, and the Worshipful Society of Apothecaries. All three organizations were concerned with setting the educational and licensing requirements for medical practice rather than the actual standards of care. As a result, they were constantly battling for priority and trying to establish the boundaries between surgery, physic, and pharmacy.[23]

Founded in 1518, the Royal College of Physicians (RCP) represented the top of the medical hierarchy and was comprised of learned physicians. By the beginning of the eighteenth century, to practice in London, its members had to obtain an MD degree from a university and complete an oral exam in Latin. Full voting membership, however, was only given to the fellows (men who had acquired a degree from either Cambridge or Oxford and passed an additional exam in Latin). Fellows were defined not only by their qualifications, but also by a ban on participating in trade (as such, fellows did not wield the knife in surgery, dispense medicine, or engage in midwifery).[24] In April 1712, Andrew Beach entered into his training for the trade of surgery, typically seen as a manual skill acquired through apprenticeship rather than university education and, as such, it ranked below *physic* in status. Andrew, however, was learning his craft at the moment that surgery was changing and increasing in prestige, in part due to alterations in professional structures as well as developments of new surgical methodologies.[25]

---

22 "Sir I desire you (if you can spare so much time) to write to my mother about my coming into the country, if you would be pleased to write as soon as you can, and desire him [Ferne] to tell me whether he can spare me or not." "Andrew Beach, Esq. to William Beach Esq. at Fittleton, 30 July 1715."

23 The Worshipful Society of Apothecaries was chartered in 1617 and required a seven-year apprenticeship, followed by an oral examination and certification by the Court of Assistants to become a member. Susan C. Lawrence, *Charitable Knowledge: Hospital Pupils and Practitioners in Eighteenth-Century London* (Cambridge University Press, 1996), 77, 80.

24 Lawrence, *Charitable Knowledge*, 77. The distinctions between physician and surgeon could sometimes be fluid, as there were doctors who practiced surgery. For instance, Joannes Groenevelt, also known by the name John or James Greenfield, was a licentiate of the Royal College of Physicians and was one of London's premier surgeons specializing in the removal of bladder stones in the early eighteenth century. See Philip K. Wilson, "Acquiring Surgical Know-How: Occupational and Lay Instruction in Early Eighteenth-Century London," in *The Popularization of Medicine 1650–1850*, ed. Roy Porter (Routledge, 1992), 55. For more on Groenevelt, see Harold J. Cook, *Trials of an Ordinary Doctor: Joannes Groenevelt in Seventeenth-Century London* (Johns Hopkins University Press, 1994).

25 Particularly in the techniques for the removal of bladder stones, see Roy Porter, *Blood and Guts: A Short History of Medicine* (W.W. Norton & Company, 2002), 115.

The surgeons in London organized into a guild beginning in the fourteenth century, but it wasn't until 1540 that they founded the Worshipful Company of Barber-Surgeons. To apprentice to a surgeon, men were to register with the Barber-Surgeons' Hall and either pass an exam or provide proof of their command of Latin as well as their broad education. After seven years under the tutelage of a member of the company, the applicant would register at the Barber-Surgeons' Hall and then undergo another examination. The board of examiners was effectively in charge of the Barber-Surgeon's Company and had been established by a royal charter in 1629 (granted by King Charles I at the urging of William Harvey). This group established the criteria for moving beyond the apprenticeship and was also responsible for certifying surgeons for naval service.[26]

Andrew's master, James Ferne, had become a surgeon at St. Thomas' Hospital in 1703, specializing in lithotomy (the surgical removal of bladder stones), and served in this capacity until his death in 1741. He also became a warden of the Barber-Surgeons in 1728 before promotion to the post of master in 1733.[27] Andrew Beach was in good company, as Ferne had also served as the master to William Cheselden (1688–1752), who had completed his apprenticeship in 1710 and was admitted to the company a little over a year before Andrew began his training.[28] Cheselden, like Ferne, became a surgeon at St. Thomas' Hospital, specializing in the removal of bladder stones, then in 1727 was made surgeon to Queen Caroline. Cheselden's success was due in part to his mastery of the new and improved technique for excising bladder stones called the lateral cystotomy, introduced at the turn of the century.[29]

---

26 Lawrence, *Charitable Knowledge*, 78–9; Zachary Cope, *The Royal College of Surgeons of England: A History* (Anthony Blond, Ltd., 1959), 3; John P. Blandy and John S.P. Lumley, eds., *The Royal College of Surgeons of England: 200 years of History at the Millennium* (Royal College of Surgeons of England and Blackwell Science, 2000), 6.

27 *Saint Thomas' Hospital Reports*, Vol. 28 (J.A. Churchill, 1901), 447–8; Sidney Young, *Annals of the Barber-Surgeons of London* (East & Blades, 1890), 11–12.

28 Ferne would continue at St. Thomas' until his death in 1741. *Saint Thomas' Hospital Reports*, 437, 447–8; John Kirkup, "Cheselden, William (1688–1752), Surgeon and Anatomist," *Oxford Dictionary of National Biography*, November 12, 2018, http://www.oxforddnb.com/view/10.1093/ref:odnb/9780198614128.001.0001/odnb-9780198614128-e-5226.

29 Porter, *Blood and Guts*, 115. For more on the particulars of the operation, see Cheselden's own, very brief account, in William Cheselden, *The Anatomy of the Human Body*, 4th ed. (W. Bowyer, 1730), 343. For an in-depth description from an observer, see James Douglas, MD, *The History of the Lateral Operation* (G. Strahan, 1726), 83–8. Cope also summarizes the procedure in Zachary Cope, "William Cheselden and the Separation of the Barbers from the Surgeons," *Annals of the Royal College of Surgeons of England* 12, no. 1 (1953): 1–13, 4.

The surgeon was so good with the knife he could perform the painful operation in a few minutes, while other practitioners took closer to twenty.[30] One witness saw him complete the operation in fifty-four seconds, while physician James Douglas stated, "he has been seldom above a Minute (sometimes less) between the Beginning of the first Incision and Extraction of the Stone."[31] Beyond speed, his success rate was very high, as he lost less than 10 percent of the 213 patients on whom he performed the technique at St. Thomas' Hospital. This speed and skill were, not surprisingly, prized by those who had to undergo the procedure in the era before the invention of anesthesia. As a consequence, Cheselden's fees were as big as his reputation and ran upwards of 500 guineas. He was a prominent member of the Barber-Surgeon's Company, rising to the post of master in 1746.[32] Cheselden published a number of works, including *The Anatomy of the Human Body* in 1713, a popular book targeted to students that provided the basics of operative surgery, accompanied by instructive plates and coupled with information on human physiology. He also published a beautifully illustrated and detailed investigation of the human bones and skeleton called the *Osteographia*.[33]

Like he would have for William Cheseleden, when taking on Andrew Beach as an apprentice, James Ferne promised to instruct him in the art of surgery. Historian Celeste Chamberland has argued that apprentices were instructed in a mixed manner, one that combined the textual and theoretical basis of the discipline with hands-on experience.[34] Andrew's requests for funds reveal some of the training

---

30 Description of the procedure: The patient was put on their back with their hands and ankles bound and their legs bent so their feet were at their buttocks. The patient was held down by two assistants, who ensured the knees stayed open by holding them and the ankles, then a third person stabilized the neck and head. The patient was prepped by filling the bladder with water, at which point a fourth assistant inserted a catheter and then the surgeon made a lateral perineal incision following the catheter, inserted a finger or guide, then removed the stone with the assistance of forceps. Spyros N. Michaleas, Gregory Tsoucalas, Halil Tekiner, and Marianna Karamanou, "William Cheselden (1688–1752): 18th-Century Pioneer of Lateral Lithotomy and Iridectomy," *Surgical Innovation* 27, no. 5 (2020), 547.

31 Cope, "William Cheselden and the Separation," 5; Douglas, *The History of the Lateral Operation*, 86.

32 Cope, "William Cheselden and the Separation," 5; Porter, *Blood and Guts*, 117; Kirkup, "Cheselden, William (1688–1752)." For other aspects of Cheselden's surgical career, particularly his controversial ophthalmological career, see Christopher Mounsey, *Sight Correction: Vision and Blindness in Eighteenth-Century Britain* (University of Virginia Press, 2019).

33 From 1713 to 1792, the book had thirteen editions published in London, its popularity possibly aided by Cheselden's successful private school of anatomy. Lynda Payne, *With Words and Knives: Learning Medical Dispassion in Early Modern England* (Routledge, 2016), 88; Kirkup, "Cheselden, William (1688–1752), Surgeon and Anatomist"; Allister Neher, "The Truth about Our Bones: William Cheselden's *Osteographia*," *Medical History* 54, no. 4 (2010), 517. For more on the afterlife of *Osteographia*, see Nico Bertoloni Meli, "Visual Representations of Disease: The *Philosophical Transactions* and William Cheselden's *Osteographia*," *Huntington Library Quarterly* 78, no. 2 (2015): 157–86.

34 Chamberland, "From Apprentice to Master," 22.

he received. In February 1716, he wrote his father mentioning he had gone over his allowance and needed to borrow money to pay for his texts and a "case of dissection knives."[35] The books in question were James Drake's *Anthropologia Nova, or, A New System of Anatomy*, first published in two volumes in 1707; Thomas Fuller's *Pharmacopoeia Extemporanea* (1702, written in Latin), first English translation (1710); and Joseph de La Charrière's *A Treatise of the Operations of Surgery*.[36] The books reflect the various practical aspects of the training Andrew was receiving – anatomy, surgery, and pharmacology. Andrew would have attended lectures and demonstrations of techniques at the Barber-Surgeons' Hall and in surgical shops and would also have been allowed to practice hands-on treatments under the eye of his master.[37]

Beyond instructing his charge, James Ferne also promised to provide Andrew with "Meat, Drink, Apparel, Lodging, and all other Necessaries." In exchange, the young boy was fully under his master's control, was not permitted to "absent himself from his said Master's Service Day or Night unlawfully" and was charged with serving his master "faithfully" and keeping his secrets. The sixteen-year-old also promised not to marry or "commit Fornication" while an apprentice and was prohibited from playing "Cards, Dice, Tables, or any other unlawful Games" or frequenting "Taverns or Play-houses."[38] These were standard conditions, and were practical rather than moral in nature, protecting both master and apprentice.

Since the apprentice lived in the master's house, marriage was out of the question, and sex could lead to unwanted pregnancy. Andrew would not have had the money to support a child or a wife and he would not have been permitted to bring them to reside in his master's house. Gambling, it was thought, could lead to a temptation to dip into his master's pockets unlawfully, while taverns and playhouses were believed to be frequented by undesirable persons, not just the unsavory, but also other apprentices. There was a fear these men would come together and compare living and working situations or, even worse, disclose their master's secrets.[39]

On May 5, 1719, Andrew Beach was officially admitted into "freedom of the Company" by virtue of his service.[40] Despite concluding his apprenticeship, the newly minted surgeon would still be obliged to continue his education and refine

---

35 "Andrew Beach, Esq. to William Beach Esq. at Fittleton, 18 February 1715/6," D2455/F2/2/8, Gloucestershire Archives, UK.
36 "Andrew Beach, Esq. to William Beach Esq. at Fittleton, 18 February 1715/6."
37 Chamberland, "From Apprentice to Master," 23, 26.
38 "Andrew Beach Indenture."
39 Lane, "The Role of Apprenticeship," 58–9.
40 *Court Minutes* (1707–1731), May 5, 1719, folio 199, Worshipful Company of Barbers, UK.

his skills by attending semi-weekly lectures on surgery and anatomy lectures four times a year.[41] Andrew became a full livery man on June 7, 1723, when he passed an examination of his "skill in Surgery."[42] As a freeman he first established a medical practice on Lawrence Street, where he remained until 1727, when he moved to Queen Street in Cheapside.[43] Three years after becoming a fully vested member of the Barber-Surgeons' Company, the now thirty-year-old bachelor finally met a woman he wished to wed, Mary Wansborough. She was from his home county of Wiltshire, and the couple married in Salisbury Cathedral on December 22, 1726. Andrew's father settled £1,000 on the pair and Mary's father gave them £700, put a further £300 in trust, and then provided £1,200 that would go to support the surviving partner should one predecease the other.[44] Well provided for, the newlyweds moved to London where they settled in the parish of St. Mary Aldermary's and St. Thomas the Apostle. This awkward arrangement of names was a product of the Great Fire of London in 1666, which damaged both churches. In 1674, Sir Christopher Wren undertook the task of rebuilding the tower of the guild church St. Mary Aldermary, and when it reopened in 1682 it had been combined with St. Thomas the Apostle to avoid to cost of rebuilding both structures.[45]

Mary and Andrew began attending the church in Bow Lane, near where he had moved his practice in 1729, and they rang in the new year in 1732 by baptizing their daughter Jane there in a private ceremony on January 2. Unfortunately, their good fortune was brief – in March 1734, just two short years later, both Andrew and Jane died, leaving Mary Beach a widow.[46] With no real ties to London, Mary returned to Wiltshire, where she remained very close with her husband's family,

---

41 Chamberland, "From Apprentice to Master," 32.

42 *Court Minutes* (1707–1731), May 5, 1719, folio 272, Worshipful Company of Barbers, UK.

43 *Daily Journal* (London, England), Tuesday, October 31, 1727, Issue 2121, 17th–18th Century Burney Newspapers Collection, Gale Document Number: Z2000244562.

44 *Wiltshire, England, Marriages, 1538–1837* [database online], Provo, UT: Ancestry.com Operations, Inc., 2013; "Release, Andrew Beach to William Beach of Fittleton, concerning money to be paid on the latter's marriage to Mary Wansbrough, 1727," D2455/F2/2/15, Gloucestershire Archives, UK; "Marriage Articles between Andrew Beach and Mary Wansborough, November 1726," 377/12, Wiltshire and Swindon History Centre, UK.

45 Howard Colvin, "The Church of St. Mary Aldermary and Its Rebuilding after the Great Fire of London," *Architectural History* 24 (1981), 26, 28.

46 For the last year of his life, Andrew was practicing in Garlick Hill. Unfortunately, there is no evidence of what led to Andrew and Jane's deaths. "Lists of Court and Livery, 1711–1751," MS5276, Worshipful Company of Barbers, UK; "Jane Beach Burial," London Metropolitan Archives, London, England; *Church of England Parish Registers, 1538–1812*, Reference Number: P69/MRY3/A/002/MS08991 [database online], Provo, UT: Ancestry.com Operations, Inc., 2010; Joseph Lemuel Chester, *The Parish Registers of St. Mary Aldermary London Containing Marriages, Baptisms and Burials from 1555 to 1754* (London, 1880), 223.

particularly Sophia Beach and her nephew-in-law's wife, Anne, married to the son of Thomas Beach, Esq.

Thomas Beach, Esq. (1684–1753), the second son of William Beach of Fittleton was, like Andrew, sent away for improvement. Rather than an apprenticeship, at the age of twelve he was enrolled at Winchester College, founded in 1382 by William Wykeham, the Bishop of Winchester, and situated less than forty miles from Fittleton. Here he joined the other eighty-five gentlemen commoners at the school.[47] Like Andrew, Thomas was bound by rules, though those laid down in the *Table of the Scholastic Laws* were certainly less restrictive than those of apprenticeship and focused on grooming the behavior of the elder Beach son. Thomas was to "behave with modesty" while in town, he was to "Worship God" and "Read nothing profane." Additionally, he was instructed to "be diligent in his studies," spelling his themes correctly and having his "school implements in constant readiness." Young Thomas was also charged with attending to his personal cleanliness. There was one rule, however, that was routinely flouted at Winchester: the prohibition against graffiti. The *Laws* stated, "Let not the building be defaced with writing or carving upon it."[48] Although expected to make a mark once they left, it seems Wykhamists also wanted to leave their mark on the institution itself, as the cloisters are littered with student carvings. This graffiti also provided an important link between generations of attendees, especially for the homesick George Bruce, who found the entire experience of entering Winchester College unpleasant. On his very first day he wrote that "[a]ltogether I find it very uncomfortable here as yet" and complained of his cold room that lacked shutters or curtains. However, one of his very first acts as a Wyckamist revolved around graffiti, as he sought out his father's name carved into the fabric of the College. He wrote, "went into the School Room where we could not find your name written" but later that day he found the marks "wrote up near my Window."[49] A month later he wrote again that "Dear Father ... I saw your Name written up on the Window in the Room you used to lay in."[50] Standing as more than a mark of presence, the graffiti at Winchester also served a transgressive purpose – not just for breaking rules, but as a mechanism by which these boys made themselves heard, expressing their opinions as well as their anger. For instance, in April 1777, the student body protested the expulsion of one of their

47 Arthur F. Leach, *A History of Winchester College* (Charles Scribner's Sons, 1899), 65; Clifford Wyndham Holgate, ed., *Winchester Long Rolls, 1653–1721* (P. & G. Wells, 1899), 72.

48 Rev. Dr. Milner, *Winchester College, with Additional Notes* (Winchester: D.E. Gilmour, 1826), 26.

49 "George Bruce to Lord Ailesbury, 21 January 1777," 1300/4142, Wiltshire and Swindon History Centre, UK.

50 "George Bruce to Lord Ailesbury, 26 February 1777," 1300/ 4158, Wiltshire and Swindon History Centre, UK.

FIGURE 3. Student graffiti, Winchester College. (Author photograph.)

own by writing his name "upon the Walls & Places & about the Hall" and scrawling the words "Vengeance Fury & many other things."[51]

Thomas Beach's arrival at Winchester seems to have been easier than George Bruce's and he began his time there just six years after the completion of the new school room (housed in a brick building to the west of the College's cloisters). The large room was ornamented by dark wainscoting and here the students completed their work under the watchful eye of a bronze statue of William Wykeham. The headmaster, William Harris, was a man particularly enthusiastic about the study of Greek and Latin, which dominated the curriculum. By the time he left

<hr>

51 "George Bruce to Lord Ailesbury, 16 April 1777," 1300/4165, Wiltshire and Swindon History Centre, UK.

the College in 1698, Thomas's training for gentry life included learning Greek and Latin and having read Homer, Ovid, Pliny, Virgil, Juvenal, and Erasmus.[52]

Beyond a command of the classics, the school was thought to instill a "gentry manliness" that permitted the transition from a "domestic dependence" to a prescribed notion of "masculine autonomy and judgment."[53] This, according to historians Henry French and Mark Rothery, "was acquired through practical experience in 'the world,' which provided lessons in how to handle authority responsibly, deal with different social ranks, discern (and anticipate) an individual's 'ruling passion,' and to identify and learn from virtuous companions."[54] Thomas would be able to demonstrate these skills when he eventually inherited the family estate, as his elder brother William (1682–1708) predeceased their father by thirty-three years. Here Thomas collected rents on the lands owned by his family, oversaw the growing of wheat and beans, along with the maintenance of cows, horses, and donkeys. Additionally, the Beaches kept their house well provisioned with bacon, cheese, and strong beer.[55]

Thomas's fortunes were also improved by a very advantageous marriage to the only sister of a wealthy wool and linen merchant, James Harding of Mere.[56] Harding had extensive business interests: selling tick, broad cloth, and lightweight woolen fabrics all over the continent, including the German states, Austria, Portugal and even trading with the American colonies.[57] Thomas Beach and Jane Harding (1695–1735) married in 1718, and in the first year of their marriage had an heir they named William Beach (1719–1790) [of Netheravon]. Their new son was baptized on New Year's Day 1719 in his uncle's parish in Mere.[58] This connection

52 B.B. Woodward, *A History and Description of Winchester* (J. Wells, 186?), 191; Holgate, *Winchester Long Rolls*, 73; *Index to Commoners 1653–1800*, Winchester College Archives; "Curriculum," Business at Winton College, *Winchester College Archives*, UK.

53 Henry French and Mark Rothery, *Man's Estate: Landed Gentry Masculinities, 1660–1900* (Oxford University Press, 2012), 3.

54 French and Rothery, *Man's Estate*, 3.

55 "Account Book detailing the distribution of property after the death of Ann Beach in 1742," D2455/ F2/2/18, Gloucestershire Archives, UK.

56 Thomas received a marriage portion of £4,000 from James Harding Senior, and as James Harding Junior never married there remained the potential of an inheritance from that quarter. "Marriage Settlement between Thomas Beach & James Harding, Senior of Mere," D2455/ F2/3/2 Gloucestershire Archives, UK.

57 J. Smail, *Merchants, Markets and Manufacture: The English Wool Textile Industry* (Springer: 1999), 60; M.F. Tighe, "Silver Threads: A Study of the Textile Industries of Mere" (Mere, 1997); "Account Books of the East India Company, IOR/L/AG/1/1/15/f. 183 (6) and IOR/AG/1/1/16/f.118(2), British Library, UK; "Account Books James Harding of Mere," D2455/B1/2 Gloucestershire Archives, UK.

58 "Christening of William Beach," Reference Number: 2944/2, *Wiltshire, England, Church of England Baptisms, Marriages and Burials, 1538–1812* [database online], Lehi, UT: Ancestry.com Operations, Inc., 2017.

to Harding would continue throughout William's life, as his uncle would eventually split his vast fortune between William Beach of Netheravon and his maternal cousin, Thomas Mansel Talbot, the son of Jane Beach (the only daughter of Thomas and Jane) and Reverend Thomas Talbot. This enormous windfall in 1775 amounted to £120,000.[59]

William Beach of Netheravon would follow his father's example, attending Winchester College from 1736 to 1738.[60] Then in May 1739, Thomas Beach took the nineteen-year-old to university, writing on May 14, "I arrived with my Son att [sic.] Oxford."[61] Two days later he remarked "entered my Son att [sic] new College" paying a total of £38, 10s, 10d in fees and in acquiring the necessities to ensure William's comfort (this included caution money, servants' fees, student robes, and even a new tea kettle).[62] William Beach would likely have been one of the approximately 1,800 students at Oxford, which matriculated around 200 students per year during this period.[63]

By the early eighteenth century, Cambridge and Oxford had become the haven of the gentry, as titled families moved away from these institutions and toward private tutoring and a European tour to give their noble sons polish. The Oxbridge institutions increasingly educated the sons of the gentry, but by the turn of the eighteenth century the two institutions had diverged in curricular focus. Cambridge began to emphasize mathematics at the same time Oxford prioritized the traditional subjects, promoting ethics, humanities, logic as well as Greek and Latin. Despite these differences, a large number of students at both institutions would go on to find livings as clergymen in rural parishes.[64]

The Inns of Court and the Oxbridge universities trained not only lawyers and the clergy; they were also tasked with polishing the sons of well-bred families, despite their less than savory reputations, with both being notable for the consumption of alcohol.[65] For instance, the prestigious Dr. Warren, when asked advice by a mother on whether she should send her son to Oxford or Cambridge

---

59 *Public Advertiser* (London, England), Tuesday, March 14, 1775, Issue 14180, Gale Document Number: Z2001153281; "Salisbury, March 13. James Harding, Esq; of Mere, whose death was mentioned lately, died possessed of three hundred thousand pounds of property, one hundred and twenty thousand of which we hear he has left to William Beach, Esq; at Fittleton, in this county." *London Chronicle or Universal Evening Post* (London, England), March 14, 1775–March 16, 1775, Issue 2850, Gale Document Number: Z2000608495.

60 *Index to Commoners 1653–1800.*

61 "Misc. Receipts," D2455/F2/5/2/1, Gloucestershire Archives, UK.

62 "Misc. Receipts," D2455/F2/5/2/1.

63 L.W.B. Brockliss, *The University of Oxford: A History* (Oxford University Press, 2016), 159.

64 Brockliss, *The University of Oxford*, 137, 139, 163–4.

65 Langford, *A Polite and Commercial People*, 88.

replied, "Madam, I believe they drink an equal quantity of port at each."[66] The accounts of Reverend James Woodforde's time at Oxford are also filled with mentions of evenings in the Bachelor's Common Room, "with Wine and Punch," and repeated diary entries speak of consuming a full bottle of wine and of his dwindling supplies of port.[67]

After leaving New College, William returned to Wiltshire, where his father helped orchestrate his marriage by recommending to Mrs. Wither "a match between my son & her daughter Miss Nancy."[68] The young lady was his second cousin, Anne Wither (c. 1718–1788), the daughter of Charles Wither, Esq., of Hall Place in Hampshire.[69] The couple courted through letters, which reveal something of their dynamics from the very beginning of their relationship. The seventeen-year-olds exchanged inquiries about fishing, and Anne, much to William's delight, asked after his horse.

Anne seems to have had the upper hand in the financial negotiations and came with the potential of an enormous settlement of £7,000 from her deceased father, Charles Wither, while William's tone was often pleading and obsequious.[70] He repeatedly circumvented his father and aunt and went straight to Anne with his queries: "I Should have waited on your Mama but thought proper to know what you would have done before I proceeded any farther.... I shall be very glad to do whatever you think fit."[71] He also placed the choice of his wedding clothing firmly in her hands, asking, "If it be not too much trouble please to [sic] let me know what such a wastcost [sic] as you think proper for me will cost ... & whether I must send up a whole suit to have it made by; as soon as you think fit." William also professed his desire "that we may find nothing more to obstruct our mutual happiness is dearest Miss the sincerest wish of your Humble Servant, who whenever you come into the country will think it the greatest happiness in the world to wait on you."[72] The couple would, after a lengthy financial negotiation, marry on June 29, 1746.[73] They had a son the following year, whom they named William Wither

---

66 "News." *Oracle*, May 4, 1798. Seventeenth and Eighteenth Century Burney Newspapers Collection (accessed May 22, 2020).

67 James Woodforde, *The Diary of a Country Parson: The Reverend James Woodforde, 1758–1781*, ed. John Beresford (Humphrey Milford, Oxford University Press, 1924), 17.

68 "Thomas Beach to Mrs. Wither, Hall Place, 1745," D2455/F2/5/1/8, Gloucestershire Archives, UK.

69 Burke, *A Genealogical and Heraldic Dictionary*, 73.

70 "An Act for vesting the settled Estate of Edmund Bramston, Esquire, and Henrietta Maria his Wife, in Trustees, for raising several Sums of Money, for discharging Portions charged upon the Same; and for other Purposes therein mentioned," 21M58/ Z1, Hampshire Archives and Local Studies, UK.

71 "William Beach to Anne Wither, 22 March [1745]," D2455/F2/5/1/10, Gloucestershire Archives, UK.

72 "William Beach to Anne Wither, 17 March [1745]," D2455/F2/5/1/10, Gloucestershire Archives, UK.

73 "Marriage of William Beach to Anne Wither, Deane, Hampshire," *Wiltshire, England, Marriages, 1538–1837* [database online], Provo, UT: Ancestry.com Operations, Inc., 2013.

Beach (1747–1829) but called Billy. He was followed by another son, James Harding, named after his great uncle; unfortunately, this infant perished the year he was born, in 1748. The following year they were blessed with their first daughter, whom they named Anne Beach (1749–1771) – further confusing the family tree, but they called her Nanny to distinguish her from her mother.

There was certainly joy at the birth of these children, but they also took a toll upon the body. The numerous pregnancies that were a part of married life came with real consequences to life and health and, even with access to the best medical personnel, fatal complications were not uncommon. Women's writing on the subject often highlights the perils, fears, and costs of repeated pregnancies, speaking of ill health, exhaustion, and other physical consequences.[74] Anne's sister-in-law, Jane Talbot, in her congratulations on the birth of another child, wrote to her brother on February 28, 1754, about her own struggle to regain her strength after childbirth. She lamented the length of her recovery and expressed hope that Anne would not suffer as she had, although she was cheered at her returning strength, writing, "I thank God I begin now to get a little strength & can walk across my room but not up or down stairs." Jane also expressed her happiness at Mrs. Beach's giving birth, stating:

> I have this morning recd ... the agreeable news of my dr sister being safely brought to bed with a daughter I beg you both will accept of my sincere congratulations.... Pray my love to Mrs Beach & Master & Miss Beach not forgetting the little stranger.[75]

Sadly, these happy times were short-lived, as the three children that followed Anne died – including young Jane, the subject of this letter.

The deaths, one after the next, of Frances Beach (born and died 1752), Jane Beach (born and died 1754) and Thomas Harding Beach (born and died 1758), may explain Mrs. Beach's attachment to her youngest child, born in 1760, Henrietta Maria Beach (1760–1837, later Henrietta Maria Hicks-Beach).[76] Her "dearest Henny" received every attention, and the anxious parents even took the child to the spa town of Bath in the first year of her life to ensure her well-being. A letter to Mrs. Beach from Jane rejoiced in the baby's health, stating, "dear little Henny

---

74 Katherine Glover, *Elite Women and Polite Society in Eighteenth-Century Scotland* (Boydell Press, 2011), 22; Porter, *English Society in the Eighteenth Century*, 27.

75 "Jane Talbot in Bath to William Beach at Fittleton 28 Feb. [1754]," private collection.

76 Administrative history, Beach Family of Fittleton, Keevil, and Netheravon, Gloucestershire Archives, UK.

FIGURE 4. Map of Steeple Ashton and Keevil. ("Keevil and Steeple Ashton," Plate No. 10, *Andrews' and Dury's Map of Wiltshire, 1773: A Reduced Facsimile*, ed. Elizabeth Crittall [1952] [The Wiltshire Record Society, 1952]. Image courtesy of the Wilshire and Swindon History Centre.)

is perfectly so & much improved by change of air."[77] The Beach family letters that have survived show a deep preoccupation with Henny's health, but there are very few mentions of Billy and Anne or of concerns for their health in the correspondence.[78] Their father even singled out his youngest daughter in his letters to his wife, while lumping the elder two together, "Love to Henny & dear children give them a kiss apiece with my love."[79]

William Beach of Netheravon settled into gentry life, splitting his time between his estate in Fittleton and the Manor House in Keevil, about five miles to the east of Trowbridge and next to the village of Steeple Ashton. The Beach Family had acquired the Keevil estate in 1680 from Thomas Lambert, but the house was already a century old by that point, having been built around 1580. The three-story stone building had four windows across the front façade and three windows on the sides. The symmetrical four-gable design was interrupted in 1611 when the center of the front façade acquired a two-story porch courtesy of Edward Lambert, who had his initials and the date of construction inscribed.[80] This porch connected to a front bedroom and was decorated with Tuscan columns, had a large front window and two small trefoil side windows that were repurposed from an earlier construction, and the whole was decorated with shell-headed niches.

---

77 "Jane Talbot at Lacock [1760–1] To [Mrs.] Beach at Mr. Hortons in Westgate Street, Bath," private collection.

78 This could simply be a result of the letters that survive, or an artifact of the differences in age as high infant mortality would necessitate vigilance for young children. It could also be the result of the intentional wiping of the archive, or an actual indication of familial sentiment.

79 "William Beach to Anne Wither, Wednesday night," D2455/F2/5/1/10, Gloucestershire Archives, UK.

80 Rev. A.T. Richardson, *Annals of Keevil and Bulkington*, Add MS 42048, British Library; Hicks, *A Cotswold Family*, 296; Victor and Marjory Manning, "Anne Beach – A Keevil Tragedy," in *A Book of Keevil*, Vol. 2 (The Keevil Society, 1998), 7; "Keevil," in *A History of the County of Wiltshire: Vol. 8, Warminster, Westbury and Whorwellsdown Hundreds* (London, 1965), 250–63.

From the large center window of the porch, the family could see an archway, built around the same time, and similarly appointed with shell-headed niches.[81] The house was extensively remodeled c. 1625, and the inside was richly decorated with dark carved oak paneling and plaster ceilings with geometrical designs. The outside was equally remarkable, as the garden was distinguished by large topiaries dubbed the Twelve Apostles. These yew trees had been styled after a chess pieces, approximating the shape of the pawn.[82] These sorts of formal gardens were popular during the seventeenth and early eighteenth centuries, not just for their aesthetics or for adding a majesty to formal country homes, but they were also thought to enhance status by demonstrating the personal authority of the family to the local community.[83]

William Beach of Netheravon and his father, Thomas, continued to manage their lands and acquire new properties, while discharging their duties as land-owners and men of standing in the community.[84] The 1730s brought changes to the Beach family, when Andrew's widow remarried. After her husband's death in 1734, Mary Beach left the bustle of London and took refuge in the quiet of Wiltshire, returning to the bosom of Andrew's family. Mary Beach did not stay single long; her marital prospects improved the year after her return, when an eligible bachelor moved into the neighborhood. On August 7, 1735, a new vicar, Richard Wainhouse, was appointed to serve at St. Leonard's Church in Keevil, just a short walk from the front door of the Manor House. Although there is no record of their courtship, the strong-willed Yorkshireman evidently appealed to Mary, and the two married with the approval and support of both Thomas and William Beach. They wed in Richard's church on December 16, 1736, and a year later welcomed a son they named William. Mary would also give birth to another son, named Richard, after his father.[85] Though she remarried, the Beach and Wainhouse families remained close throughout Mary's life.

---

81 Pevsner, *The Buildings of England: Wiltshire*, 278; "Keevil," in *A History of the County of Wiltshire*, 250–63.

82 Andor Gomme and Alison Maguire, *Design and Plan in the Country House: From Castle Donjons to Palladian Boxes* (Yale University Press, 2008), 206–7; Pevsner, *The Buildings of England*, 278; "Keevil," in *A History of the County of Wiltshire*, 250–63; *A Book of Keevil*, Vol. 3 (Wiltshire: The Keevil Society, 2001), 64–5.

83 Julian Hoppit, *A Land of Liberty? England 1689–1727* (Oxford University Press, 2000, reprint 2010), 368, 373.

84 They even controlled the lease for Angel Inn in New Sarum. This "commodious large well-accustom'd House" had "very good Stabling, a handsome Garden, and all Manner of Conveniences." Classified ads, *London Evening Post* (London, England), June 5, 1731–June 8, 1731, Issue 550. Gale Document Number: Z2000632228.

85 Robert Forsyth Scott, ed. *Admissions to the College of St. John the Evangelist in the University of Cambridge*, Part III, July 1715–November 1767 (Printed for the College at Cambridge University Press, sold by Deighton Bell and Co., 1903), 326; "Marriage Records," *Wiltshire, England,*

FIGURE 5. Manor House, Keevil. *Top*: View of seventeenth-century garden entrance with shell-headed niches in front of Keevil Manor. *Bottom*: Side view of Keevil Manor showing the Twelve Apostles and the two-story porch added in 1611 (photographs by author).

The Beach family was disrupted yet again in 1752 when the patriarch, Thomas Beach, took ill. In August, James Harding received the following account of his brother-in-law:

> I am sorry to acquaint you that Mr. Beach is in a very declining way, he was last Wednesday night taken in another fit & that worse than the former, the Physician says, another plunge may carry him off. I hope for the best for a better man never existed, or can ever tread on English Ground, but we must all submit to the divine Will.[86]

These fits were severe enough to warrant a visit from a medical professional, although the use of the term *physician* does not necessarily denote a trained and licensed doctor but could also refer to others within the medical marketplace. For instance, since 1704 apothecaries (pharmacists) had the legal right to dispense medical advice as well as medicine, and by the 1730s many began to adopt the sobriquet of "doctor," taking on the task of treating patients without physician oversight.[87]

It is likely Thomas was treated in the home first, as was common in the eighteenth century. As historian Elaine Leong has argued, "householders were not only quick to combine self-diagnosis and self-treatment with commercially available medical care but many also produced their own homemade medicines."[88] Family recipe books from the period are littered with formulas for curing sore throats, gout, consumption, and ague, and some even purported to defend against the plague. These medical prescriptions were often nestled next to recipes for cosmetics, calves' foot jelly, carrot pudding, spitchcock eels, potted venison, jams, and plumb cakes. For instance, a mid-eighteenth-century example from the Vernon Family has a wound and eye water next to directions for making stewed venison and "fried Chickens … Boiled in butter."[89] The Beach family recipe book has instructions for French rolls on the same page as a concoction to thicken the hair and one to treat consumption.[90]

Marriages, 1538–1837 [database online], Provo, UT: Ancestry.com Operations, Inc., 2013; "Christening Records," Reference Number: 653/5, *Wiltshire, England, Church of England Baptisms, Marriages and Burials, 1538–1812* [database online], Lehi, UT: Ancestry.com Operations, Inc., 2017.

86 "Thomas Talbot at Keevil to James Harding Esqr at Mere 11 August 1752," private collection.

87 T.D. Whittet, "Apothecaries and their Lodgers: Their Part in the Development of the Sciences and Medicine," *Journal of the Royal Society of Medicine Supplement* 76, no. 2 (1983), 1; Geoffrey Holmes, *Augustan England: Professions, State and Society, 1680–1730* (George Allen & Unwin, 1982), 168.

88 Elaine Leong, "Collecting Knowledge for the Family: Recipes, Gender and Practical Knowledge in the Early Modern Household," *Centaurus* 55, no. 2 (2013): 81–103, 82.

89 Vernon family recipe book, mid-eighteenth century, private collection.

90 Beach family recipe book, D2455/F2/5/3/5, Gloucestershire Archives, UK.

As historian Ann Hobart has argued, recipe collections "could have provided a basis for much self-help in early modern household healthcare."[91] These often took the form of handwritten assemblages gathered from friends and even culled from the growing number of printed sources offering practical medical advice and concoctions for home use. Recipes were traded between family members and friends and even handed down from generation to generation or given as gifts.[92] The Beach family's recipe books certainly illustrate friendships and familial relationships. For instance, it contains offerings from Mrs. Wainhouse (the former Mary Beach) alongside those from family members like "My Coz. Wither," "Cousin Eliza Beach," "My Coz Wansbrough," and "my Aunt Wither." Friends, notables, and physicians were also represented. The book contains recipes like "The Duke of Norfolk's Punch," "Dr. Nichols Receipt for Burn, Scald or Inflammation," "Dr. Halsey's Receipt for a Strain," and "Dr. Savery's Rect for the pain in ye Stomach." Tucked into the recipe book there were examples cut from printed sources, including "Directions for Taking the Convulsion Lozenges" and "An Excellent RECIPIE for preventing the dreadful Consequences arising from the BITE of a MAD DOG."[93] There were also recipes that may have proven useful in Thomas's case, including one for Fitt Drops.[94] Once things progressed beyond the capabilities of family remedies and the skill of locals, the next step would be to send to another town for assistance.[95]

People in the rural countryside had a number of options when it came to treating disease, taking advantage of the medical marketplace – and not just to purchase nostrums for self-dosing.[96] Wiltshire's proximity to the spa town of Bath

---

91 Ann Hobart, *Household Medicine in Seventeenth-Century England* (Bloomsbury, 2016), 29. Similarly, Elaine Leong has argued that "[r]ecipes, both medical and culinary, were the main medium for the recording and transmission of information and knowledge in pre-modern households." Leong, "Collecting Knowledge for the Family," 83.

92 Hobart, *Household Medicine in Seventeenth-Century England*, 30.

93 "*Beach Family Recipe Book*," D2455/ F2/2/3 and D2455/ F2/2/4, Gloucestershire Archives, UK.

94 "Take one Large Spoonfull of the Glaz'd Wood Soot, one Large Spoonful of new Laid egg shell both finely Beat, Half an Ounce of Assafatida sliced thin, a little Saffron, a few Anniseeds & Corriander Seeds little Bruised, put all these ingredients into a Quart of the best Brandy and let it stand Ten Days shaking the Bottle well ev'ry Day then pour of the Clear from the ingredients and Bottle it for Use keep it close Stop'd & it will keep a great while you are to put as much of each sort of the seeds as will Lay on a Crown piece and as much Saffron as will Colour the Brandy of a Bright yellow." "The Fitt Drops Mrs. Beach," in the Beach family recipe book, D2455/ F2/2/4, Gloucestershire Archives, UK.

95 Mark S.R. Jenner and Patrick Wallis, eds., *Medicine and the Market in England and its Colonies, c. 1450–c. 1850* (Palgrave Macmillan, 2007), 76.

96 For more information on the medical marketplace, see Harold. J. Cook, *The Decline of the Old Medical Regime in Stuart London* (Cornell University Press, 1986); Harold J. Cook, *Trials of an Ordinary Doctor: Joannes Groenevelt in Seventeenth-Century London* (Johns Hopkins University Press, 1994); Anne Digby, *Making a Medical Living: Doctors and Patients in the Market for*

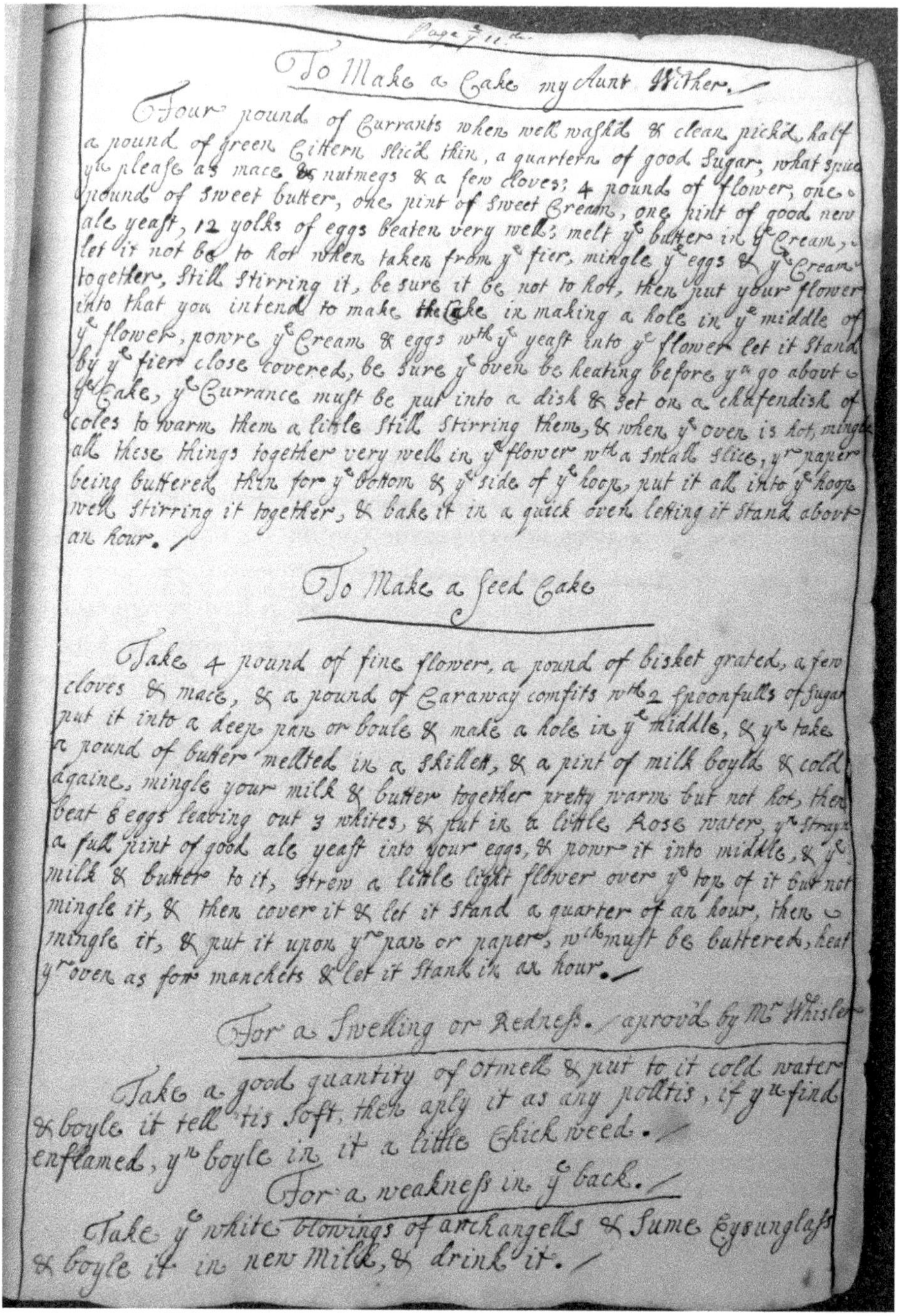

Page y 11th

To Make a Cake my Aunt Wither.

Four pound of Currants when well washd & clean pickd, half
a pound of green Cittern slic'd thin, a quartern of good Sugar, what spice
yu please as mace & nutmegs & a few cloves; 4 pound of flower, one
pound of sweet butter, one pint of sweet Cream, one pint of good new
ale yeast, 12 yolks of eggs beaten very well; melt ye butter in ye Cream,
let it not be to hot when taken from ye fier, mingle ye eggs & ye Cream
together, still stirring it, be sure it be not to hot, then put your flower
into that you intend to make the Cake in making a hole in ye middle of
ye flower, powre ye Cream & eggs wth ye yeast into ye flower let it stand
by ye fier close covered, be sure ye oven be heating before yu go about
ye Cake, ye Currance must be put into a dish & set on a chafendish of
coles to warm them a little still stirring them, & when ye oven is hot, mingle
all these things together very well in ye flower wth a small slice, yr paper
being buttered thin for ye bottom & ye side of ye hoop, put it all into ye hoop
well stirring it together, & bake it in a quick oven letting it stand about
an hour.

To Make a Seed Cake

Take 4 pound of fine flower, a pound of bisket grated, a few
cloves & mace, & a pound of Caraway comfits wth 2 spoonfulls of sugar
put it into a deep pan or boule & make a hole in ye middle, & yn take
a pound of butter melted in a skillet, & a pint of milk boyld & cold
againe, mingle your milk & butter together pretty warm but not hot, then
beat 8 eggs leaving out 3 whites, & put in a little Rose water, yn strain
a full pint of good ale yeast into your eggs, & powr it into middle, & ye
milk & butter to it, strew a little light flower over ye top of it but not
mingle it, & then cover it & let it stand a quarter of an hour, then
mingle it, & put it upon yr pan or paper, wch must be buttered, heat
yr oven as for manchets & let it stank in an hour.

For a Swelling or Redness. aprov'd by Mr Whisler

Take a good quantity of otmell & put to it cold water
& boyle it tell 'tis soft, then aply it as any poltis, if yu find
enflamed, yn boyle in it a little Chick weed.

For a weakness in ye back.

Take ye white blowings of archangells & Sume Eysunglass
& boyle it in new Milk, & drink it.

FIGURE 6. Page from the Beach family recipe book. (D2455/F2/2/4, Gloucestershire Archives,
UK. Image courtesy of the Gloucestershire Archives, UK.)

vastly increased the options available to the Beaches, as apothecaries and trained physicians were drawn to the town by the potential client base. Thankfully, those in search of assistance would not need to travel as far as Bath, because the market towns and larger villages also drew medical practitioners. The Beaches turned to the market town of Devizes, which lay approximately twenty kilometers northeast of Fittleton, along the main road that ran along the west bank of the Avon River.[97] From Devizes, they employed apothecaries John Richards and Richard Griffiths, who had an established practice, even taking on apprentices like Jordon Hatt in 1754; Hatt paid £8 for training that lasted for a period of eight years.[98] Richards and Griffiths not only sent medicines but also made twenty-five separate trips to see Thomas between October 4, 1752, and February 27, 1753 (charging five shillings per visit).[99] The prescriptions provide an indication that they were seriously concerned about the patient's stomach, fluid buildup, and heart. Initially, in October 1752, the apothecaries sent eight prescriptions based on the information they had received, whether from the patient himself or family members, but did not make their first visit until the following month.[100]

These treatments drew on the contemporary understanding of the body and disease, one steeped in the humoral approach to illness. Humoralism was a pervasive medical system that viewed illness as the inevitable result of a disruption, or imbalance, in the humors – either in a single part of the body or in the person as a whole. The theory held that the combination of the humors (blood, yellow bile, mucus, and black bile), as well as environmental concerns such as cold, damp, dryness, and warmth, provided a barometer by which the health of an individual could be measured, quantified, and adjusted. This complexion of humors was unique to each individual and a lack of balance in any one of them could lead

---

Medicine, 1720–1914 (Cambridge University Press, 1994); Mary E. Fissell, Patients, Power and the Poor in Eighteenth-Century Bristol (Cambridge University Press, 1991); Jenner and Wallis, eds., Medicine and the Market; Margaret Pelling, Medical Conflicts in Early Modern London: Patronage, Physicians and Irregular Practitioners 1550–1640 (Oxford University Press, 2003); Charles Webster and Margaret Pelling, "Medical Practitioners," in Health, Medicine and Mortality in the Sixteenth Century, ed. Charles Webster (Cambridge University Press 1979).

97 Dorothy Porter and Roy Porter, Patient's Progress: Doctors and Doctoring in Eighteenth-Century England (Stanford University Press, 1989), 18–19; A.P. Baggs, Elizabeth Crittall, Jane Freeman, and Janet H. Stevenson, "Parishes: Fittleton," in A History of the County of Wiltshire: Vol. 11, Downton Hundred; Elstub and Everleigh Hundred, ed. D.A. Crowley (Victoria County History, 1980), 142–51.

98 "Indenture for Hatt Jordan to John Richards, 21 September 1754," UK, Register of Duties Paid for Apprentices' Indentures, 1710–1811 [database online], Provo, UT: Ancestry.com Operations, Inc.; Christabel Dale, ed. Wiltshire Apprentices and Their Masters 1710–1760 (Devizes, 1961), 85.

99 "Bill from J. Richards & R. Griffiths Apoth., 20 March 1753," Misc. Receipts, D2455/E3/2/4/3, Gloucestershire Archives, UK.

100 For more on the practice of diagnosis by letter, see Wayne Wild, Medicine-by-Post: The Changing Voice of Illness in Eighteenth-Century Consultation Letter and Literature (Rodopi, 2006).

to disease. As a scheme, it emphasized the harmony and unity of the body and elevated the importance of the relationship between the physical and the mental. Health was tenuous and easily overset, meaning physicians had to account for complex and myriad factors (both internal and external) in treating illness.[101]

It was within this framework that the family understood Thomas's affliction and from which Richards and Griffiths derived their treatments. The apothecaries provided an aggressive combination of therapies that grew in frequency and scope as the illness progressed. Thomas was treated with laxatives, and sweet iced cakes (called savoy biscuits) were sent to tempt his appetite; however, the majority of their prescriptions were substances with diuretic properties.[102] Early in Thomas's illness, Richards and Griffiths relied heavily on Pyrmont water, a carbonated mineral water with "a subtile acrid, sulpherous spirit" but not a "sulphurous smell."[103] It was thought to cause the body to release its fluids through evacuation and sweating. *A Treatise on the Nature, Properties and Medicinal Uses of the Waters of Pyrmont, Spa, and Seltzers* stated that "[a]ll physicians agree, that this water … commonly proves diuretic, frequently sudorific, even to such as otherwise sweat with difficulty." The water was thought effective in correcting "all disorders of the Stomach and Bowels" and was also believed to dissolve "all obstructions of the Lungs, Kidneys, and small Vessels" and prevent "the fresh accumulation of bad humours."[104] The Pyrmont water was not without side effects and was purported to cause the stool to blacken and the skin to break out.[105] Concern over Thomas's stomach and bowels lessened, as Pyrmont water was only prescribed for the first two months, and afterwards attention turned to his heart, with consistent prescriptions of "cardiac boluses." For instance, in December he was given forty cardiac boluses over a total of seven days. All in all, cardiac juleps and boluses accounted for 35 percent of all the treatments prescribed by the apothecaries.[106]

---

101 Vivian Nutton, "Humoralism," in *Companion Encyclopedia of the History of Medicine*, Vol. 1, eds. W.F. Bynum and Roy Porter (Routledge, 1993), 281–2.

102 "To Make Savoy Biscuits. Take eight eggs, part the yolks from the whites, beat your whites till they be very high; then put your yolks in with a pound of sugar; beat that for a quarter of an hour, and when your oven is ready, put in one pound of fine flour, and just stir it, till 'tis well mixt; lay your biscuits upon the paper, and ice them, which will be infallibly effectual: only take care your oven be hot enough to bake them speedily." See Charles Carter, *The London and Country Cook or Accomplished Housewife*, 3rd ed. (Charles Hitch, 1749), 49. Other recipes can be found in works like *The Compleat Confectioner; or the Art of Candying and Preserving*, 3rd ed. (R. Montagu, 1742).

103 John George Keysler, *Travels Through Germany, Bohemia, Hungary, Switzerland, Italy and Lorrain*, Vol. II, 2nd ed. (A. Linde, 1757), 440.

104 *A Treatise on the Nature, Properties and Medicinal Uses of the Waters of Pyrmont, Spa, and Seltzers* (W. Owen, 1762), 6–7.

105 *A Treatise on the Nature*, 6.

106 Dr. Thomas Willis defined boluses and juleps in the following manner: "Bolus is a medicine made up into a thick substance to be swallow'd, not liquid, but taken on a Knives point," and "Julap, A

Even more interesting was the heavy use of viper wine for Thomas's illness – approximately 23 percent of the treatments were concoctions containing viper flesh.[107] These were prescribed in heavy doses from the beginning and continued for the entirety of his illness. John Quincy's 1739 *Pharmacopoeia Officinalis & Extemporanea, or a Complete English Dispensatory* provides the following recipe for the restorative viper wine:

> Take live Female Vipers in the Spring-time, No 6; put them alive into 6 pounds of Canary, and let them stand close stopt without any Heat for six months. This ... will occasion the whole substance of the vipers to be almost taken up by the wine, which must be strain'd off thro' a thick Flannel, or filter'd for Use; it is a wonderful Restorative, and greatly invigorates the whole Constitution.[108]

Richard Brookes's *The General Practice of Physic* stated that viper flesh was "a strong diuretic."[109] There were numerous recipes for viper wine and discussions over whether or not live or dried vipers were best. The gender of the vipers was also important in some preparations.[110] *Pharmacopoeia Universalis* acknowledged the debate, stating, "There has been some dispute whether living or dryt'd Vipers are best for Viper wine, or whether a cold or hot infusion is preferable" but it determined that there was very little difference in the efficacy.[111] Viper wine was considered an important tonic, one that could be purchased or made, to be kept on hand in the medicine chest, a conviction that even lasted into the nineteenth century when *The Family Herbal* recommended viper wine as one of those "tinctures and wines that need to be kept in

---

cooling Cordial, or a mixed Potion to cool and refresh the heated spirits, used in Fevers." See "A Table of all the hard words derived from the Greek and Latin, of all Terms of Art and other words not vulgarly received, with the explanation of them," in *The Remaining Medical Works of that Famous and Renowned Physician Dr. Thomas Willis*, English by S.P. [Samuel Pordage] (T. Dring, C. Harper, J. Leigh, and S. Martyn, 1681), 108, 112.

107 "Misc. Receipts," D2455/E3/2/4/3, Gloucestershire Archives, UK.

108 John Quincy, *Pharmacopoeia Officinalis & Extemporanea, or a Complete English Dispensatory* (Thomas Longman, 1739), 562.

109 Richard Brookes, *The General Practice of Physic*, Vol. II, 5th ed. (J. Newberry, 1765), 153.

110 Edward Strother's 1727 *Materia Medica* describes the poisonous snakes in question, stating "Vipers – Whether Male or Female, are serpents of a cubit in Length, of a yellowish, palish red colour on the upper part, and speckled greenish." Edward Strother, *Materia Medica: Or a New Description on the Virtues and Effects of All Drugs, or Simple Medicines*, Vol. II (Charles Rivington, 1727), 153.

111 R. James, *Pharmacopoeia Universalis, or A New Universal English Dispensatory* (J. Hodges, 1747), 686.

a family."[112] This may explain the shipment of "6 Vipers sent to Fiddleton [sic]" sixteen days after Thomas's funeral.[113]

William Beach of Netheravon was at his father's side during this trying time, writing to his wife, Anne: "My Father is so very ill we don't expect he can hold above two or three days which makes me unwilling to be from here tho I wish my self home with you."[114] Unfortunately, Thomas succumbed to his illness and was buried on March 5, 1753.[115] His death elevated the status of his son, making him an independent man of means in gentry society, a trend he continued in November 1753 when he gained the title of Esquire and became a member of Gray's Inn.[116] In 1760, William increased his family's holdings when he purchased Netheravon House, just a mile from his Fittleton estate.[117] In the decade that followed, the family continued to split most of their time between Fittleton and Keevil Manor, which, by 1762, had been vacated by his aunts Dorothy, Joan, and Sophia. William even went so far as to purchase close to £20 worth of household goods from these ladies to furnish the home.[118] The time spent at Keevil also permitted a rekindling of the relationship with the Wainhouses.

❊ ❊ ❊ ❊ ❊

I am always amazed when things come full circle. My search for Princess Amelia brought me to Anne Beach and my search to uncover this tragic story led me right back to Princess Amelia. When I was kindly allowed access to the Manor House and met the proprietor, I was chatting about my work and as I hobbled up the stairs

---

112 John Hill, *The Family Herbal, or an Account of All Those English Plants, Which Are Remarkable for Their Virtues, and of the Drugs Which Are Produced by Vegetables of Other Countries, with Their Descriptions and Their Uses, as Proved by Experience: by Sir John Hill* (C. Brightly and Co./ T. Kinnersley, 1812), *Nineteenth Century Collections Online*, Gale Document Number: GALE| BMUYUR373151124, 27.

113 "Misc. Receipts," D2455/E3/2/4/3, Gloucestershire Archives, UK.

114 "William Beach to Anne Wither," D2455/F2/5/1/10, Gloucestershire Archives, UK.

115 "Burials," Reference Number: 653/5 Source Information: Ancestry.com, *Wiltshire, England, Church of England Baptisms, Marriages and Burials, 1538–1812* [database online], Lehi, UT: Ancestry.com Operations, Inc., 2017.

116 Ralph Houlbrooke, *Death, Ritual, and Bereavement* (Routledge, 1989), 33; Kristen Olsen, *Daily Life in 18th-Century England* (Greenwood Press, 1999), 275; "Misc. Receipts," D2455/E3/2/4/3, Gloucestershire Archives, UK; Ralph Houlbrooke, *Death, Religion, and the Family in England, 1480–1750* (Oxford: Clarendon Press, 2000), 292; Joseph Foster, *The Register of Admissions to Gray's Inn 1521–1889* (privately printed, 1889), 379.

117 There are conflicting accounts; the estate of Netheravon was sold either in 1758 or in 1760. Hicks, *A Cotswold Family*, 300.

118 "Septm ye 29 1762 – recvd of my cousin Beach my share of ye household goods he bought of us when we left Keevill – £19 11s 2d," Misc. receipts Dorothy, Jane, and Sophia Beach, D2455/F2/4/2/3, Gloucestershire Archives, UK.

behind her, I mentioned my other project. I was surprised when she responded, "I have a portrait of Princess Amelia." It seemed odd, but it turns out the family that had purchased the house in the early twentieth century had been well connected in the Court of King George III and Queen Charlotte. We moved to examine the room above the porch, where I had to do some quick thinking to figure out the dimensions. I ended up photographing my overlapping crutches, which I later lined back up and measured. Necessity is the mother of invention, and I sometimes think I need to create a "historian kit," one that has more than the things I need for taking notes and photographing. I usually bring a measuring tape when I know I will be looking at historic clothing, but not when I go to other places. It just didn't cross my mind that I might want to measure the room until I was standing in the tiny space imagining poor Anne. Like many other things about this project, I have once again changed my approach and now I always keep a measuring tape in the stuff I take to libraries and archives. You just never know when understanding the materiality of an object, book, or space will enhance your understanding of the history you are investigating. After we finished in the room, I assumed she would escort us to the front door, but instead she took us to the stairs again, where there were empty rooms along the hall with windows overlooking the grounds. When we reached the third doorway, we walked in, and I saw a yellow floral bedsheet draped over something against the wall. The owner carefully removed the cover, and I was stunned. In this otherwise empty room, under a sheet being used as a dust cover, were four eighteenth-century pastel portraits! One of George, Prince of Wales (eldest son of King George III, who later became King George IV); one of his secret Catholic wife Maria FitzHerbert (that was also a whole secret marriage mess); one of Frederick, Duke of York (second son of George III), and then the elusive Princess Amelia portrait. This one was different from the others, and not just because it had fallen in the frame, so was only partially visible behind the glass. I stood there in shock. The name plate on the frame clearly said Princess Amelia, but I was in disbelief. It felt like this was the Beach family problem all over again. My Amelia had been named for her father's sister, also called Princess Amelia ... surely this was the elder woman? But the elder Amelia had died in 1786, and the Prince of Wales's portrait was a copy of one painted in 1787. The delicate face in the painting was young, and George III's daughter was only twenty-seven when she died and would have been a teenager when this portrait was painted. There are many portraits of her as a teenager – so why, you might ask, would I not take it at face value, especially since it was with the portraits of her brother? Why was I shocked? The reason was her clothing, or lack thereof. It was missing – okay, not really – but there was more than a wardrobe malfunction happening on that canvas. Her breasts were completely exposed, nipples as well, not just a little peek but they were front and center on full display, framed by a wispy ruffle. I knew this sometimes happened with portraits exchanged between lovers, but this sitter was young, and this portrait was in the hands of possible court friends, but not ones known to be close to Princess Amelia. Was this naked Amelia in fact my Amelia? If so, what was happening with this portrait? How did it end up in this place? Now I have yet another mystery to unravel! Anne Beach and Princess Amelia were not just connected by their tragic early deaths from consumption, but also by a stroke of luck and a weird archival synergy that kept bringing me back to both women at the same time.

CHAPTER TWO

Marriage

William Wainhouse

Mary and Richard Wainhouse remained in Keevil with their two sons, and they were frequent callers to the Beaches' house while the maiden aunts resided there, living "on the most friendly terms."[1] Although nine years older than the Beaches' son, Billy, and eleven years older than Anne, it is likely the children interacted, as William Wainhouse had been a visitor to their home since his infancy.[2] Life in Keevil, however, was not always quiet or without controversy. The village certainly had its share of characters, particularly Thomas Gilbert and his son George. These men had taken an intense dislike to Reverend Richard Wainhouse. The clergyman had apparently drawn their ire early in the 1740s when the Gilberts began a smear campaign, posting anonymous notes around the village with nasty comments about their minister. In 1741, Richard claims, they had posted a sign saying "scurrilous Things" and calling him "the <u>little Levite</u>."[3]

Wainhouse was plainly afraid of the Gilberts, fearing they would "do me or my Family some mischief tho ... I never did any Thing to injure or affront either of them in my Life." The Reverend was convinced their hatred stemmed from his attempts "to confirm my parishioners in their allegiance."[4] The allegiance mentioned was to both the church and the Crown. Wainhouse had a reputation for

---

1 *Narrative*, folio 5.
2 *Narrative*, folio 6.
3 "Reverend Richard Wainhouse to the Secretary of State, 25 November 1745," SP 36/75, *The State Papers*, National Archives, UK.
4 "Reverend Richard Wainhouse to the Secretary of State, 25 November 1745," SP 36/75.

preaching against Catholicism, something he continued throughout his life, even publishing a sermon in 1755 in which he claimed, "The God of the Papists may be eaten by a Mouse; [and] that the Doctrine of Transubstantiation is the most absurd, ridiculous, stupid, and impious Tenet that was ever maintain'd in the World."[5] The Gilberts' reaction to the anti-Catholic rhetoric came at a particularly precarious time – there was a serious Jacobite uprising in 1745 that threatened the stability of the state.[6]

In 1701, the royal succession had been settled upon the Protestant descendants of Sophia, Electress of Hanover, to prevent the return of the exiled Catholic Stuarts, who had been removed from the English throne in 1688.[7] This led to the establishment in 1714 of the Hanoverian dynasty after the death of Queen Anne, who, despite seventeen pregnancies, had no children who survived to adulthood. There had been unsuccessful Jacobite uprisings in the early part of the century, but in 1745 a far more serious threat emerged in the form of Charles Edward Stuart, the grandson of James II. The handsome Bonnie Prince Charlie was in his early twenties and although blessed with charm, he was less well-endowed in the in the intelligence department. He landed in Scotland with a small contingent in July 1745 and quickly took advantage of a bump in his numbers from members of the Scottish Highland clans. His cause was also aided by the fact that Britain was embroiled in the War of the Austrian Succession (1740–1748) and their experienced troops were busy fighting on the European continent. Charles was able to defeat the British at the Battle of Prestonpans in September 1745, and the day before the battle, he wrote his father:[8]

> Sir, since my landing everything has succeeded to meet my wishes, it has pleased God to prosper me hitherto even beyond my expectation, I have got together about 3000 (and am promised more), brave and determined men who are resolved to die or conquer with me.[9]

The Jacobites followed this victory by moving into England. By November 1745, when Richard Wainhouse was reporting the troublesome Gilberts, England

---

5 Richard Wainhouse, "Proposals for Printing by Subscription A SERMON Preach'd in the Abbey-Church, Bath November 5, 1755," 0557, Bath & Northeast Somerset Record Office, UK.

6 The Jacobites were followers of the exiled Stuarts.

7 James II and his descendants.

8 Thomas William Heyck, *The Peoples of the British Isles: A New History, From 1688–1870* (Lyceum, 2002), 36, 110–12. For more on the '45 see Jacqueline Riding, *A New History of the '45 Rebellion* (Bloomsbury, 2016).

9 "Charles Edward Stuart at Perth to his father James Stuart, 20 September 1745," SP 54/26/32, National Archives, UK.

had been invaded by the "rebels" who were marching south. In December, they reached Derby, approximately 130 miles from London, before they lost their nerve and retreated north, eventually being defeated in a complete rout in April 1746 at the Battle of Culloden.[10]

The Jacobite uprising was a precarious time for the Hanoverian monarchy, and Wiltshire did not escape the preparations or fear, as the uprising provoked an anti-Catholic panic.[11] In Exeter, Bristol, and neighboring Gloucestershire troops were raised, while the lord-lieutenant of Dorset saw to the defense of the coast. Though things were mostly quiet in the county, a few occurrences sparked alarm. For instance, in Salisbury in October 1745 there was reportedly a mysterious man thought to be "some Priest or Spie."[12] This tense climate provided Richard Wainhouse an opportunity to rid Keevil of the persistent thorns in his side.

The clergy played a central role, both spiritually and socially, in the eighteenth century. They were responsible for not only ministering to souls by officiating burials, weddings, and baptisms but among their duties they also tended to the mechanics of parish life, functioning as landlords – collecting tithes, rents, and offerings – as well as supervising charity.[13] Beyond their local religious role, eighteenth-century clergy also played an administrative role, providing the main link between the population and the government, with the responsibility for reading proclamations and participating in the ecclesiastical courts, which oversaw cases related to defamation. They also increasingly took on a governmental role, providing oversight of the poor law, sitting as justices of the peace and in mediating disputes; however, Richard Wainhouse's actions in Keevil extended beyond his clerical responsibilities and verged on the personal.[14]

It is not clear whether the Gilberts' behavior was personal or religious, but in November 1745 the pair apparently decided to needle the vicar again. Wainhouse was convinced they were responsible, despite admitting "I can get no direct proof of their being so."[15] He reported the men to Secretary of State Thomas Pelham-Holles, Duke of Newcastle, suggesting they were a menace that needed to be

---

10 Heyck, *The Peoples of the British Isles*, 112.

11 Colin Haydon, *Anti-Catholicism in Eighteenth-century England, c. 1714–80: A Political and Social Study* (Manchester University Press, 1993), 260.

12 J. Anthony Williams, *Catholic Recusancy in Wiltshire 1660–1791* (Catholic Record Society, 1968), 63–4.

13 W.M. Jacob, *The Clerical Profession in the Long Eighteenth Century, 1680–1840* (Oxford University Press, 2007), 2, 9–10.

14 Jacob, *The Clerical Profession*, 10.

15 "Reverend Richard Wainhouse to the Secretary of State, 25 November 1745," SP 36/75, *The State Papers*, National Archives, UK.

curtailed, particularly during this period of uncertainty. He wrote that the inhabitants of Keevil were as convinced as he was

> That ye Gilberts are ye disaffected persons here, & wish that they were secur'd, at least till our Troubles are over; For They all agree that they wou'd be ye first men to head a mob of Scriblers, Weavers, &c. Shd ye Rebels succeed wch God Forbid.[16]

Wainhouse then detailed a "treasonable paper & threatening Letter" that was tacked to the door of St. Leonard's Church. This had been followed by a second, similar letter left on the church porch, and then what he termed a "silly Paper" attached to the east end of the church. This was a drawing, ostensibly representing Wainhouse as a crudely drawn figure with horns and a shepherd's crook labeled "Bully Dick the Bullard." Although insulting, it was the rest of the sketch that caused concern. There was a picture of a bull and a dog with a scrawled threat stating "By the Popes Authority, This is to give notice, That the popes Bull will, Play his Old Dogs over agen [sic] to begin about, Ten a Clock this morning."[17] Although he called it treasonable due to its Catholic references, Wainhouse interpreted the document as wanting him to continue preaching about Catholicism, writing: "When he says that ye pope's Bull will play his old Dogs over again, I suppose he means that I shou'd proceed to preach against popery; for I have preached against the Errors of the Church of Rome, & ye unnatural rebellion (one Sunday excepted) ever since ye 15th of Sept."[18]

It seems that the furor over "the silly paper" did not end the feud, nor did Wainhouse's anti-Catholic and anti-Jacobite sermons. In December, he again wrote to Pelham-Holles, prompted perhaps by yet another paper – this one affixed to a post in Keevil. It once again devolved into a personal attack, but one the reverend felt was also aimed at the British Constitution, stating, "But surely ye author's design was to wound our Constitution, as he makes a Jest of my two discourses published in Defense of it."[19] The "discourses" published in 1745, *Two Sermons*

---

16 Wainhouse is also likely alluding to the uprising of Wiltshire weavers in 1738. "Reverend Richard Wainhouse to the Secretary of State, 25 November 1745," SP 36/75. For more information, see J. de L. Mann, "Clothiers and Weavers in Wiltshire during the Eighteenth Century," in L.S. Presnall, ed. *Studies in the Industrial Revolution* (Oxford University Press, 1960).

17 "Reverend Richard Wainhouse to the Secretary of State, 25 November 1745," SP 36/75.

18 "Reverend Richard Wainhouse to the Secretary of State, 25 November 1745," SP 36/75; J. Anthony Williams, "Catholicism and Jacobitism: Some Wiltshire Evidence," *The Dublin Review* 485 (Tablet Publishing Company, Ltd., 1960), 252.

19 "Reverend Richard Wainhouse to the Secretary of State, 21 December 1745," SP 36/77/2/169, *The State Papers*, National Archives, UK.

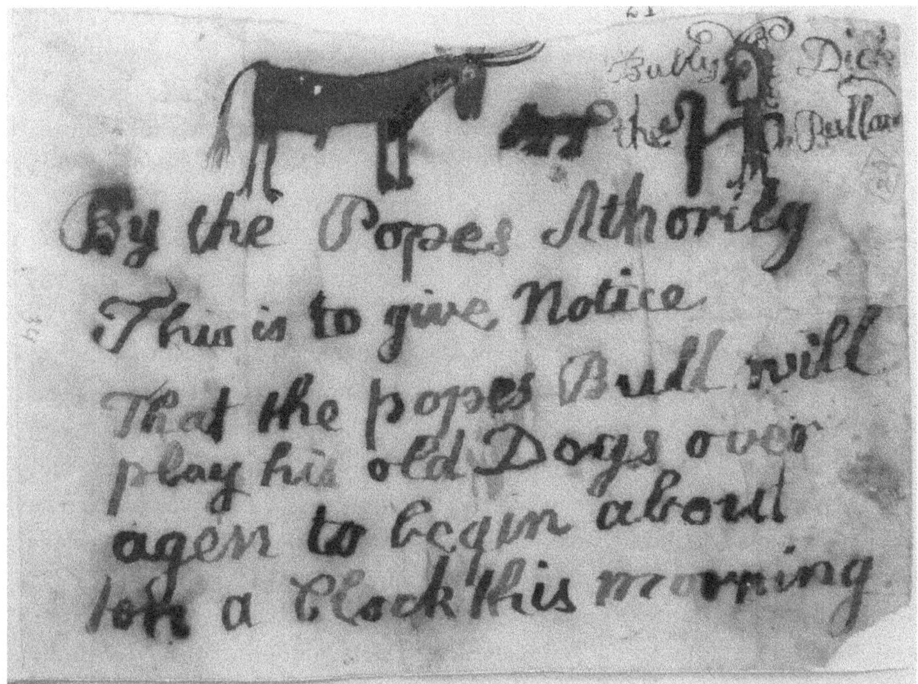

FIGURE 7. The silly paper (sent by Reverend Richard Wainhouse to Secretary of State Thomas Pelham-Holles, Duke of Newcastle). ("Reverend Richard Wainhouse to the Secretary of State, 25 November 1745," SP 36/75, *The State Papers*, The National Archives, UK. Image courtesy of The National Archives, UK.)

Preached in the Parish-Church of Keevil, Wiltshire (In September and October, 1745), laid out a case against the young Scottish Pretender (Bonnie Prince Charlie). In them, Wainhouse charged his fellow clergy members "to make the People committed to their Care sensible of the many Errors of the Papists" in light of the fact that "foreign Powers are making such Efforts in favour of a Popish Pretender, and consequently are for introducing Popish Superstition."[20]

This recounting of evidence against the Gilberts was accompanied by news of a possible witness to their perfidy. One of the parishioners said they had seen George Gilbert and William Garret standing by the east end of the church the morning the offensive papers were affixed to the door.[21] Garret, however, was

---

20 Richard Wainhouse, *Two Sermons Preached in the Parish-Church of Keevil, Wiltshire (In September and October, 1745) on the Occasion of the Rebellion in Scotland* (J. Jolliffe, 1745), 27.
21 Wainhouse, *Two Sermons Preached*, 27.

away serving in the Duke of Bolton's regiment, which had been raised in Hampshire late in 1745 to deal with the Jacobite threat.[22] Undaunted, Wainhouse wrote that if he "was severely threatened wth punishmt wou'd probably make a Discover of the author, or authors of ye seditious & treasonable papers."[23] This recommendation may have been motivated out of fear for his safety rather than personal vindication. The vicar characterized the Gilberts as "turbulent & cruel men," going so far as to compare them to the Jacobites and stating that they were "as savage as ye rebellious Highlanders"; this was particularly the case for "ye old Man," who possessed "a very black Character."[24]

Although it is not clear what happened to the Gilberts, it is clear that Richard Wainhouse was unwilling to tolerate attacks on his reputation, given that he raised this personal feud to the level of national threat. Reputation, as historian Faramerz Dabhoiwala has argued, was connected not only to the idea of an individual's character, but also to the ways in which they projected themselves publicly; as such, reputation was heavily tied to social status and often zealously guarded.[25] It was this environment and upbringing that helped forge the personalities of the vicar's sons, William and Richard. William Wainhouse (1738–1797) was raised in a household with a father who was not afraid to take on his detractors and to punish those who sullied his reputation – a lesson his son learned well and would emulate in his own career. William even admitted that he was "seldom mute" and although he had a warm personality, was "eager at Dispute."[26]

William also followed his father in other crucial ways, particularly in his choice of profession. This was not surprising given that much of the clergy came from the better-off "middling sort" of British society and in Wiltshire it was increasingly popular for the sons of clergymen to follow their fathers into the profession. By 1730, one-third of the clergy in that county came from clergy families. There was also a large increase in the number of those clergymen who styled themselves as gentry, with the number doubling from 1683 to 1730. As we have seen, *gentry* was a fluid category that lacked clear and distinct criteria.[27]

---

22 S. Boyse, *An Impartial History of the Late Rebellion in 1745 from Authentic Memoirs* (Edward and John Exshaw, 1748), 79; *Journals of the House of Commons*, Vol. 25, 12–13, 67; Stuart Reid, *Cumberland's Culloden Army, 1745–46* (Bloomsbury, 2012), 38.

23 "Reverend Richard Wainhouse to the Secretary of State, 21 December 1745," SP 36/77/2/169.

24 "Reverend Richard Wainhouse to the Secretary of State, 25 November 1745," SP 36/75.

25 Faramerz Dabhoiwala, "The Construction of Honor, Reputation and Status in Late Seventeenth- and Early Eighteenth-Century England," *Transactions of the Royal Historical Society* 6 (1996), 201. For more on reputation, see also Linda A. Pollock, "Honor, Gender, and Reconciliation in Elite Culture, 1570–1700," *Journal of British Studies* 46, no. 1 (2007).

26 "William Wainhouse, Verses on the Marriage of Miss Beach & Mr. Richardson, 20 November 1767," D2455/F2/5/3/3, Gloucestershire Archives, UK.

27 Jacob, *The Clerical Profession*, 39–41, 45.

Although William followed in his father's professional footsteps, he did diverge in his choice of university. Richard had attended St. John's College Cambridge; however, in 1755 his son went off to Queen's College, Oxford, matriculating at the age of sixteen. The universities funneled students into the clergy, and in the early eighteenth century 70 percent of the students graduating from Oxford went into that profession.[28] William received his BA in 1759, and the following year he was ordained as a deacon in the Chapel Royal at Whitehall by the Bishop of Salisbury.[29] William was lucky to already have an established clerical network, as newly ordained men tended to obtain their first jobs through their personal connections. Nine days after his ordination, on September 29, 1761, he took up a position as a curate in his father's parish. This sort of arrangement was common and would certainly have helped defray costs, as a clergyman living with his family minimized his expenses. William would not work for his father long, as Reverend Richard Wainhouse died in December 1761, just a few months after his son was ordained. Although a blow to the family, the Reverend's death did not bring any immediate alteration to William's personal or financial circumstances. He remained the curate at Keevil and his mother, Mary, inherited all of his father's property and goods.[30]

What of the Wainhouse's second son, Richard? There are very few records related to him, but it is clear that by the time of his father's death, his relationship with his family had soured. Young Richard was set aside "for his general bad incorrigible Behavior." Although there were consequences for the young man and serious familial disapproval, his mother pushed back against relatives who suggested he be completely cast out, replying, "still he is my Child."[31] Whether it was due to Mary's influence or Reverend Wainhouse's belief in Christian duty, their son was not completely abandoned. Although his father did label him his "undutiful son" in his will, he did not cut him off entirely; instead he provided his wayward son

---

28 This was a little early to enter Oxford, as the standard age in this period was closer to seventeen or eighteen. Brockliss, *The University of Oxford*, 166; Scott, *Admissions to the College of St. John the Evangelist in the University of Cambridge*, Part III, 326; Joseph Foster, *Alumni Oxonienses: The Members of the University of Oxford, 1715–1886*, Volume IV (Parker and Co., 1888), 1480; Jacob, *The Clerical Profession*, 44.

29 He was ordained on September 20, 1761. Foster, *Alumni Oxonienses*, Vol. IV, 1480; William Wainhouse, W&SRO D/1/2/27 (Register 1756–76) (Episcopal Register), *The Clergy Database*, https://theclergydatabase.org.uk/.

30 Jacob, *The Clerical Profession*, 61; "Mr. Wainhouse's Testimion for Priest's Orders Sep 1763," D1/14/1/ 13, Wiltshire and Swindon History Centre, UK; *Narrative*, folio 5; "Will of Reverend Richard Wainhouse, 11 Feb 1762," PROB 11; Piece: 873 Ancestry.com. *England & Wales, Prerogative Court of Canterbury Wills, 1384–1858* [database online], Provo, UT: Ancestry.com Operations, Inc., 2013.

31 "William Wainhouse to William and Ann Beach, 27 September 1770," D2455 Box 8/4, Gloucestershire Archives, UK.

an annuity of £30.[32] Mary also continued some limited support for Richard, who relocated to London, giving him a further £10 in her will. Considering his brother William stood to inherit thousands of pounds worth of stock and property, this was a pittance. Despite Richard's disgrace, his bad behavior did not seem to damage the family's reputation in the neighborhood, as Mary and William continued to remain "altogether sociable & agreeable" with the Beaches and "frequent Visits were paid & receiv'd."[33] The Beaches once again closed ranks around Mary, as they had after her first husband's death, and her son Richard's annuity was even witnessed and "Sealed & delivered in the presence of Sophia Beach [and] Ann Beach."[34]

Things soon changed rapidly for twenty-four-year-old William Wainhouse. He not only had to deal with the death of his father and the estrangement from his brother, but his mother, Mary, would also leave his orbit. She moved to Bath to live with Sophia Beach, who split her time between that city and her house in Kelston.[35] William remained in Keevil as curate, while at the same time laying the groundwork for the advancement of his career by paying fees to Queen's College and progressing towards a master's degree, which he gained in 1762.[36] He also had to adjust to his new working situation and quickly developed good rapport with the new vicar of Keevil, James Richardson, who was described by friends as "chaste, pacific, meek" and as a man who never "meant & ne'er suspected Harm."[37]

Richardson, like Richard Wainhouse before him, would find a bride from within the ranks of the Beach family.[38] He fell for the charms of Anne Beach (yes, another one), the niece of Mrs. Beach of Netheravon and cousin of her daughter

---

32 "Will of Reverend Richard Wainhouse, 11 Feb 1762," PROB 11; Piece: 873, Ancestry.com. *England & Wales, Prerogative Court of Canterbury Wills, 1384–1858* [database online], Provo, UT: Ancestry. com Operations, Inc., 2013.

33 *Narrative*, folio 6.

34 "Will of Reverend Richard Wainhouse"; "Copy of an Assignment of an Annuity of £30 per Annum on the Life of Mr. Richard Wainhouse," DD/DP/ 21/1, Somerset Record Office, UK.

35 "Recvd of Mrs. Wainhouse my share of one quarters board," Miscellaneous Receipts Sophia Beach 1762–1767, D2455/F2/4/2/3, Gloucestershire Archives, UK.

36 The term *curate* covered a great deal of ground in the eighteenth century, serving as a descriptor for those newly ordained clergymen learning their profession, but it could also be a parish assistant. It likewise referred to those who were effectively running the parish if the incumbent vicar was indisposed or not in residence. Finally, the term could mean those who were working as incumbents in specific positions as "chaplains of chapelries" or those labeled as "perpetual curates." Jacob, *The Clerical Profession*, 64; "Battel and Rental Books Queens College Oxford 1756–1764," Queens College Archives, Oxford, UK; Foster, *Alumni Oxonienses*, Vol. IV, 1480.

37 "Wainhouse, Verses, 20 November 1767," D2455/F2/5/3/3.

38 James Richardson would be vicar at Keevil from his appointment on December 15, 1761, until his death on January 15, 1783. *The Clergy Database*, https://theclergydatabase.org.uk/.

(also called Anne Beach). William Wainhouse, by then a close friend of the groom, described her as "chearful, witty, wise, good-natur'd, kind" but didn't neglect a nod to her fine tapering waist.[39] Her cousin's characterization, however, was less admiring, writing that she thought the wedding "must be a curious one" but she hoped "matrimony will alter her temper, or I shall pitty [sic] Mr. Richardson."[40] Wainhouse was far more complimentary of the match, describing James as "An honest grave, & guileless Man of God" who had long resisted marrying "Till his fair Consort glanc'd her fatal Eyes, Shot though his Soul" and "Love-struck & suppliant at her Feet he fell ... [and] In Love's sweet Converse glides each welcome Day, Both now are blest & innocently gay."[41]

The pair's 1767 wedding, hosted by Mrs. Beach and officiated by William Wainhouse, provides a glimpse of the personalities of various attendees, including Billy, Anne, Henrietta Maria, and Mrs. Beach. Interestingly, there is no mention of Mr. Beach in William Wainhouse's "heroic poem" dedicated to Mrs. Beach, and his absence perhaps speaks to the dominant personality of his wife. Billy is styled a "comely Youth" and praised for his scholarly acumen. He was "Of sterling Worth ... Noble his Aspect, nobler is the Soul, Sense & Good Nature animate the Whole." The eighteen-year-old Anne Beach (daughter of William Beach of Netheravon and Anne Wither Beach) served as bridesmaid. Dark haired, the lady in red was blessed with rosy cheeks and an unaffected smile, though she was lumped together with the other bridesmaid, Miss Talbot of Margam, when the pair were both praised for their graceful demeanor and expression. Anne is only mentioned in passing, as it was Miss Talbot that stirred the affections of the gentlemen, leading to a battle of bewigged guests vying for her attention. Anne was dismissed in silence but Miss Talbot, "the green-rob'd Bridemaid shoots through all by Heart." One would-be suitor, a lawyer in an "umbrageous Peruke," was in competition with a "sprucer Beau ... In Wig his Equal." The second gentleman cut quite a figure in his outdated formal coat "Chequer'd with Lace" and paired with a cherry-colored silk vest.[42] It seems, however, that the lady in green was unmoved by the displays of either of the men.

The youngest Beach child, Henrietta Maria (age seven) garnered the most attention; she is described as having "cheeks [where] The Rose & Lily ... join ... azure Eyes ... Cherubick Smiles ... the Charms of Youth & Innocence ... her Temper sweet indears, Her dulcet Prattle charm our list'ning ears." She was styled "a

---

39 "Wainhouse, Verses, 20 November 1767," D2455/F2/5/3/3.
40 Jane Talbot at Margam to Mrs. Beach at Fittleton October 26 [c. 1767 or later], private collection.
41 "Wainhouse, Verses, 20 November 1767," D2455/F2/5/3/3.
42 "Wainhouse, Verses, 20 November 1767," D2455/F2/5/3/3.

precious Jewel ... sweet & fair." Even in this accounting, her place in Mrs. Beach's affections shines clear, as she was styled as her mother's "joy, her Blessing, her delightful Care!" Mrs. Beach was likewise praised for possessing "a precious Mind, A Gem by liberal Culture well refin'd, Poised by skillful[sic] Hands, she shines in Life. A tender Mother, & a loving Wife." The poem even provides a glimpse of the curate himself, who, at twenty-nine, was "smooth-chinn'd" with "amber locks" that curled "like Tendrils of the spreading Vine." He possessed a "nimble Tongue" and was charming enough to be styled by the ladies as a "teasing Thing." William nonetheless lamented his own inability to secure a wife, stating, "Women & Marriage are his fav'rite Themes, By Day his Talk, by Night I ween, his Dreams."[43] In the 1760s, securing both his career and a wife would consume William's attention and animate his actions.

Although he had become friends with his father's replacement, William remained in close contact with his father's friends, depending upon them as character witnesses when he applied to take his priest's orders. In his "Testimion" for career advancement, he is listed as "Mast of Arts & Curate of Keevil," and his witnesses paint a picture of a sober and honest young man who "diligently applied himself to his Studies" and stayed firmly within the Church of England's teachings. These men, Edward Batten, vicar of North Bradley, which lies just a few miles from Keevil, along with the vicar and curate of the neighboring parish of Steeple Ashton – Robert Foulkes and Griffith Griffith, respectively – judged him "worthy" to join their ranks, which he did in September 1763.[44] These connections were of particular importance for newly ordained ministers, who often went back to where they grew up or went to school to obtain a position. Often their first job resulted from familial, educational, or social networks and William Wainhouse certainly used his family and social connections to obtain his post as curate in his hometown.[45]

These relationships continued to prove of value as William's career advanced; he would remain especially close to Robert Foulkes, who had, in 1747, been appointed vicar of Steeple Ashton by Magdalene College, Cambridge (which controlled the living). Foulkes had been a fellow of Magdalene College since 1719 and even served as its president. The Welshman, whose father had been a grocer in Denbigh, was in his late fifties when he resigned from his other posts, a stipulation laid down when the vicarage was willed to the College and moved to Steeple

---

43 "Wainhouse, Verses, 20 November 1767," D2455/F2/5/3/3.
44 "Mr. Wainhouse's Testimion for Priest's Orders Sep 1763," D1/14/1/13.
45 Jacob, *The Clerical Profession*, 61.

Ashton. The £200 per annum living was unusual as it required the office holder to "be daly [sic] resident."[46]

Beyond his career, William was also searching for love, though he would have less success on that front than in his professional endeavors. As historian Sally Holloway has argued, "Courting couples were painfully aware that matrimony was by no means a fait accompli, with a significant proportion of relationships stalling before they reached the altar."[47] This was certainly the case in William's search. In 1767, he lamented that "with the Fair contending oft he's foil'd."[48] The pursuit and achievement of marriage was a marker of adult status and an important component of masculine identity in the eighteenth century. As historians Henry French and Mark Rothery have argued, "Above all, it offered emotional security and support, rather than just transient sexual gratification, and provided the final component of adult autonomy – the creation of an independent, financially secure household and nuclear family."[49] Historian Karen Harvey has also asserted the centrality of marriage in the eighteenth-century conception of masculinity, as "the house and its social relationships were critical to men's wider social status," and "men's governance in the household was deemed one important route to early modern manly honour."[50]

Early in the 1760s, William's attentions were caught by "a Fair One in the Neighbourhood," and although there is no record of who she was, he was serious in his pursuit and saw himself as "entangled" in her "Charms." After several months, however, the budding romance fizzled and William "disengag'd himself from this Attachment." It seems the curate's lack of fortune proved a sticking point as, shortly before his mother's death, the woman delivered "in the public Streets, what he [William] conceiv'd to be a design'd Slight & Indignity."[51] Offended, and certainly not one to shy away from a confrontation, William sent her a letter conveying his hurt but never received an answer. This ill treatment fostered his

---

46 "West & Steeple Ashton Tithes," 730/45, Wiltshire and Swindon History Centre, UK; Ged Martin, *Magdalene College Cambridge and Steeple Ashton, An Exploratory Essay* (Copy of record for the Magdalene College Archives, 2016); "Opinion of E. Simpson on the living, 2 January 1748," A/29/2/7, Magdalene College Archives, Pepys Library, Cambridge, UK; "Steeple Ashton Bond of Foulkes to reside 1747," A/29/2/8, Magdalene College Archives, Pepys Library, Cambridge, UK. This stipulation was likely an attempt at preventing non-residence, which often attended the problem of clerical pluralism, the practice of holding more than one living at a time. Jacob, *The Clerical Profession*, 95.

47 Sally Holloway, *The Game of Love in Georgian England: Courtship, Emotions, and Material Culture* (Oxford University Press, 2019), 118.

48 "Wainhouse, Verses, 20 November 1767," D2455/F2/5/3/3.

49 French and Rothery, *Man's Estate*, 197.

50 Karen Harvey, *The Little Republic: Masculinity and Domestic Authority in Eighteenth-Century Britain* (Oxford University Press, 2012), 2, 4.

51 *Narrative*, folio 7, 9.

resolve to "never to court her good Graces again," although the lure of love would prove irresistible.[52]

While dealing with his familial and romantic woes, William was forced to re-evaluate his relationship with the Beach Family. At the end of 1766, he became concerned about a perceived "Coldness" from Mrs. Beach. This was disturbing, considering the closeness of their families. Perhaps with marriage on the mind, given his pursuit of "other objects," Wainhouse came to believe Mrs. Beach thought he had "some Design on her eldest Daughter." Seeking to diffuse this tension he sent her a letter, alluding to his suspicions and "disclaiming all Design on the young Lady."[53] William stated that although he had "often cast an Eye of Delight, akin to Affection, on the eldest Daughter, in the Bloom of Youth, lovely in Person & Temper, but he encourag'd no Thought of addressing her, as a Lover."[54] Wainhouse went so far as to assure Mrs. Beach that "on his Honour & the Word of a Clergyman, he wou'd never make any private Attempt on her Affections." He did, however, state that, "were their respective Fortunes & Circumstances suitable, he shou'd esteem her an eligible Partner for Life."[55] With things settled, the Beaches continued their intimacy with the family, as Mary Wainhouse remained with Sophia Beach until her death, and by November 1767 William Wainhouse was once again speaking of Mrs. Beach in glowing terms.

William Wainhouse was not the only inhabitant of Keevil concerned with love and matrimony; these were also preoccupations for the Beach family, who sought to consolidate their social gains and advance their family fortunes. Marriage remained an important consideration for gentry families, although scholars have debated the shifting nature of this institution in the eighteenth century. Some argue the century was dominated by the rise of romantic love, while concerns for alliances, family advancement, land acquisition and social mobility were downplayed. This simplistic dichotomy ignores the social realities and wide variety and styles of courtship. Marriage was a mix of practicality and sentiment.[56] There was, however, a growing acceptance among the gentry of marrying for more than social and familial advantage. There was a growing celebration of love and its role in companionate marriage during the eighteenth century. This is not to suggest that love became the primary

---

52 *Narrative*, folio 9.
53 *Narrative*, folio 7.
54 *Narrative*, folio 6.
55 *Narrative*, folio 7.
56 Vickery, *The Gentleman's Daughter*, 40; Holloway, *The Game of Love*, 9–10; Porter, *English Society in the Eighteenth Century*, 26; Ingrid H. Tague, *Women of Quality: Accepting and Contesting Ideals of Femininity in England, 1690–1760* (Boydell Press, 2002), 73; Linda Pollock, "Review Article: 'An Action Like a Stratagem': Courtship and Marriage from the Middle Ages to the Twentieth Century," *Historical Journal* 30 (1987): 483–98.

motivation in marriage, but rather that it rose in prominence as a factor. Despite this, the social appropriateness of the match remained paramount.

There needed to be some equity in status no matter the romantic feelings and, generally, the decision to marry was rooted in an established affection rather than simply in romantic desire. Marriage was a complex social process as well as a legal and religious one, and orchestrating a match among the propertied classes often involved intricate negotiations and the cooperation of family and friends. It was a key component of maintaining and advancing social status and procuring property. The right marriage elevated opportunities for the whole family, but it could also be a volatile and competitive enterprise.[57]

The Beaches first turned their attention to settling their middle child, Anne, and selected a possible spouse from a wealthy family of clothiers in Westbury – the Gaisfords. Westbury, situated near Trowbridge and Warminster, had emerged as a cloth-manufacturing center in the fifteenth century and by the eighteenth century it was known for the making of medley cloth. Although there were a number of successful clothiers who had acquired estates and property, by the mid-eighteenth century the inhabitants of the town still had a reputation for being "rough [and] turbulent."[58] It is likely the families came to each other's attention through their business dealings, as the Beaches had sold some of the 100 acres of property they owned in West Ashton, known as Dunge Farm, to William Gaisford in 1741.[59]

---

57 Vickery, *The Gentleman's Daughter*, 45; Lawrence Stone, *Uncertain Unions: Marriage in England 1660–1753* (Oxford University Press, 1992), 8, 12; Langford, *A Polite and Commercial People*, 112–13. For more on marriage see Joanne Bailey [Begiato], *Unquiet Lives: Marriage and Marriage Breakdown in England, 1660–1800* (Cambridge University Press, 2003); Katie Barclay, *Love, Intimacy and Power: Marriage and Patriarchy in Scotland 1650–1850* (Manchester University Press, 2011); Katherine Crawford, *European Sexualities, 1400–1800* (Cambridge University Press, 2007); David Cressy, *Birth, Marriage and Death: Ritual, Religion and the Life-Cycle in Tudor and Stuart England* (Oxford University Press, 1999); Anthony Fletcher, *Gender, Sex and Subordination in England 1500–1800* (Yale University Press, 1995); John R. Gillis, *For Better, For Worse: British Marriages, 1600 to the Present* (Oxford University Press, 1985); Glover, *Elite Women and Polite Society*; Holloway, *The Game of Love*; Judith Schneid Lewis, *In the Family Way: Childbearing in the British Aristocracy, 1760–1860* (Rutgers University Press, 1986); Diana O'Hara, *Courtship and Constraint: Rethinking the Making of Marriage in Tudor England* (Manchester University Press, 2000); Lawrence Stone, *Road to Divorce: A History of the Making and Breaking of Marriage in England 1530–1987* (Oxford University Press, 1995); Lawrence Stone, *The Family, Sex and Marriage in England 1500–1800* (Weidenfeld and Nicholson, 1977); Stone, *Uncertain Unions*; Naomi Tadmor, *Family and Friends in Eighteenth-Century England: Household, Kinship and Patronage* (Cambridge University Press, 2004); Amanda Vickery, *Behind Closed Doors: At Home in Georgian England* (Yale University Press, 2009).

58 "Westbury: Industry and Trade," in *A History of the County of Wiltshire: Vol. 8, Warminster, Westbury and Whorwellsdown Hundreds* (London, 1965), 168–72.

59 "Conveyance to William Gaisford of Dunge Farm in West Ashton, Purchased from the Beach Family," 1494/4 Wiltshire and Swindon History Centre; "Steeple Ashton," in *A History of the County of Wiltshire: Vol. 8, Warminster, Westbury and Whorwellsdown Hundreds* (Victoria County History, 1965), 198–218.

After identifying an appropriately wealthy suitor, the Beaches arranged an offer of marriage, though they seem to have been more concerned with their prospective son-in-law's financial viability than the possible romantic connection, or even the basic rapport between Anne and "Young Gaisford of Westbury." William Wainhouse certainly believed that "Money alone was predominant" in their deliberations, particularly as "the Family, the Connexion, the Occupation, the Education, the Endowments of the Lover, were not great, shining, estimable, [or] recommendatory."[60] In this assessment Wainhouse was correct, as the Gaisfords would have brought material gain, but not much else.

They were engaged in commercial enterprise and lacked gentry status; as such, they would not bring any elevation to the Beaches' social standing. Even more shocking were the family's nonconformist leanings. They were Congregationalists, not members of the Church of England, and were part of the Upper Congregational Chapel founded in 1751. The Gaisfords were prominent members of the congregation and made bequests to support the ministry.[61] As nonconformists, the men of the family would have been barred from attending Oxford, Cambridge, or the Inns of Court, excluding them from those avenues for improving their standing. William Wainhouse's accusations are given credence by the fact that the marriage between Anglican and nonconformist families was not common, and it is unlikely the Anglican Beaches marrying their daughter to someone outside of the Church of England would have been seen as anything other than a mercenary step, as it would not improve the family in any way, except financially.

Beyond the economic viability of the match (which seems to have been the paramount concern) it remained undetermined whether the couple would suit, and the match also seemed to lack this virtue. The decision to marry was the most important one a woman could make – there was no way out once the vows had been said.[62] As historian Amanda Vickery has argued, the seriousness of the choice weighed heavily, as a good union brought contentment and familial stability. Temperament and the disposition of the parties were important considerations in determining a good match, and making a careful assessment of the

---

60 *Narrative,* folio 20.

61 "Westbury: Protestant Nonconformity," in *A History of the County of Wiltshire: Vol. 8, Warminster, Westbury and Whorwellsdown Hundreds* (London, 1965), 181–5. For more information, see David W. Bebbington, *Evangelicalism in Modern Britain: A History from the 1730s to the 1980s* (Routledge, 1989); Reginald W. Ward, *Early Evangelicalism: A Global Intellectual History 1670–1789* (Cambridge University Press, 2006).

62 Divorce was not generally possible, except in rare cases that earned parliamentary approval, until the passage of the Matrimonial Causes Act in 1857. However, it still remained an expensive and onerous process as a woman needed to prove adultery and another transgression (either cruelty, rape, incest, bestiality, or bigamy) to obtain a divorce.

individual's personal character was key.[63] When Anne met the young man her parents had secured for her, the results were not fortuitous, as the temperaments of the two could not have been more different.

Anne was shy and her brash suitor set her back up almost immediately. She took an instant dislike to him. Mr. Beach tried to convince his reticent daughter by speaking at length "about living <u>grandly</u>, & what a fine <u>Settlement</u> she wou'd have!"[64] This, however, proved insufficient enticement to a young woman who was "us'd to a retir'd Way of Life."[65] She even went so far as to run from the room at the first opportunity, leaving the hapless young man to give his "Sighs & Soliloquies to the Air."[66] Anne's personal aversion, however, was not enough to put an end the match. In the face of parental pressure, the young woman crumpled. Fearing the "ill effects of their displeasure" she was extremely hesitant to declare "her Dislike to this Suitor." In the end, she was only saved from the disagreeable fate of "a forc'd Union with the Man she dislik'd" by the objections of a wealthy relative (possibly James Harding of Mere), upon "whom their [The Beaches] grand monied Expectations were built."[67]

In the late 1760s Anne Beach's matrimonial struggles would intertwine with those of William Wainhouse. The bachelor began to spend more time at Keevil Manor, and the pair got to know each other while her parents and brother were away in London for several weeks. Anne and Henrietta Maria were left behind, in the care of the Beaches' niece.[68] The tacit approval of vicar James Richardson and his wife (the former Anne Beach) proved decisive, and beginning in June 1767, William and Anne were repeatedly in each other's company in various social settings, affording them the opportunity to speak freely and get to know one another.[69]

The curate proved to be a fun, witty conversationalist with a confident laugh and penchant for singing. He was described as being "jocose & free" and it seems his "fond, playful, [and] merry" personality brought the shy Anne out of her shell.[70] Although neither party had any plans beyond simple conversation, their feelings deepened as they spent time together. It is not clear when his feelings changed from polite regard to affection and then to love, but Wainhouse certainly began to see Anne Beach as more than a neighbor or someone he had known since

---

63 Vickery, *The Gentleman's Daughter,* 39–40.
64 *Narrative,* folio 19.
65 "Wainhouse to William and Ann Beach, 27 September 1770," D2455 Box 8/4.
66 *Narrative,* folio 19.
67 *Narrative,* folio 20.
68 *Narrative,* folio 9; "Wainhouse to William and Ann Beach, 27 September 1770," D2455 Box 8/4.
69 "Wainhouse to William and Ann Beach, 27 September 1770," D2455 Box 8/4.
70 "Wainhouse, Verses, 20 November 1767," D2455/F2/5/3/3; "Wainhouse to William and Ann Beach, 27 September 1770," D2455 Box 8/4.

childhood. Mrs. Richardson proved an unreliable, or at least complicit, chaperone, even permitting Anne and William to spend time alone.[71] The couple's fondness for each other grew by accident, as William admitted those things that in the moment "appear[d] quite trivial & innocent," had "future serious Consequences we were not at first aware of." The more time they spent together, the more affected he became. Anne's "Person & Temper" made a deep "Impression" upon the curate and "Friendship soon gr[ew] into Love."[72] Anne "was of the most sweet, obliging, meek, patient Temper & Manners that ever bless'd & adorn'd the softer Sex."[73] The lovesick Wainhouse claimed, "My Love stole upon me insensibly, & grew into a confirm'd settled Regard & Esteem."[74] As historian Sally Holloway has argued, during this period, "love was understood as a long-lasting and intangible passion, and celebrated as an almost spiritual experience that went beyond words."[75]

The young couple was now faced with a serious dilemma, as the differences in their financial situations loomed large, as did William Wainhouse's rash promise long before his eyes turned to Anne to "never make any private Attempt on her Affections." His caveat, "that, were their respective Fortunes & Circumstances suitable, he shou'd esteem her an eligible Partner for Life" seemed his out, particularly as the romance did not develop until after an improvement in his fortunes upon his mother's death in May 1767.[76] William, however, still struggled with this situation, remembering "the Mother's Declaration, that it wou'd never do for the Clergyman to think of gaining her Daughter in Marriage." Given the closeness of the families, William believed Mrs. Beach's objections were simply a consequence of his estate and not to him personally. His intimacy with the family, their support of him, and their favorable characterization of his character convinced him that their objection was the "Inequality of Fortune, & Inability to make an adequate Settlement," knowing this "weighs heavily with the Generality of Parents" and "wou'd have render'd the Clergyman Light in the Balance."[77]

Despite his newly found financial solvency, William suppressed any idea of courtship and the couple put aside their feelings. For two years they stayed apart, but by spring of 1769 the clergyman could deny his feelings no longer and "ventur'd on an offer to <u>Miss Beach</u>, private indeed, but honourable." Anne, perhaps out of duty or fear, remained silent and William, concerned that his pursuit would

---

71 "Wainhouse to William and Ann Beach, 27 September 1770," D2455 Box 8/4.
72 "Wainhouse to William and Ann Beach, 27 September 1770," D2455 Box 8/4; *Narrative*, folio 10.
73 *Narrative*, folio 93.
74 "Wainhouse to William and Ann Beach, 27 September 1770," D2455 Box 8/4; *Narrative*, folio 10.
75 Holloway, *The Game of Love*, 8.
76 *Narrative*, folio 7.
77 *Narrative*, folio 10.

put her in a difficult position with her family, decided to abandon any "thoughts of offering fresh Overtures to <u>Miss Beach</u>." Once again, the clergyman submitted to "Prudential Considerations," but remained desperate for marriage.[78] More than anything, William wanted to be "By Spouse well-managed, noos'd in Wedlock's Yoke" and his "Heart panted after a Companion loving & belov'd, 'to fill up the uncomfortable Blank of Solitude.'"[79]

With Anne lost to him, the unattached clergyman went looking for "a Partner in social Felicity, which his sociable Nature yearn'd after."[80] In the summer of 1769, the lonely bachelor once again turned his attention to the woman who had previously caught his heart.[81] His desire for companionship trumped his personal pride over her earlier treatment, as he was "determin'd (if possible) not to live & die in single Blessedness." Sadly, his former beloved proved as unreliable as ever, though she did finally provide him closure by confirming that his earlier offer of marriage "was not after the Lady's Heart."[82]

After another year, William's loneliness and longing for Anne Beach got the best of him, and in April 1770, he slipped a message into her hand "containing an Offer of his Services, & a Proposal of a secret Marriage."[83] Anne had remained aloof until this moment, despite their convivial interactions three years earlier, but she finally confessed her love and openly returned his affection. She remained wary, however, and was terrified of the possible consequences. She knew that to pursue him would have a calamitous outcome, particularly in light of her parents' earlier matchmaking attempts with the Gaisfords and their attitudes toward her brother's romance in 1769 (to be discussed later).

Given these experiences and fearing parental disapproval, it is not surprising that Anne was extremely apprehensive and was certain she would be cut off financially if she wed without her parents' approval. William was undaunted, and assured her he would "behave well & honourably," promising that even if she never saw another penny from her family he would "settle one hundred Pounds a Year" on her. This assurance seems to have won Anne over and she agreed to undertake "a matrimonial Excursion to <u>Scotland</u>."[84]

It may seem odd that a clergyman in good standing in the community, who had had the assistance of the vicar's wife in his romance, would seek to flee to

---

78 *Narrative*, folio 11.
79 "Wainhouse, Verses, 20 November 1767," D2455/F2/5/3/3; *Narrative*, folio 11.
80 *Narrative*, folio 12.
81 *Narrative*, folio 12–13.
82 *Narrative*, folio 12.
83 *Narrative*, folio 13.
84 *Narrative*, folio 14.

Scotland to marry. However, "The Act for the better preventing of clandestine Marriages," more often called the Hardwicke's Marriage Act, passed in 1753 and ensured that William and Anne had no other choice but elopement.[85] The Act was intended to end the practice of clandestine marriage, and it invalidated all nuptials not subscribing to the stipulated procedures. A clandestine marriage was one that occurred outside the home parishes of the couple and "with no prior public notification."[86] Henceforth, marriages could only be performed after the banns (the statement of a couple's intention to marry) had been publicly declared three times. The only way around this procedure was to procure an expensive special license either from the bishop or an approved surrogate. The ceremony could be held afterward, but only if officiated by an Anglican minister and occurring in a church.[87]

Crucial in Anne and William's case, the Marriage Act also stipulated that minors under the age of twenty-one (which applied to Anne) had to obtain parental consent or the marriage was null and void. So, even if William had convinced someone to perform the ceremony (an unlikely situation, as a clergyman who performed an illegal marriage was subject to prosecution and transportation to the Americas for fourteen years), the marriage would have been declared invalid. The bill only applied to England and Wales, however, which permitted underage individuals to still get married in Scotland, where a witnessed vow was considered a lawful marriage.[88] This loophole was left in place by Lord Chancellor Hardwicke to get the Scottish lords to sign on to his bill. This left them to create their own for the Church of Scotland; however, it didn't materialize as the Scottish Court of Sessions refused to overturn the existing marriage laws. After the Marriage Act, then, couples lacking parental consent had no other choice than a costly and lengthy trip to Scotland, where a marriage industry had developed, one that provided the service with no questions. As a consequence, Gretna Green, standing as it did just over the border on the main road, became the premier destination for those seeking a clergy member willing to marry a couple with no notice.[89]

---

85 David Lemmings, "Marriage and the Law in the Eighteenth Century: Hardwicke's Marriage Act of 1753," *Historical Journal* 39, no. 2 (1996): 339–60, 340. The law went into effect March 25, 1754. See also Rebecca Probert, "The Impact of the Marriage Act of 1753: Was It Really 'A Most Cruel Law for the Fair Sex'?," *Eighteenth-Century Studies* 38, no. 2 (2005), 254.

86 Newton, "Clandestine Marriage," 248.

87 Gillis, *For Better, For Worse*, 140.

88 Rebecca Probert and Liam D'Arcy Brown, "The Impact of the Clandestine Marriages Act: Three Case-studies in Conformity," *Continuity and Change* 23, no. 2 (2008), 309; Gillis, *For Better, For Worse*, 140–1, 195.

89 Scotland had a system that permitted marriage simply by the consent of eligible parties, which allowed for flexibility in the wake of Hardwicke's Act, and it became a growing site for irregular

The couple planned to elope and on May 6, 1770, at midnight Anne tried to sneak out of Keevil Manor to meet William, who had arranged a post-chaise and four for their journey. Unfortunately, she was sharing a room with her younger sister, Henrietta Maria, who though usually a sound sleeper, woke up, forcing Anne to abandon the attempt. Despite fizzling, the plan did not go unnoticed, as the carriage raised suspicion when it barreled through the tollgate with its blinds closed at such a late hour and the astonished gatekeeper wasted no time in spreading the gossip around the neighborhood.[90]

These events raised Mrs. Beach's suspicions and she took Anne to task, abandoning any charitable thoughts of the young man who had been so close to her family. The conversation between mother and daughter was fraught, and an enraged Mrs. Beach heaped invective upon William, calling him "the vilest of Names" and going so far as to say that she had rather follow her "Daughter to the Grave, or see her married to a Shoe-Black, than to such a Villain."[91] One can imagine a mother's anger at her child's disobedience, but none of the parties knew how prophetic this statement would prove to be.

In the face of Anne's resolve, Mrs. Beach tried another tactic, saying she would intervene with her father if her daughter disclosed her elopement plans. This was a double-edged offer, as she said she would only do so if Anne truly "cou'd not be happy without him," but in the next breath she stated that "she thought it impossible to bring her Father into it." It seems that Anne was not taken in by this tactic, particularly as her mother had just moments before called her love "a Villain," and the young woman remained steadfast in her denial she had any plans to marry. Curiously, "though [he was] violently suspected," William Wainhouse was still allowed free access to Keevil Manor.[92] Perhaps the Beaches felt they could exert control over the parties and, through heavy surveillance, prevent any further attempts at elopement. Despite this, the pair were able to plot yet another trip to Scotland. This time Anne planned to sneak away from the house during the hustle and bustle of the day, then hide in a place known only to her; then, at midnight, she would make her way to meet William at a prearranged spot.

---

marriage after 1753 – particularly at Gretna Green, which lay just over the border from England. See Leah Leneman and Rosalind Mitchison, "Clandestine Marriage in the Scottish Cities 1660–1780," *Journal of Social History* 26, no. 4 (1993), 845–6; Stone, *Road to Divorce*, 130–31; Stone, *The Family, Sex and Marriage*, 122, 130–1, 135.

90 *Narrative*, folio 14–15.
91 *Narrative*, folio 15.
92 *Narrative*, folio 16.

On May 28, 1770, just before supper, Anne disappeared. As dinner approached, her absence was noticed, and her mother sent a search party to find her.[93] Mrs. Beach and two of her friends then stormed the vicarage looking for her wayward daughter. Upon entering William Wainhouse's parlor, Mrs. Beach dropped to her knees and begged for information on her daughter, but just as quickly her performative distress turned to rage. Wainhouse denied knowing Anne's whereabouts, which at that moment was accurate since only Anne knew where she planned to hide herself before their rendezvous. Although he later admitted that "[h]ad he known, he certainly wou'd not have discover'd her."[94]

Mrs. Beach wasted no time in bringing up the clergyman's honor and "upbraided him with his former Promise & the Breach of it." William immediately acknowledged his fault, but retorted that she was only concerned about money and that her only real objection was to "Inequality of Fortune."[95] Mrs. Beach was enraged by the accusation and tried to counter it by bringing up the failed matchmaking attempt with the Gaisfords. Mrs. Beach stated that "her Daughter had an Offer long before, where there was no Want of Money. Why then was it not embrac'd?" Knowing there was an objection from a wealthy family member to the match, William reminded her that, despite the lackluster endowments of the suitor, the family had tried to convince Anne by extolling "what a fine <u>Settlement</u> she wou'd have!"[96]

Outmaneuvered and incensed, Mrs. Beach changed tactics and moved to assassinate her own daughter's character, calling Anne "endutiful & obstinate."[97] She then told William that "he wou'd have no Catch in her Daughter, as she was of an obstinate Temper" to which the curate replied "that was his Business, not her's [sic]." Mrs. Beach then rushed out of the parlor, but not before delivering her parting shot that she never wished "to see the Clergyman's Face any more" and furthermore stating "she did not care much whether she ever saw her Daughter's."[98] Anne, knowing nothing of what had transpired, would be forced to deal with the fallout from this altercation when she was eventually located around midnight, hiding in the shrubbery on the estate.[99] She was brought by the searchers to her mother (her father was away from the estate during the dramatic events of the

---

93 *Narrative*, folio 17.
94 *Narrative*, folio 18.
95 *Narrative*, folio 18
96 *Narrative*, folio 19.
97 *Narrative*, folio 20.
98 *Narrative*, folio 21.
99 Hicks, *A Cotswold Family*, 299.

day), who "talk'd very lovingly ... in the Presence of the Company; but ... her Tone chang'd when she had her Daughter alone."[100] Then Mrs. Beach and several others took turns berating her.

One can imagine the pressure Anne was under, after having spent hours hiding outside, only to have her plans frustrated once again, and then being lectured by multiple individuals about her behavior and duty. It is unsurprising, then, that after she was repeatedly berated and pushed "to promise, that she wou'd never make any such Attempt to go off again," that she eventually gave in. William ascribed her capitulation to her confusion in that moment, but her mother interpreted this "as a serious Promise to give the Lover up." A few days later, however, Anne backpedaled and when her father confronted her and asked "whether or no she wou'd go away with her Gentleman, if she shou'd have an Opportunity? She coolly & resolutely answer'd, Yes."[101]

The Beaches, determined to prevent the match, took drastic action to cure "her Passion" and on June 6, 1770, they imprisoned their daughter in a small room located above the porch in Keevil Manor.[102] Anne's incarceration had the reverse effect, confirming her resolve and love for William "& a Dislike of Home & her Parents."[103] Here Anne remained for over five months, her parents only permitting her to leave her prison for short periods of time. The room overlooked the village church and it is possible that it was during her imprisonment that she scratched a message into the windowpane: "Remember Ann Beach."[104] Once she reached twenty-one years of age, Anne's family could no longer legally detain her, although William claims they did so illegally for twelve days after her birthday (November 1, 1770).[105]

Her parents, out of options, provided her with a difficult choice. She could remain in the family and be exiled to another family estate, or she could marry the clergyman and be cast out. They were willing to give her the hundred pounds' legacy left to her by her grandfather, Thomas Beach, which they were obligated to do by law, but not a penny more.[106] Her father stated if she chose to marry Wainhouse she would be turned away if she ever tried "to set her Foot within the Gate afterward." According to Wainhouse, Mr. Beach followed with the proviso that

---

100 *Narrative*, folio 22.
101 *Narrative*, folio 23.
102 *Narrative*, folio 25.
103 *Narrative*, folio 29.
104 In the documentary evidence, her name is alternately spelled Ann or Anne, but in the window the "e" is absent.
105 *Narrative*, folio 51.
106 *Narrative*, folio 51.

Anne could travel the following day with her mother "to <u>Fittleton</u>, & be <u>damn'd</u>, or stay here, & go to the <u>Devil</u>."[107]

We will never know what went through Anne's mind at this ultimatum, but what is clear is that whether out of love or in a response to her family's treatment, she chose William Wainhouse. Anne asked her mother if she might stay for a few days so she could make arrangements with the clergyman, but her mother refused to even let her write to William or contact him in any way, putting her daughter in an untenable situation.[108] This would force her "before Marriage, to go for her Protection to the Lodgings of a single Man," which would ruin her reputation. William Wainhouse characterized it as "such a Breach of common Decency, as well as Humanity, that it rais'd the Surprise & Censure of all who thoroughly knew, or dar'd speak freely of the Matter."[109]

Cast out, with only the clothes on her back Anne made her way to William's lodgings on November 14, 1770. The curate immediately moved houses and arranged a chaperone to prevent sullying her reputation, and the very next day he made the trip to Bath to secure a special license. They settled on a date for the ceremony, invited guests, and planned a honeymoon. It took a full week to draw up the marriage settlement and sort out the paperwork, but William made good on his promise to look out for Anne and "settled on her two thousand Pounds in Money, & forty Pounds a Year beside." The couple was married by special license in November 1770 "in the Face of a large Congregation."[110]

Sadly, Anne's trials were just beginning. When she came to William, she was already plagued by "a very bad, deep, hollow, ill-sounding Cough."[111] As her illness progressed, her husband grew in certainty that her condition originated not only from her family's neglect of a cold she had before their botched elopement, but also from their long-term abuse of his delicate wife. This notion that harsh treatment, grief, and even failure in love could have medical consequences, creating consumption, was entirely in keeping with contemporary understandings of the etiology of the disease.

Despite every attempt at intervention, "the Cough, from the Beginning, gain'd Ground. A Symptom, that now alarm'd, was a very troublesome Shortness of Breath. She was bled." William states that the "Bleeding gave little or no Relief. Other Medicines were taken without any visible good Effect. Not only Difficulty of breathing, but a Fever & Drowsiness began to accompany her Cough."[112] By

---

107 *Narrative*, folio 52, 54.
108 *Narrative*, folio 54–55.
109 *Narrative*, folio 55.
110 *Narrative*, folio 56–57.
111 *Narrative*, folio 60.
112 *Narrative*, folio 60.

January, Anne was in desperate straits and was growing weaker every day. She "was very visibly alter'd in her outward Appearance."[113]

In early February all hope was lost, and "She seem'd to approach hastily to her Dissolution."[114] Her physician, recognizing the peril, took it upon himself to write to her father, informing him that she "lay dangerously ill, that there was not the least Probability of her Recovery."[115] Mr. Beach responded that he was "sorry to hear Mrs. Wainhouse is ill, but as her friends used their utmost endeavours to save her and in return she repeatedly gave her family up I'm convinced she can receive no pleasure in seeing any of e'm [sic] her ill behaviour has hurt us all, if our Blessing and wishes for her recovery will be any consolation she has it."[116] Anne's family never saw her again and she succumbed to consumption two days after her father wrote his letter.

William Wainhouse made good on this threat to have the Beaches brought to account for Anne's illness, producing "A NARRATIVE, Exemplifying the Cruelty of Mr. and Mrs. B– –CH ... A Tale of domestic and uncommon Parental Barbarity." Although, initially prepared for print and advertised, the Beaches were able to stop its publication. Undaunted, William sought to vindicate his late wife "by a proper Circulation of her Story in Manuscript."[117] William's accounting draws heavily on the contemporary understandings of disease to cast blame upon the Beach family; in doing so, he relies on emerging medical models of the nervous system positing that health and disease were the result of the connection between the mind and body.

* * * * *

So, I know people have this idea historians sit in neat libraries, wearing white gloves while working in total silence. I am here to let you know, it is not that kind of a sterile profession and can sometimes be a very dirty job. First, the white glove thing is not true; often it is safer for the documents that you have clean hands, but full dexterity. It is easy to accidentally tear a page while turning it if you are wearing gloves because you can't feel it. Gloves are sometimes used, but more often with photographs and certain material objects. Just like you shouldn't wear white gloves, you definitely shouldn't wear a white shirt. I only made that mistake once. I was searching for corset patterns for my first book and between the patent rolls (which are filthy) and the

---

113 *Narrative*, folio 67.
114 *Narrative*, folio 67.
115 *Narrative*, folio 68.
116 "William Beach to Anne Wainhouse's Physician, 8 February 1771," D2455/F2/5/1/22, Gloucestershire Archives, UK.
117 *Narrative*, folio ii.

register books whose bindings were crumbling, I came out with rust-colored stripes across my upper body from carrying a book that was bigger than my torso and whose cover was leaving powered leather everywhere. I figured those days were behind me and that I would be dealing with letters and some deeds and maps (mostly clean documents) while doing the research for this book (but I still don't ever wear white to a record office, library, or archive). There were some other elements of danger, too – I had to climb a ladder in one archive to photograph the Map of Keevil because it was over ten feet long and six feet tall, and although I broke my leg during this project, it didn't happen in an archive. However, the hunt for Anne Beach turned out to be a dirty job after all. I ended up in a church with a bat infestation and then had to rescue a baby bat in the chapel. I crawled through attics covered in feathers and bird poo and even a house with a rat infestation. I seriously wanted to call a chapter "Rats, Bats, and Pigeon Poop," but lost my nerve. Being a historian is far more active and exhausting than most suppose. Getting up early to make it to where you are going, extensive travel, and spending all day in an archive, museum, library can be both physically and mentally draining. There have been so many times that I have been the first person in and last person out of a place, taking only a quick break to scarf down a hasty lunch, before heading back to the piles of documents. I have spent countless hours looking for anything that might just be even remotely useful and there have been many days that were just pure frustration, that after hours of work I still didn't find a single useful thing. Though seriously annoying, this is also an important part of the process. Knowing you checked and that there wasn't some valuable document you ignored, that some later person could point out you missed, is a good thing. Don't get me wrong, I have to remind myself about this constantly when I have those days. The most important thing is to not get discouraged, even when you think you don't have anything, or the right documents. As you sit down to write, things often become apparent. I spent so much time photographing stuff I didn't think I would even use – like receipts, so many boxes of receipts. If you think photographing is tedious, just wait until you have to transcribe pages and pages of handwritten receipts. Let me tell you, receipts are not filled with juicy gossip – or are they? They may seem boring, until they divulge that people were sending poisonous snakes through the mail, or they reveal what happened to someone who was intentionally wiped out of the archive. Receipts finally provided clues to the archival silences surrounding another member of the Beach family, Billy. Just because a source looks useless or doesn't tell you exactly what happened, doesn't mean that valuable information can't be gotten from it. Don't discount something that might seem trivial, like a receipt. Because it was only as I began to write, and I trolled back through my transcriptions, that I actually realized I had struck archival gold in the most mundane scraps of paper.

CHAPTER THREE

"The Rest of His Life … Is a Dreadful Silence"

Anne was cast out of her family and the remains of her life erased, but she was not the only victim of the Beaches' machinations, as William Wainhouse also claimed: "the Mother did cruelly & wilfully [sic] render the Lives of two of her Children unhappy."[1] Who was the second child made cruelly unhappy? Anne's brother Billy provides yet another archival silence that must be reckoned with, as his presence likewise became murky and obscured – this time due to disability and not disobedience. Unlike his sister, although he fades from the archive, becoming a shadowy figure, he was not deliberately cast out of the family. William Wither Beach (1747–1829) was the eldest Beach child and only son. He was the pride of the family and had a promising start as a scholar, but early on his mother's heavy hand was apparent. For instance, she ordered her fourteen-year-old son to share his unrefined poetry about furniture with other members of the family. Billy's letter to his aunt about his verses on "the glittering sideboard" is cringing, hinting both at his discomfort and at his mother's overbearing personality. He wrote "The enclosed is a Specimen of my Poetry which on shewing to my Mama, she commanded me to send to you otherwise shou'd not have taken the Liberty of offering Advice (at so young an age) to one who knows so much better than I can be supposed to do."[2]

The tight control Mrs. Beach exercised over her family seems to have been more than a mother simply bragging about her child's accomplishments. Billy, however, managed to escape from under his mother's thumb when he, like his

---

1 *Narrative*, folio 50.
2 "W.W. Beach to Mrs. Bramston, 15 January1761," D2455/F5/5/13, Gloucestershire Archives, UK.

father, attended Winchester College. Then at the age of eighteen, in December 1764, he "subscribed the Articles of Religion on his admission as a gentleman Commoner at New <u>College</u>, Oxford."[3] This shift from the household to school was considered an important transition for developing manliness in the gentry, and as Henry French and Mark Rothery have argued, the move to a residential school, like Winchester, and then to university was essential. It was seen as a mechanism for breaking a son's dependence upon his mother, as the female influence was thought to stunt "the development of 'proper' masculine autonomy and judgment," which could have both social and familial consequences.[4]

Billy was a good-natured if serious boy, described as "comely" with a noble aspect, animated by a sense "of sterling Worth & wealth."[5] A young intellectual of great promise and extremely dedicated to his studies, he was particularly enamored of ancient Greece and Rome. He even published a book, translated from the Greek, in his first year at Oxford.[6] The work, *Abradates and Panthea, A Tale, extracted from Xenophon* (1765), received charitable praise from critics who made allowances for Billy's youth in his "first essay."[7] They were mixed, however, in their reaction to his subject matter. One reviewer characterized the work as "a pathetic and interesting tale, in which the best and noblest passions are exercised."[8] Another questioned the taste level of the story, because the romance climaxed with a woman who stabbed herself while lying across her dead lover.[9] Billy's attraction to such a melodramatic tale for his first authorial enterprise provides a glimpse into his personality and, like the lovers he wrote about, the young man's own romance would eventually face tragic consequences.

Billy was a credit to his family, a worthy heir whom they were concerned to preserve, both in health and for the dynastic opportunities he presented. Perhaps this is the reason the Beaches became increasingly concerned about the scourge of smallpox as it raged in the areas around their estates, and they acted to shield their son from this illness. Although smallpox had been present in England since the Middle Ages, in the seventeenth century a more virulent form of the illness

---

3 A *gentleman commoner* was a student not on scholarship. "William Wither Beach Articles of Religion for admission to Oxford," Gloucester Record Office D2455/F2/7/1; Beach, William Wither, s. William, of Fiddleton, Wilts, arm. NEW COLL, matric. 1 Dec., 1764, aged 18; Foster, *Alumni Oxonienses*, Vol. I, 81.

4 French and Rothery, *Man's Estate*, 3.

5 "Wainhouse, Verses, 20 November 1767," D2455/F2/5/3/3.

6 "Wainhouse, Verses, 20 November 1767," D2455/F2/5/3/3; *The Universal Magazine of Knowledge and Pleasure*, Vol. 36 (John Hinton, 1765), 223.

7 Tobias Smollet, *The Critical Review or Annals of Literature*, Vol. 19 (A. Hamilton,1765), 394.

8 *The Monthly Review; or Literary Journal*, Vol. 32 (R. Griffiths, 1764), 393.

9 Tobias Smollet, *The Critical Review or Annals of Literature*, Vol. 19 (A. Hamilton, 1765), 394.

took hold and became endemic, affecting not only children but also the adult population. By the early eighteenth century, smallpox had become a significant cause of death, and as Gareth Williams argued, "a fact of life and a rite of passage that nobody could ignore."[10]

Highly contagious, the disease could be transmitted through bedding and clothing that came into contact with the sores or, more commonly, through the mouth and/or mucosal lining of the nose. After an incubation period of approximately twelve days, the individual was suddenly struck with a headache and backache accompanied by a fever.[11] Richard Holland's 1755 *Miscellaneous Reflections on the Smallpox* describes the symptoms in the following manner:

> At the beginning a general chilness [sic], as in intermittent Fevers, then shivering, yawning, &c. Afterwards feverish heats, great thirst, violent pains in the head, back or loins, restlessness and tossing about with uneasiness, sickness, nauseas and vomiting.[12]

The fever was followed by the appearance of the red spots or "pocks" within a few days, hard swellings that burned and spread all over the body. As Holland stated, "the pimples, which are hitherto white, begin to be red and swoln, and affected with a stretching pain."[13] The pocks were extremely painful, filled with a greenish

---

10 The disease caused extensive mortality in the period 1717–30, and the number of smallpox deaths rose from approximately 5 percent to more than 10 percent by mid-century. The mortality rate ranged from 15 to 25 percent, but these numbers could grow to 40–50 percent, especially when the disease affected children. The epidemics that struck London were particularly bad; for instance, smallpox claimed more than 3,000 lives both in 1710 and in 1719. For more on smallpox, see Deborah Christian Brunton, "Pox Britannica: Smallpox Inoculation in Britain 1721–1830" (PhD dissertation, University of Pennsylvania, 1990); Jennifer Lee Carrell, *The Speckled Monster: A Historical Tale of Battling Smallpox* (Plume, 2004); Elizabeth A. Fenn, *Pox Americana: The Great Smallpox Epidemic of 1775–82* (Hill and Wang, 2001); Ian Glynn and Jenifer Glynn, *The Life and Death of Smallpox* (Cambridge University Press, 2004); Donald R. Hopkins, *Princes and Peasants: Smallpox in History* (University of Chicago Press, 1983); Donald R. Hopkins, *The Greatest Killer in History: Smallpox, with a New Introduction* (University of Chicago Press, 2002); David Koplow, *Smallpox: The Fight to Eradicate a Global Scourge* (University of California Press, 2003); S.L. Kotar and J.E. Gessler, *Smallpox: A History* (McFarland & Company, 2013); Joanna Marschner, David Bindman, and Lisa Ford, eds. *Enlightened Princesses: Caroline, Augusta, and the Shaping of the Modern World* (Yale Center for British Art, 2017); Susan Scott and Christopher J. Duncan, *Human Demography and Disease* (Cambridge University Press, 1998); David E. Shuttleton, *Smallpox and the Literary Imagination 1660–1820* (Cambridge University Press, 2007); Mary L. South, *The Inoculation Book: 1774–1783*, Southampton Records Series 47 (4word, 2014); Gareth Williams, *Angel of Death: The Story of Smallpox* (Palgrave Macmillan, 2010).
11 South, *The Inoculation Book*, 47–8.
12 Richard Holland, *Miscellaneous Reflections on the Smallpox* (W. Owen, 1755), 65–6.
13 Holland, *Miscellaneous Reflections*, 33–4.

yellow pus and broke open easily, emitting a foul odor and at their full size they had a "bigness (which equals that of the greater sort of Pease [sic])."[14]

For those with a mild case, recovery took a month or so. Even if one survived, however, they were usually left with permanent scarring. If the pocks had erupted near the eyes, blindness could result, and in those cases with nervous system involvement the patient could be left with permanently weakened limbs. Many people were afflicted with poor health for years afterwards, with some even becoming invalids for the rest of their lives. Other survivors suffered from infertility, respiratory and neurological problems, and even arthritic difficulties.[15] In 1747, Charles Perry argued of smallpox that "it is a disease which is the Produce of every Country and Climate; and that it is the Lot of almost every Person to have once."[16]

The inhabitants of Wiltshire certainly did not escape the scourge, as there was an epidemic between 1740 and 1741 in Westbury, not far from Keevil. It was significant enough that after the death of two of his neighbors, Jeffery Whitaker wrote in November 1740: "was ill and low Spirited. thought I was going to have the Small pox. Sign'd my Will."[17] Further, in December 1742, George Wansey of Warminster was unable to bring his new bride home because she had never had smallpox and it was "at present ... in the Town."[18] It would be another nine months before the married couple could live together safely, and in August 1743 George wrote, "The Small pox being now almost out of the Town, & our Neighbourhood round about us being very clear; I brought my Wife home from her Brother's."[19]

The smallpox epidemics continued in Wiltshire. Salisbury was repeatedly afflicted during the 1760s, with effects beyond the human toll – these outbreaks also impacted the city's economy and stifled trade, so much so that in 1763 one author complained in the *Salisbury Journal* that "[t]he long and repeated continuance of the Small-pox for years past has ... quite impoverished many honest, tho small tradesmen."[20] The newspapers were not the only source of remark; there were numerous mentions of the outbreaks by the Beach and Talbot families.

The disease featured as a consistent concern, with family members tracking its progress in their letters. In November 1764, Jane Talbot wrote fearfully that "I hear

---

14　Holland, *Miscellaneous Reflections*, 34; Brunton, "Pox Britannica," 10; South, *The Inoculation Book*, 46.

15　Brunton, "Pox Britannica," 11; South, *The Inoculation Book*, 42–3.

16　Charles Perry, *Essay on the Small Pox* (A. Long, 1747), 3.

17　Entry November 18, 1740, *The Diaries of Jeffery Whitaker Schoolmaster of Bratton, 1739–1741*, ed. Marjorie Reeves and Jean Morrison (Wiltshire Record Society, 1989), 56.

18　"14 December 1742, Family Book of George Wansey of Warminster, Clothier," 314/16, Wiltshire and Swindon History Centre, UK.

19　"3 August 1743, Family Book of George Wansey of Warminster, Clothier," 314/16, Wiltshire and Swindon History Centre, UK.

20　*Salisbury Journal*, April 25, 1763, quoted in South, *The Inoculation Book*, 44.

every body at Bath is not quite free from the small pox, I wish poor Mr. Cooke is not past recovery, I pray God spare his life."[21] A year later, she wrote to her sister-in-law, Mrs. Beach, that "I am very glad to hear that the small pox has stopd at Haxton."[22] Her relief would have been very real, as Haxton was close to the Beach estates in Fittleton and Netheravon. Then in July 1766, she once again lamented the disease's approach, but also hinted at its toll upon her own family, writing:

> I am sorry the small pox proceeds so round you but hope it will not come nearer to you indeed it is a desease [sic] much to be dreaded & the late experience I have had of it has made me very thankful to the almighty for preserving my dear children hit.[23]

In the 1760s, perhaps motivated by the illness of his sister's children, or maybe by the numerous discussions of smallpox in print, William Beach demonstrated a growing interest in the prevention of the disease by inoculation.

In 1748, physician Richard Mead defined inoculation as the custom of "transferring the small pox from an infected person to one that is sound."[24] The term, borrowed from the procedure for the grafting of plants in horticulture, involved making an incision then deliberately introducing pus taken from a smallpox pustule to induce a more controlled and milder infection than the one in naturally occurring smallpox.

One of the early proponents of smallpox inoculation in England was Lady Mary Wortley Montagu (1689–1762), who herself had suffered and been scarred by the illness and had lost a brother to the disease.[25] She had observed the procedure while living in Constantinople and chose to have her young son inoculated in 1718. Upon her return to England she became a prominent member of the court and close friend of the Princess of Wales, Caroline of Ansbach (1683–1737). In 1721, when there was an epidemic of smallpox, she chose to have her daughter inoculated by Scottish surgeon Charles Maitland, who had been previously stationed in Turkey. Word of the successful procedure spread and inspired Princess

---

21 Jane Talbot to Mrs. Beach 15 November [1764], private collection.

22 Jane Talbot to Mrs. Beach at Widcomb [c. 1762 or 1765], private collection.

23 Jane Talbot at Margam to Mrs. Beach at Fittleton July 12, 1766, private collection.

24 Richard Mead, *A Discourse on the Smallpox and Measles* (John Brindley, 1748), 82. Mead had been an avid supporter of the early investigations into inoculation conducted in Newgate prison by Sir Hans Slone in 1721. See Anita Guerrini, "Mead, Richard (1673–1754), Physician and Collector of Books and Art" *Oxford Dictionary of National Biography*, 2003 (accessed February 27, 2019), http://www.oxforddnb.com/view/10.1093/ref:odnb/9780198614128.001.0001/odnb-9780198614128-e-18467.

25 Gavin Weightman, *The Great Inoculator: The Untold Story of Daniel Sutton and his Medical Revolution* (Yale University Press, 2020), 2.

Caroline to push forward further investigation of inoculation. She, like Montagu, had personal experience with smallpox, and her eldest daughter had almost died from the disease, so she was personally invested in attempts to combat the illness. Further experimentation with the technique ensued, and in August 1721, six condemned prisoners were used as test subjects, with additional experiments performed the following February, and then in March five orphans were successfully inoculated, paving the way for several of the royal children to receive protection from smallpox through inoculation.[26]

There were numerous arguments over the effectiveness of inoculation, and discussions were not just found in medical treatises but also increasingly seen in popular literature, making them accessible to people like Mr. William Beach of Netheravon. For instance, *The Gentleman's Magazine* and *The Scots Magazine* often published articles from physicians and patients, as well as editorials discussing inoculation (generally in favorable terms).[27] Rising circulation numbers, and the expansion of newspaper and periodical readership, meant these sources assumed a growing importance in communicating public opinion. These sorts of popular publications were also accompanied by a proliferation of medical treatises on the topic by mid-century.[28]

William Beach was interested in the procedure and even purchased his own copy of John Zephaniah Holwell's *On Inoculation* just one month after it was published in 1767.[29] Holwell is perhaps more famous for his writings on his experiences in India and his naming of the Black Hole of Calcutta, but he also wrote treatises on crime and disease.[30] *On Inoculation* was an assessment of the procedure in India, placed into conversation with contemporary practice in Europe,

---

26 Marschner et al., *Enlightened Princesses*, 429–30.

27 South, *The Inoculation Book*, 57–8; Brunton, "Pox Britannica," 72. Variolation was not without risks, as it could lead to a serious case of the illness that could prove disfiguring or fatal. Most individuals, however, only experienced a mild case. Another problem attendant to variolation was that those undergoing the procedure could pass the disease to the uninoculated, making isolation key if an entire town was not being inoculated. See Kotar and Gessler, *Smallpox: A History*, 12–13.

28 Karl W. Schweizer, "Newspapers, Politics and Public Opinion in the Later Hanoverian Era," *Parliamentary History* 25, no. 1 (2006), 32; Brunton, "Pox Britannica," 72.

29 "Miscellaneous receipts William Beach, Esq., 1760s," D2455/E3/2/4/6, Gloucestershire Archives, UK. For more on Holwell's work see: Sudip Bhattacharya, *Unseen Enemy: The English, Disease, and Medicine in Colonial Bengal, 1617–1847* (Cambridge Scholars Publishing, 2014).

30 D.L. Prior, "Holwell, John Zephaniah (1711–1798), East India Company Servant," *Oxford Dictionary of National Biography*, 2008 (accessed November 6, 2018). http://www.oxforddnb.com/view/10.1093/ref:odnb/9780198614128.001.0001/odnb-9780198614128-e-13622. John Zephaniah Holwell had commanded a garrison of East India Company men in Calcutta that was overthrown by Siraj ud-Daula in 1756. Initially the men were permitted to remain free after the taking of the city, but after a drunken Company soldier shot one of the Mughul soldiers, the garrison was rounded up and placed in a small cell, fourteen feet wide and eighteen feet long, with only a tiny window. Many died from suffocation in the night. The actual numbers of those incarcerated are in

and its author stated that the "Brahmins" practiced "nearly the same salutatory method, now so happily pursued in England."[31] The technique in question was one originated by the Sutton family and popularized during the 1760s.

Surgeon Robert Sutton created a standardized methodology for the procedure not based on the individual constitution but one that instead applied to everyone. This was a serious departure from the traditional humoral approach, and as historian Deborah Christian Brunton has argued, it "was the first explicitly disease-centered, rather than patient-centered inoculation technique."[32] Historian Gavin Weightman has likewise asserted that "Suttonian inoculation ... was a genuine breakthrough, and was recognized as such at the time by most medical authorities."[33] Under this system, everyone underwent a month-long period of preparation and took the same medications. The Suttons also shifted the mechanics of the procedure, making a smaller incision, and carefully choosing the matter used in an effort to reduce the severity of the reaction. They also endorsed isolation to prevent the spread of infection from the recently inoculated to the uninoculated. This approach was incredibly successful, producing a reliably mild presentation of the smallpox; as a consequence, the Sutton method increased the numbers of those willing to undertake the procedure.[34]

In 1763, Daniel Sutton, second son of Robert, set up his own practice and refined his father's method by trimming the period of preparation to between eight and ten days and encouraging the patient to spend time outside.[35] In the next four years he amassed a fortune and developed a reputation as the premier Suttonian inoculator. Then he expanded his practice to the capital, acquiring a

---

dispute, as are the deaths. Holwell stated that 145 men and one woman were jailed and that 123 of them died, and these are the numbers generally given in British history textbooks; see, for instance, Stephanie Barczewiski et al., *Britain Since 1688: A Nation in the World* (Routledge, 2015), 51. William Dalrymple argues that Holwell's account "was clearly an exaggeration" but that his "highly coloured account of the Black Hole," written two years after the event, had a lasting legacy. A re-examination of the event, using both British and Mughul sources, put the numbers at sixty-four people incarcerated and forty-three dead. More significant than the actual numbers are the ways in which Holwell's accounting of the event has been used, as Dalrymple states the Black Hole raised ire for generations "and 150 years later was still being taught in British Schools as demonstrative of the essential barbarity of Indians and illustrative of why British rule was supposedly both necessary and justified." See William Dalrymple, *The Anarchy: The East India Company, Corporate Violence, and the Pillage of an Empire* (Bloomsbury, 2019), 104–6.

31 J.Z. (John Zephaniah) Holwell, *An Account of the Manner of Inoculating for the Small Pox in the East Indies. With Some Observations on the Practice and Mode of Treating that Disease in Those Parts* (F.R.S. London, 1767), Gale Eighteenth Century Collections Online.

32 Brunton, "Pox Britannica," 98. For more on these developments, see Weightman, *The Great Inoculator.*

33 Weightman, *The Great Inoculator*, 33.

34 Hopkins, *The Greatest Killer*, 59; Brunton, "Pox Britannica," 98.

35 Hopkins, *The Greatest Killer*, 59–60; Weightman, *The Great Inoculator*, 37.

mansion he called Sutton House in March 1767.[36] The following month, he began advertising his large, newly established inoculation house located on the border between Knightsbridge and Kensington Gore.[37] Mr. Beach became so enamored of the technique that he took Billy to be inoculated by no less than Daniel Sutton himself.

The Beaches certainly did not have to go as far as London to have the procedure, as their own physician, Dr. Abel Moysey of Bath, was well known as an expert inoculator.[38] Mr. Beach, however, was "inclin'd to the <u>Sutton</u> Method" and was interested in having Billy "inoculated by one of the Principals." In May 1767, he took his wife and son (but not his daughters) to London, where they "hir'd a House at <u>Knights-Bridge</u>."[39] It is clear they intended to be gone for some time, as Mr. Beach hired the coach for a month.[40]

In addition to the cost of travel and the hire of a house, the services and attendance of the famous inoculator came at a premium. On June 21, 1767, Mr. Beach paid £20 "to Mr. Sutton" for the procedure.[41] This was certainly more than they would have paid had Billy been inoculated on the premises. The fees varied, but in 1765 those inoculated at Sutton's house paid between three to six guineas. This covered room, board, and the requisite medications; however, the attendance of the man himself depended upon what level of service the individual paid for.[42] Well-off patients could, for an extra expense, be attended in their own homes or in a home they hired near the inoculation house (as the Beaches did). The elevated price of Billy's procedure reflects the level of personal attention he received, and the luxury of having it performed in the comfort of the family's rented establishment.

36 Weightman, *The Great Inoculator*, 38, 44, 52.

37 "The Gazebo House at Kensington Gore, built by the late Mr. Mitchel, is purchased by Mr. Sutton, and, as we hear, for the purpose of inoculation," *London Chronicle*, April 7, 1767–April 9, 1767, 1608, 17th–18th Century Burney Newspapers Collection, Gale Document Number: Z2001685151; "Inoculation. Mr. Daniel Sutton, surgeon, of Ingalestone, Essex, informs the public; that he has purchased the Cupola House, between Knightsbridge and Kensington, for the purpose of Inoculation; which will be fit for the reception of patients as soon as they can be prepared. After the 12th instant, his friends are desired to direct their favours to Mr. Sutton, at the above place." *Gazetteer and New Daily Advertiser* (London, England), Friday, April 10, 1767, 11 887, Seventeenth and Eighteenth Century Burney Newspapers Collection, Gale Document Number: Z2000357848; Daniel Sutton, *The Inoculator; or, Suttonian System of Inoculation* (T. Gillet, 1796), xiii.

38 "Misc. Receipts," D2455/E3/2/4/5, Gloucestershire Archives, UK; "Julia Trevelyan in Bath to her father John Trevalyan, February 1752," DD/WO/56/4/58, Somerset Record Office, UK.

39 *Narrative*, folio 10.

40 "Receipts William Beach, Esq., 1767," D2455/E3/2/4/11, Gloucestershire Archives, UK.

41 "Receipts William Beach, Esq., 1767," D2455/E3/2/4/11.

42 Brunton, "Pox Britannica," 106.

Although there is no record of Billy's treatment, and Robert Sutton kept his technique a secret, we can get some idea of the ordeal from the writings of other patients and practitioners who observed the method or learned from Sutton, as the beauty of the method was its uniformity.[43] Other clues come directly from Daniel Sutton, who, in 1796, towards the end of his career – as his method was being superseded by Edward Jenner's introduction of vaccination – finally published the methodology.[44]

Daniel Sutton argued his preparatory measures were "anti-variolous" and "calculated to resist the violence of the disease."[45] The medications were to intended "to clear away all redundancies and indigestible impurities ... thereby securing a regular and good digestion."[46] Because, as Thomas Thompson argued in 1752, it was believed that smallpox was "an inflammatory disease, it is most certain that the body must be disposed to receive an inflammation."[47] Since, in the humoral system, inflammation was seen as heating, Daniel Sutton recommended a purging powder and a purging syrup containing mercury, which caused a desirable perspiration and reduced "preternatural heat."[48] It also had the added benefit of "destroying worms" that would hamper the success of the inoculation process.[49] These medications were accompanied by a strict diet, once again targeted at reducing heat. Sutton argued that a diet "restricted in quantity and nutritious quality" would attenuate the blood and remove "its influence to induce or support an undue heat and irritation on the surface of the body, [and] a mitigated disease will naturally be the result."[50]

Billy would have undergone preparation before he was inoculated. For a period of eight to ten days he would not have been allowed to consume alcohol, cheese, meat, or butter, and patients were only allowed to drink skimmed milk. They were to consume vegetables, fruit, or pudding and were allowed to drink water, tea, or gruel.[51] On May 27, Mr. Beach acquired milk and tea, and then on June 4 purchased "strawberrys," "collyflowers," and pears for Billy, who would then have undergone the sequence of purging medications.[52]

---

43 Brunton, "Pox Britannica," 100.
44 Jenner's procedure used the related and comparably milder cow pox virus to induce immunity to smallpox.
45 Sutton, *The Inoculator*, 80.
46 Sutton, *The Inoculator*, 80.
47 Thomas Thompson, *An Enquiry into the Origin, Nature and Cure of the Small-Pox* (A. Millar, 1752), 39.
48 Sutton, *The Inoculator*, 81–3.
49 Sutton, *The Inoculator*, 83.
50 Sutton, *The Inoculator*, 80.
51 Brunton, "Pox Britannica," 100.
52 "Receipts William Beach, Esq., 1767," D2455/E3/2/4/11.

Once Billy had completed his preparation, the procedure would commence. Daniel Sutton instructed that the inoculation site should be "not more than two or three inches above the joint of the elbow, on the upper part of the arm of an adult." This was to avoid any inconvenience in examining the site as pushing a tight sleeve repeatedly over the wound might remove the head of the pock "and a considerable inflammation and sloughing may take place in consequence, creating unnecessary pain and trouble."[53]

With the site chosen, the inoculator would make a small cut or puncture with a lancet "barely sufficient to draw blood, and not deeper than the sixteenth part of an inch."[54] The lancet was "charged with the smallest perceivable quantity (and the smaller the better) of unripe, crude, or watery matter."[55] The procedure was followed by further medications intended to promote sweating and cool the patient, with the doses determined by the patient's reaction. Sutton believed in an inverse relationship between the redness surrounding the puncture site and the severity of the corresponding case of smallpox (the more inflamed the arm, the weaker the smallpox). The patient would not have been allowed to languish in bed, but instead would have been encouraged to get up and move around outside and may have also been given cold water to drink or a special restorative punch.[56]

By June 27, Billy was recovered enough to get a visit from the barber, and then he traveled to spend time at Hall Place in Hampshire before continuing his studies at Oxford. In 1767, he again followed in his father's footsteps, becoming a member of Gray's Inn, after which William Beach signed over his London lodgings and Billy took possession of "his Ground Chamber No. 17 In Coney Court with a Cellar."[57] In that same year observers remarked on his dedication to his "Mind's Improvement" and the "intense grave studies he pursues."[58] Perhaps it was his intense application to study, a sensitive soul, or a broken heart (all of which were thought to cause madness in the eighteenth century), but within a few years of this description, the twenty-year-old lost his wits.

A broken heart emerges as the culprit, as multiple accounts laid Billy's condition at the door of a frustrated matrimonial connection; less charitable accounts cast his mother as the architect of his disappointment.[59] We do not have explicit

---

53 Sutton, *The Inoculator*, 78.
54 Sutton, *The Inoculator*, 77.
55 Sutton, *The Inoculator*, 77.
56 Brunton, "Pox Britannica," 102–3.
57 "Receipts William Beach, Esq., 1767," D2455/E3/2/4/11; Foster, *The Register of Admissions to Gray's Inn 1521–1889*, 385; "27 Nov 1767," *Gray's Inn Book of Orders*, Vol. 3 (December 1730–June 1785), folio 338, Gray's Inn, London, UK.
58 "Wainhouse, Verses, 20 November 1767," D2455/F2/5/3/3.
59 *Narrative*, folio 46–8.

accounts of Billy's situation, as his illness and his life after this moment is shrouded in mystery. He, like so many others in the same predicament, fell victim to what Allan Ingram argues is "the history of silence" surrounding madness, making it difficult to recover the thoughts and feelings of those who experienced mental illness, and Billy's case is no exception.[60] As Mrs. William Hicks Beach wrote in *A Cotswold Family*, "the rest of his life ... is a dreadful silence, for he went out of his mind."[61] Careful archival research, however, has uncovered a few glimpses of Billy's predicament and his family's hopes for his recovery.

The only direct account of the events surrounding the onset of Billy's condition comes in the form of accusations from William Wainhouse, who obviously did not provide a charitable account of the role of Mr. and Mrs. Beach. He made strong allegations, stating that he had witnessed the harsh treatment of Anne, whom he claimed Mrs. Beach "lov'd very little." However, Wainhouse was shocked "that this same Mother cross'd the Son of her Love in his Inclinations." Billy had apparently fallen for "a truly amiable young Lady," and unlike Anne's attachment to Wainhouse, this woman was "a very equal & proper Match." Despite this equity, when Mrs. Beach was informed, she refused to consent to the marriage. A clue to the identity of Billy's beloved is neatly penned in the margins, in Wainhouse's hand – "Miss Talbot."[62]

Was this the same Miss Talbot of Margam, the bridesmaid in green, who garnered such attention at the wedding of James Richardson and Anne Beach? One can imagine that the lady's sweet temper and demeanor could turn the head of the studious Billy, who was also known to have a bit of a romantic predilection, courting the Muse in his "gayer Hours." Miss Talbot was certainly lauded for her "Fair Virtue ... [and] Charm" and had won widespread approbation during the wedding.[63] Miss Ann Talbot (1752–1771) was the daughter of Rev. Thomas Talbot (1719–1758) and Jane Beach (1725–1768), and she was the sister of Thomas Mansel Talbot (1747–1813). She was also a close friend to Billy's sister, Anne Beach.[64] Aligning with William Wainhouse's account, Ann Talbot herself provides a few fragmentary pieces of evidence, and she also points to a broken heart as the originator of Billy's condition. Hers is the most comprehensive explanation that remains, and it is also the only surviving letter addressed to Billy's sister, Anne.

---

60 Allan Ingram, *The Madhouse of Language: Writing and Reading Madness in the Eighteenth Century* (Routledge, 1991), 17.

61 Hicks, *A Cotswold Family*, 297–8.

62 *Narrative*, folio 46.

63 "Wainhouse, Verses, 20 November 1767," D2455/F2/5/3/3.

64 The other sisters had died before this time: Jane Talbot (1750–1758) and Mary (1753–1762); "Outline Pedigree of the Mansel and Talbot Families," Martin, *The Penrice Letters*, 179.

Miss Talbot provides the only assessment by a family member of Billy's illness. She articulates a cause for his condition, one intimately entwined with his emotions, writing that "they say in Wilts the occasion of it was the forcing him to marry Miss B – whom he said he never would like as his affections were settld on another lady, pray who is it?"[65] This question could be interpreted in a variety of ways; perhaps she did not know she was the object of his affection, or maybe she was seeking confirmation that she was, or perhaps it was someone else entirely. Sadly, the response did not survive, and this letter leaves us with more questions than answers. Who is the mysterious Miss B? Why would Mrs. Beach have forced Billy to marry her? Was this another situation like the debacle of the botched match between their daughter and Gaisford of Westbury? What objections did she have to the "other lady"? For the first three questions, we may never know; for the last, Wainhouse provides a possible motive.

What could be objectionable about a match with Miss Talbot? The young woman was from a good family and would likely have brought "a very good Fortune" to the marriage. Wainhouse purports Mrs. Beach's motive was revenge. She had taken an extreme dislike to the young woman and stated that she would "rather have him [Billy] marry the Cook-Maid." Just as she had in her daughter's case, Mrs. Beach charged that "[h]e might have any one, but the Lady he mention'd." This, Wainhouse railed, proved her perfidy, and that "her Children may have any, but those they like." Mr. Beach seems to have had no objections to Billy's ladylove, but gave in to his wife's judgment. Wainhouse further asserts that "[t]he Mother laid her Commands on the Son to think no more of his Beloved."[66] It was this "Disappointment [that] threw the Son into a low, odd & unsociable Way, in which he has continued ever since."[67]

Mrs. Beach's adamant stand against the match, according to Wainhouse, stemmed from a hostility toward the family even though they were connected through marriage. As he further asserted "This Dislike has been attributed to a Money-Rivalship, the Family being look'd on as too powerful Competitors for the Fortunes of rich Relations."[68] This assertion certainly fits with the splitting of James Harding's fortune between the Talbots and Beaches. Whether Wainhouse's account can be believed, the young woman did run afoul of Mrs. Beach at the end of 1769, which corresponds with the timing of Billy's illness. Ann Talbot wrote Mrs. Beach a letter of apology, stating,

---

65 Ann Talbot (1752–1771) at Margam, Glamorganshire, to her first cousin, Ann Beach (1749–1771) at Keevil, Wiltshire, September 25 (n.d., but c. 1769), private collection.
66 *Narrative*, folio 47.
67 *Narrative*, folio 47–8.
68 *Narrative*, folio 48–9.

> Tis with great concern I have been made acquainted that a letter of mine should be so far misinterpreted as to occasion you any uneasiness. I desire you will pardon the contents & attribute it to the giddyness of Seventeen, not to a design of disobliging you.... I hope I have express'd myself in a manner which can leave you not room to doubt that I am ever asham'd to acknowledge myself in fault or make any concession adequate.[69]

Although this is in keeping with the notion that Mrs. Beach had taken a dislike to the young woman, circumstance does not equal causation.

Wainhouse also claims that "the young Lady, the Son's Flame, had been detected in relating some unwelcome Truths that gall'd the Mother." Perhaps this was the subject of her misinterpreted letter and the reason for her apology. Wainhouse felt Mrs. Beach saw the match as "An Opportunity of Revenge," gratifying her "Pique & Spleen ... at the Expence [sic] of the Son's future Peace & Enjoyment."[70] Even if this was the case, given Billy's importance to the continuation of the family line, why wouldn't Mrs. Beach simply relent once Billy's condition became apparent? It is possible she may have had a change of heart, but in 1770 her attention would have been diverted by Anne's attempted elopement and subsequent incarceration. Even more problematic, if Miss Ann Talbot was actually Billy's ladylove, any hope in that quarter was ended when the young woman died in 1771 (the same year as his sister, Anne). Whatever the cause, Billy's unhappy state of mind continued.

Ann Talbot also provides the only other brief glimpse into the nature of Billy's affliction, asking, "pray my dr how is your brother does he still continue in the same melancholy way."[71] This mention of melancholy is a clue. In the eighteenth century, this term, along with spleen, vapors, and hypochondria, were all used to describe depression. This was a very different idea of depression than the modern clinical definition, and it was a shifting and vague concept.[72] This circumstance was acknowledged by Nicholas Robinson in 1729, when he complained of

---

69 Ann Talbot at Kelston [To Mrs. Beach], December 4, 1769, private collection.
70 *Narrative*, folio 48–9.
71 Ann Talbot to Ann Beach, September 25.
72 Clark Lawlor, *From Melancholia to Prozac: A History of Depression* (Oxford University Press, 2012), 5. For more on Madness see Jonathan Andrews, "The Lot of the 'Incurably' Insane in Enlightenment England," *Eighteenth Century Life* 12, no. 1 (1988): 1–18; Peter Bartlett and David Wright, eds., *Outside the Walls of the Asylum: The History of Care in the Community, 1750–2000* (Athlone Press, 1999); Shirley Burgoyne Black, *An 18th Century Mad-Doctor: William Perfect of West Malling* (Darenth Valley Publications, 1995); Leigh Wetherall Dickson and Allan Ingram, eds., *Depression and Melancholy, 1660–1800* (Pickering & Chatto, 2012); R.A. Houston, "Clergy and the Care of the Insane in Eighteenth-Century Britain," *Church History* 73, no. 1 (2004): 114–38; Richard Hunter and Ida Macalpine, *Three Hundred Years of Psychiatry, 1535–1860* (Oxford University Press, 1963); Ida Macalpine and Richard Hunter, *George III and the Mad Business* (Allen Lane, 1969); Alan

the difficulties of writing on a subject "where most of the Phaenomena that concern this Enquiry are deeply entrench'd in impenetrable Darkness, and where the Nature of the Subject it self scarce admits of evidence, much less Demonstration."[73]

In his treatise *A New System of the Spleen, Vapours and Hypochondriack Melancholy*, Robinson attempted to move beyond humoral explanations of madness, which saw melancholy as the product of a superfluous quantity of black bile.[74] Humoral physiology held that the spleen functioned in the absorption of this humor and when it was not equal to the task, a complaint called the spleen ensued, causing things like panic, anxiety, and lassitude, all hallmarks of melancholy (though the symptoms were legion).[75] The illness caused both psychological as well as physical symptoms, like hallucinations, due to the action of overheated black bile. Other causes of imbalance included the action of powerful emotions, which could result in melancholia, a confusing and often nonspecific term that generally referred to "unusual or *mad* behaviour."[76]

Melancholy, the spleen, the vapors, and even the Hip (Hypp) were often used interchangeably, and their definitions were not stable from treatise to treatise, although some physicians like Dr. Smith attempted to elucidate their subtle differences. He gendered the spleen and vapors, stating that "[t]he spleen and vapours are nearly synonymous terms; the symptoms and causes are the same: only the vapours sometimes bring on fits, and as these fits are most frequently observed in women, we call the same disease vapours in women and spleen in men." He further stated that if the spleen and vapors continued long enough to impact the patient's constitution they would be afflicted with the more serious condition called "hip, or hypochondrical melancholy: and is for the most part attended with a scurvy." If this continued, in men it would turn into madness and, depending

Ingram, ed. *Patterns of Madness in the Eighteenth Century: A Reader* (Liverpool University Press, 1998); Kathleen Jones, *Lunacy, Law, and Conscience 1744–1845* (Routledge, 1999); MacDonald, *Mystical Bedlam*; Chris Mounsey, *Christopher Smart: Clown of God* (Bucknell University Press, 2001); William L. Parry-Jones, *The Trade in Lunacy: A Study of Private Madhouses in England in the Eighteenth and Nineteenth Centuries* (Routledge and Kegan Paul, 1972); Roy Porter, *Madmen: A Social History of Madhouses, Mad-Doctors and Lunatics* (Tempus, 2004); Roy Porter, *Mind-Forg'd Manacles: A History of Madness in England from the Restoration to the Regency* (Athlone Press, 1987); Andrew Scull, *Undertaker of the Mind: John Monro and Mad-Doctoring in Eighteenth Century England* (University of California Press, 2001); Leonard Smith, *Lunatic Hospitals in Georgian England, 1750–1830* (Routledge, 2007); Akihito Suzuki, "The Household and the Care of Lunatics in Eighteenth-century London," in *The Locus of Care: Families, Communities, Institutions, and the Provision of Welfare since Antiquity*, eds. Peregrine Horden and Richard Smith (Routledge, 1998).

73 Nicholas Robinson, *A New System of the Spleen, Vapours and Hypochondriack Melancholy* (A. Bettesworth, 1729), 3.

74 Lawlor, *From Melancholia to Prozac*, 25.

75 Porter, *Madmen*, 55.

76 Lawlor, *From Melancholia to Prozac*, 26.

on the constitution, would manifest differently. The bilious constitution led to a "raging and furious" madness "called mania, lunacy or frenzy," but in those with a "cold and phlegmatic" constitution the madness took the form of "a settled, fixed, moaping [sic] melancholy."[77]

Insanity, like other diseases, had been anchored in the humoral system, though there was a great deal of discussion over the specific causes and nature of madness. These notions were heavily influenced by the individual constitution (the specific complexion of humors), which could be affected by a number of factors, including gender, environment, diet, and family, and could lead to an imbalance in bile, blood, and phlegm.[78] However, over the course of the eighteenth century, ideas about the cause of disease began to shift away from strict humoralism towards the concept of a nervous body. There was a corresponding change in the notion of the constitution, which remained an important consideration in chronic, difficult-to-treat illnesses like insanity, consumption, or even gout.

The concept of the constitution hardened, and instead of a complexion of humors it was now seen as "an ordered structure whose fundamental characteristics were inherited as a whole, resulting in either a strong constitution that was resistant to disease or a weak one that left an individual vulnerable to illness."[79] These ideas were increasingly anchored in the developing ideas of the nervous system promoted by a number of medical writers who saw its proper functioning as crucial for the maintenance of health.[80] The nerves assumed a greater importance in accounts of illness for people like William Cullen, who believed that a neurosis could be created particularly when the nerves were subjected to intense emotions.[81]

Strong passions had long been enumerated among the causative agents of disease, featuring in explanations of madness and, ironically, in the other affliction to hit the Beach family – consumption. The idea that a disappointment in love could lead to insanity was well accepted, and Billy was not even the only victim in Keevil. Sophia Beach received a letter complaining about the predicament of

---

77 W. Smith, *A Dissertation upon the Nerves* (W. Owen, 1768), 149–50.

78 Porter, *Madmen*, 49.

79 Carolyn A. Day, *Consumptive Chic: A History of Beauty, Fashion and Disease* (Bloomsbury, 2017).

80 Some notable seventeenth- and eighteenth-century theorists of the nervous system include Thomas Willis, Albrecht von Haller, Robert Whytt, William Cullen, Alexander Monroe II, and John Brown. For more on the nerves and the influence of these theories, see George S. Rousseau, "Nerves, Spirits, and Fibres: Towards Defining the Origins of Sensibility," in *Studies in the Eighteenth Century*, eds. R.F. Brissenden and J.C. Eade (University of Toronto Press, 1976); Clark Lawlor, "It is a Path I Have Prayed to Follow," in *Romanticism and Pleasure*, eds. Thomas H. Schmid and Michelle Faubert (Palgrave Macmillan, 2010).

81 W.F. Bynum, "Nosology," in *Companion Encyclopedia of the History of Medicine*, ed. W.F. Bynum and Roy Porter, Vol. 1 (Routledge, 2001), 346–7.

the curate Mr. Martin, who was a "very good kind of Man" but his head had been turned by "a love affair" and his pining for "Miss Long of Row Ashton" had led to a dereliction of duty. He was reported to be "out of his Mind [and] not done duty this fortnight."[82]

The family was certainly concerned with returning Billy to health. Unsurprisingly, they first sought assistance in Bath. The Beaches had long turned to Mr. Horton of Westgate Street for their medical needs, having visited him many times in the preceding decade. John Horton, apothecary, alderman, justice of the peace, and later mayor of the city offered his clients lodging as well as treatments.[83] In December 1769, he began providing a variety of medicines for Billy's affliction. Recalling the perceived connection between melancholy and scurvy, it is not surprising that "an Antiscorbutick Mixture" was prescribed alongside numerous nervous pills and juleps. Billy was also given the famous Dr. James's Fever Powder.[84] Invented by Dr. Robert James (1703–1776), a close personal friend of Dr. Samuel Johnson, and popular with the well-off and literary set, his powders were not only used to combat fevers, but because they also contained sweating agents, they were used as a general restorative. There were a number of controversies surrounding the powder, but despite objections it remained popular, even being used regularly by King George III.[85] Billy was also given Sir Walter Raleigh's cordial, which Thomas Sydenham had prescribed in the seventeenth century, "along with a restorative diet," for treating a type of madness that "at length descends into idiotism."[86]

Between December 28, 1769, and May 9, 1771, Horton sent no fewer than 144 separate prescriptions, and because in melancholy the abdomen remained an originator of the muddled senses and the perturbation of the brain, a number of the treatments were targeted at this area. The apothecary delivered purges and a vomit, as well as saline-opening draughts that would have had laxative properties

82 "Letter M. Taylor to Sophia Beach, Monday Morning, no date," D2455/F2/4/1/2 Gloucestershire Archives, UK.

83 There were fifteen apothecaries in Bath that offered lodging as well as treatment. See Whittet, "Apothecaries and their Lodgers, 15; Janet Mary Chivers, "'A Resonating Void': Strategies and Responses to Poverty, Bath, 1770–1835," doctoral thesis (Bath Spa University, School of Historical and Cultural Studies, 2006); Anne Borsay, *Medicine and Charity in Georgian Bath: A Social History of the General Infirmary c. 1739–1830* (Routledge, 2020); *The Strangers' Assistant and Guide to Bath* (R. Cruttwell, 1773), 71.

84 "Medicines deliver'd for the Use of Willm. Beach Esqr. pr Jn. Horton & Son, December 1769," D2455/E3/2/4/16, Gloucestershire Archives, UK.

85 T.A.B. Corely, "James, Robert (bap. 1703, d. 1776), Physician and Inventor of James's Fever Powder," *Oxford Dictionary of National Biography*, 2004 (accessed March 23, 2019), http://www.oxforddnb .com/view/10.1093/ref:odnb/9780198614128.001.0001/odnb-9780198614128-e-14618.

86 John Swan, *The Entire Works of Dr. Thomas Sydenham* (Edward Cave, 1742), 609.

and caused loose stools.[87] A number of the medications were soap-based preparations, including the prescribed saponaceous boluses and soap pills, believed to be capable of removing obstructions. For instance, *A Dissertation upon the Nerves* suggested that soap pills were useful in cases of patients "under nervous diseases" who are "always affected with wakefulness." The work went on to advocate that

> Soap ... is an excellent diobstruent medicine ... as soap seems to remove obstructions by melting down the morbid indurated matter ... therefore, after the use of soap ... the offending matter should be evacuated by diaphoretics and gentle emetics.[88]

Mr. Horton seems to have heeded this advice, using diaphoretics like mercury to promote sweating and perspiration.[89] Despite these and numerous other preparations, Billy's treatments did not have the desired effect. In August 1771, Sophia Beach reported that "Billy is much as usual."[90] The family then removed to Mere, which his cousin Thomas Mansel Talbot hoped was a sign of Billy's recovery, writing in October, "As you justly observe, by my cousin Beaches being at Mere he is undoubtedly better. I sincerely wish he may perfectly recover."[91] Two days later he wrote to a cousin inquiring again about Billy's health: "How is the Fittleton family? My brother sent me word that my cousin Beach was at Mere; this makes me hope to hear he is better."[92]

It is possible the family felt a sojourn in Mere would benefit the young man, by taking him away from the place where he had experienced his disappointment. William Battie's controversial, though influential, 1758 *Treatise on Madness* argued that curing madness required removing the patient "entirely from the context where he or she had become mad, including family, friends and external pressures."[93] Battie believed it was only in the asylum that this could be achieved. As he stated,

> Madness then ... requires the patient's being removed from all objects that act forcibly upon the nerves, and excite too lively a perception of things,

---

87 "Medicines deliver'd," D2455/E3/2/4/16; Porter, *Madmen*, 54; F. Penrose, *A Dissertation on the Inflammatory, Gangrenous and Putrid Sore Throat, also on the Putrid Fever* (D. Prince, 1766), 48.

88 Smith, *A Dissertation upon the Nerves*, 204, 224–5.

89 "Medicines deliver'd," D2455/E3/2/4/16.

90 "William Beach, Esq. to Sophia Beach, 13 August 1771," D2455/F2/4/1/2, Gloucestershire Archives, UK.

91 "Thomas Mansel Talbot in Milan to Christopher Mansel Talbot, 22 October 1771," in Martin, *The Penrice Letters*, 59.

92 "Thomas Mansel Talbot in Milan to Mrs. [?Anna Catharina] Beach, 24 October 1771," Martin, *The Penrice Letters*, 61. "Anna Catherine Beach (c. 1720–1804). Daughter of Thomas Beach of West Ashton, Wilts (brother of William Beach of Fittleton and Keevil, 1655–1741). She lived at Kelston and in Bath. She nursed Thomas Mansel Talbot's mother and sister Ann in their last illnesses." Martin, *The Penrice Letters*, 163.

93 Ingram, *Patterns of Madness*, 112.

more especially from such objects as are the known causes of his disorder.... The visits there fore of affecting friends as well as enemies ... ought
strictly to be forbidden. On the same account the place of confinement
should be at some distance from the home.[94]

As Billy's illness progressed, or at least failed to improve, the Beaches would have
had to determine how best to deal with the situation. What were their options,
beyond consulting the medical professionals in Bath, should the illness prove
intractable?

During the eighteenth century, options for caring for the mad were growing
but still limited, as most individuals would have been taken care of at home, sent
to board with someone else, or simply left to wander. Evidence on the subject is
spotty but indicates it was common for parishes to intervene in the case of problematic persons, and magistrates could order the family to control the individual,
or sometimes they would be sent to live with another parishioner.[95] Extant information indicates that by the end of the previous century people were sending
lunatics to board with caretakers and that there were also small private institutions that housed the mad.[96] Historian of medicine Andrew Scull has asserted
that this practice of the parish boarding out paupers "in private dwelling houses"
led to these arrangements earning "the description of 'mad' houses."[97] Rarely were
afflicted individuals sent to asylums in large towns, or admitted as pauper patients
to private madhouses. Most afflicted individuals remained in the community, as
there was not yet a system in place to efficiently care for those with mental illnesses and there were only a few institutions devoted to their care.[98]

In the seventeenth century, Bethlem Hospital in Moorfields was the only public institution charged with caring for the mad, and it was not until the eighteenth
century that there was growing "awareness of the need for public responsibility
for the care of lunatics."[99] By mid-century, some charitable hospitals, like St. Luke's
(established in 1751), were attempting to assert medical authority over the issue of
insanity. The large asylum was a rarity; even at the end of the century there were

---

94 William Battie, *A Treatise on Madness* (J. Whiston and B. White, 1758), 68–9.
95 Porter, *Madmen*, 126–7.
96 There were no legal licensing regulations, and because many of these institutions came and went
   or were desirable due to the privacy they provided, there is a dearth of records surviving that allow
   clear access to the breadth and scope of private madhouses during the eighteenth century. See
   Andrew Scull, *The Most Solitary of Afflictions: Madness and Society in Britain 1700–1900* (Yale
   University Press, 1993), 20; Porter, *Mind-Forg'd Manacles*, 137–8.
97 Scull, *The Most Solitary of Afflictions*, 21.
98 Porter, *Madmen*, 126–7.
99 Porter, *Madmen*, 128; Parry-Jones, *The Trade in Lunacy*, 1.

only three large institutions, all close to London, with Hoxton House maintaining 486 individuals in 1815. Instead, it was more common for patients to end up in small, privately owned, profit-oriented institutions.[100]

Although seen as seedy enterprises, private madhouses were lucrative and offered a solution to a community or family that did not wish to deal with a member acutely afflicted with madness. They were also extremely diverse, varying in amenities, quality and style of care, treatment options, size, and even the status of their charges. Most only housed around a dozen patients at a time, and many were even smaller. Even at the turn of the eighteenth century, outside of London most housed only twenty or less, with only seven institutions larger than thirty inmates in size.[101]

The cost of boarding an individual depended on the institution, the status of the patient, and the level of care. Some establishments only catered to a higher-end clientele, like that of Dr. Charles Best, who claimed his Yorkshire asylum at Acomb was "for persons of condition only."[102] Savvy owners also offered a menu of upgrades for wealthier clients, including access to nicer rooms, personalized attention, better food, or even greater discretion, and some even permitted patients to be attended by family servants. Others implemented high tariffs: one institution in St. Albans, Hertfordshire, charged between three to five guineas per week (this weekly charge amounted to the annual salary of someone working as a maid servant). Other places catered to the social elite – for instance, Thomas Warburton supposedly charged the Duke of Atholl £1,500 per annum to care for his son.[103] Even this steep price tag would not have put off the Beaches, as Mr. Beach put aside £1,600 annually to ensure Billy's comfort, a sum equal to the most expensive of asylums.

Not only could the Beaches afford this care for Billy, there were also options available in the vicinity of their estates and those of their family members. For instance, the Fishponds in Bristol (Gloucestershire) had been operating since 1766, and St. Mary Magdalen Hospital in Bath had been "built for the reception of Idiots." Likewise, in Wiltshire there was Fonthill Gifford, founded in 1718.[104] Even closer was the institution at Box, near Trowbridge, which was nearest to

---

100 Scull, *The Most Solitary of Afflictions*, 18; Porter, *Mind-Forg'd Manacles*, 141–2; Parry-Jones, *The Trade in Lunacy*, 1.

101 Scull, *The Most Solitary of Afflictions*, 19; Porter, *Mind-Forg'd Manacles*, 140.

102 Porter, *Mind-Forg'd Manacles*, 142.

103 Porter, *Mind-Forg'd Manacles*, 142; Charlotte MacKenzie, *Psychiatry for the Rich: A History of Ticehurst Private Asylum 1792–1917* (Routledge, 1992), 14.

104 John Wood, Esq., *A Description of Bath*, 2nd ed. (Bathoe, 1765), 306. For more on St. Mary Magdalen, see Peter K. Carpenter, "The Georgian Idiot Hospital at Bath," *History of Psychiatry* 4 (1998): 471–89.

their estates.[105] Kingsdown House had operated there since c. 1615, and this establishment was concerned not just with housing the mad but also with "the restoration of the lunatic."[106] The proximity to their estate, and the stated purpose of cure, must have been appealing, and there is evidence the Beaches may have consulted someone there in June 1771 but there is no indication that Billy was ever incarcerated.[107]

By the turn of the nineteenth century, Box was notorious and featured prominently in the 1815 investigation into private madhouses.[108] By this time the house was owned by Dr. Langworthy and was "delightfully situated, the house and ground commanding cheerful views."[109] Edward Wakefield shared the details of his visit in 1814 with the Select Committee in the House of Commons for Better Regulation of Madhouses. Wakefield provided an account of four women incarcerated in a cellar:

> lying upon straw on fixed bedsteads, two women nearly naked; around these beds was a deal partition. I heard more in similar places make a great noise; Dr. Langworthy stating that they were perfectly naked.... The room in which they were confined is entirely dark; and I think in the course of my visiting these places I never recollect to have seen four living persons in so wretched a place.[110]

There is no way to determine Mr. Beach's reaction to his visit to Kingsdown, but we do know Billy's parents made different choices for his care. In the end it appears that the attempts to cure him were for naught, but unlike their daughter Anne, Mr. and Mrs. Beach did not abandon him. They settled upon an option more common for affluent families, who tended to continue the care of their mad individually or give them over to the care of a clergyman or a medical practitioner.[111] In this case, Reverend William Williams was tasked with attending Billy, though there are no details of the attention he provided.[112]

---

105 Porter, *Mind-Forg'd Manacles*, 137–8; Parry-Jones, *The Trade in Lunacy*, 38.
106 Parry-Jones, *The Trade in Lunacy*, 38, 168.
107 "Miscellaneous Receipts, June 1771," D2455/E3/2/4/16, Gloucestershire Archives, UK.
108 Porter, *Mind-Forg'd Manacles*, 141–2.
109 *Report, Together with the Minutes of Evidence, and an Appendix of Papers, from the Committee Appointed to Consider of Prevision being Made for the Better Regulation of Madhouses in England* (Baldwin Craddock, 1815), 297.
110 *Report*, 297.
111 Scull, *The Most Solitary of Afflictions*, 21.
112 *Journals of the House of Lords* 48 (1810), 397.

Billy received long-term care at Netheravon House while his family hoped for his recovery. They acquired books for him and continued to pay for the lodgings at Gray's Inn in his name (rather than returning them to his father's control).[113] They also established a routine of care for him, ensuring his comfort, and his father even made provisions in his will for £1,600 per annum "for the maintenance and support of my said Son and his Servants" in a manner that "will conduce most to his comfort during the unhappy state of mind under which he now labours." This was to occur for the rest of his life to ensure "his comfort [was] provided always."[114] Billy was tucked away at Netheravon House, and eventually he was removed from the succession in 1790 by a codicil in his father's will and a 1797 judgment confirmed by a private act of Parliament, when the Reverend Williams provided testimony that he "has continued and still continues in the same State of Imbecility of Mind." Here we get our final glimpse of Billy when Rev. Williams "stated that he had known him for the last Twelve or Fourteen Years, and was of the Opinion, that there was no Expectation of his Recovery."[115] With Billy removed from the succession, his youngest sister, Henrietta Maria (1760–1837), and her husband, Michael Hicks (1760–1830), became the sole heirs to the Beaches' considerable fortune. Billy spent the rest of his long life at Netheravon, dying there at the age of 82 in 1829.[116]

* * * * *

One of the most frustrating aspects of this project, apart from there being nothing from Billy or Anne, was trying to corroborate or disprove the accusations surrounding the couple. Should the people of the villages of Keevil and Steeple Ashton be believed? Was William Wainhouse just a money grubber who was only after Anne for her inheritance? One of my students asked me: how do you know when to stop going down a rabbit hole, and how do you find sources when you have hit a dead end? These are huge questions without any satisfactory answers. Rabbit holes can be really productive, but you do need to realize that you can still write something even if you don't get to the bottom of a question. As someone who is stubborn and just desperately wants to know the answer even if I will never write about it, I have often fallen down a rabbit hole, and when I hit a dead end I am always trying to

---

113 William Cooke, *Poetical Essays on Several Occasions* (S. Smith, 1774), v; *Gray's Inn Book of Orders*, Vol. 3, December 1730–June 1785, folio 574, Gray's Inn, London, UK.

114 "Will of William Wither Beach, Esq. Testatm. died 9th June 1790, Attested Copy of Office Copy Will and Codicils dated 13 August 1785, 1st Codicil 21 May, 2d Codicil 22 May, 3d 23 May 1790, Proved 24th June 1790," D2455/F2/5/4/2, Gloucestershire Archives, UK.

115 "Mr. Beach's Estate Bill," HL/PO/CO/1/ 41, Parliamentary Archives, UK; *Journals of the House of Lords* 48 (1810), 397.

116 "Obituary," Sylvanus Urban, ed., *The Gentleman's Magazine* (J.B. Nichols and Son, 1829), 651.

find another way of accessing that information. This was certainly the case with the properties inherited by William Wainhouse. There was mention of two houses in Bath. If I was going to establish if there was money, I needed to find those houses. Bath is a stunningly beautiful place, so I am always happy to go, but as a historian it is also a deeply weird place. Because it was a spa town that people visited seasonally, the records related to those passing through are not actually in Bath. This means that when you are trying to find things out about the city, you need to know the family, trace them back to their home, and then hope they happened to write about the time they spent there and that those writings survived. Since I had already grabbed everything I could find from the Beaches and Wainhouses there was no more to be found in that quarter. I was stuck. At the Bath Record Office I did look for deeds for the Wainhouse properties, to no avail. I also went down to Duke Street and figured out exactly where it was, and how close it was to the fashionable places in the city. Although things have changed, I find exploring the sites of the happenings I am investigating helps me to better understand what I am reading. This whole book project really brought home to me the power of standing in the spaces and places where things happened. It helped me interpret the documents, and while standing surrounded by Georgian mansions, I got an idea. William Wainhouse certainly wasn't living in the house, but its location meant it would be a great place for people coming to Bath for the season to rent out. Ah HA! This might be the way I could get at the information through a side door. Even though there wasn't a deed for Wainhouse's property, if I could figure out how much the houses on Duke Street went for in rent, I could make an educated guess about the kind of revenue he might be making from the property. I grabbed a bite to eat and then went back to the record office. I was so excited when I found a deed for another property on the same street (they were all part of a planned neighborhood development and were of the same size). I called up the document, eagerly scanned through the legalese looking for the amount of the rent, and weirdly I didn't see a number. Annoyed, I went back and read carefully and had to resist the urge to scream in the archive in frustration. All I could think was, "Are you kidding me?!!" Oh, there was an amount listed, but it wasn't in money, instead it said "and paying therefore the rent of one peppercorn on the last day of the said term."[117] A PEPPERCORN!!! What the heck!!!! I had absolutely no idea what this was. Was this shorthand for some specific amount of money? I knew spices were at one time worth a lot, but that was in a much earlier period than the one I was studying. I thought, "How on earth am I supposed to find out the value of peppercorns in the mid-eighteenth century?" What I didn't know, and had to look up, was that this was a shorthand

---

117 "Lease James Rothey to Joseph Saughton," December 17, 1759, 928/N/4a, Bath Record Office, UK.

for indicating a nominal rent. Frustratingly, it didn't give me the amount of money William Wainhouse might have gotten from leasing out his property. I felt like a cartoon villain that had been foiled again. Sometimes you rack your brain, come up with what you think is a brilliant plan, and then you are outwitted by the archive. It happens – the key is to not get discouraged.

CHAPTER FOUR

Refutations and Reputation: The Social Uses of Disease

For his Sake she set her Health & Fortune at Stake. They were happy in each other, but alas! their social Happiness was of short Duration. The beloved Fair was cut off, in the Flower of Youth ... by repeated Strokes of parental Cruelty, under the Load of which she droop'd & died.[1]

Sickness is not simply a biological event, but also an individualized and social one, grounded in its cultural context and historical and geographic location. This connection between society and sickness means a victim of disease experiences that illness not just within the established parameters of medical knowledge and biological evidence, but also as a function of their own life circumstances and social place – these factors were incredibly important both in the progress and in the uses of Anne's illness and death.

The *Wainhouse Narrative* discusses the various possible origin points of Anne's disease, an important consideration in laying blame. It begins with the "taking cold" that was being circulated as the cause of her illness. If her disease was brought on by a neglectful husband this would lend credence to the accusations of William Wainhouse as fortune hunter, despite his providing her a portion upon their marriage. If Anne had caught her cold while attempting to elope, she would bear responsibility and consumption would be a fitting punishment for her foolishness. If, however, the disease originated from the neglect of the family or their harsh treatment, it would confirm William's accusation "that the Mother's

---

1 *Narrative*, folio 4.

cruel & continued ill Treatment of her eldest Daughter was the prime and original Cause of the Decay of her Constitution."[2]

In his very first mention of Anne's illness, William counters the accusations and lies by those he calls "his Enemies, & ignorant Tale-Bearers." For the first month of their marriage the newlyweds lived in Keevil, until Christmas Eve of 1770 when they moved into a house in nearby Steeple Ashton that had been "newly fitted up." The Beaches seized upon this move to accuse William of bringing his young bride into a deadly living situation, claiming that the "House was damp, & not well air'd."[3] This, by contemporary understandings of disease, would have been the perfect environment for her illness to develop. The Beaches did not, however, mention that they themselves had turned their daughter out into the cold night air with only the clothes on her back, another accepted route to illness in the eighteenth century. As Benjamin Marten stated in *A New Theory of Consumptions* (1720), one of the immediate causes of consumption was "for the most part, taking Cold," leading "the vitiated Humours [to] flow to the Lungs in full Stream, obstruct the Glandules, stagnate there, and form Tubercles."[4] *A New Practice of Physic* in 1753 even provided specific causes for the cough that could develop into a consumption, stating, "An accidental cough may be occasioned by a sudden alteration of weather, change of clothes, hard drinking, or the catching of a cold, as 'tis commonly called."[5]

Wainhouse acknowledged the power of "taking cold" but not as the rumored cause of Anne's. He emphatically responded that in his residence, "Fires had been kept in it for a long Time. The Parlour & Bed-Chamber ... were thoroughly warm'd, dry, & exceedingly comfortable."[6] Despite these favorable accommodations, Anne's illness rapidly progressed. John Pringle put forth bloodletting as "the chief remedy" for curing a bad cold; unfortunately, in Anne's case it was to no avail.[7] Plagued by a fever, lethargy, difficulty breathing, and a cough, Anne took multiple medicines, which had no "visible good Effect."[8]

On January 24, 1771, a concerned William convinced his wife a trip to Bath was necessary to consult her favorite trusted physician. The initial meeting was positive and the doctor thought "favourably of her Case," believing the illness was a product of "the thick State of her Blood." He recommended that once the spring

---

2 *Narrative*, folio 84.

3 *Narrative*, folio 59–60.

4 Benjamin Marten, *A New Theory of Consumptions: More Especially of a Phthisis or Consumption of the Lungs* (R. Knaplock, 1720), 44.

5 Peter Shaw, *A New Practice of Physic*, 7th ed. (T. and T. Longman, 1753), 106.

6 *Narrative*, folio 60.

7 John Pringle, *Observations on the Diseases of the Army*, 4th edition (A. Millar, 1764), 169.

8 *Narrative*, folio 60.

arrived she should undertake a regimen of "Air & exercise," and assured the worried couple her health could be restored by drinking whey and taking the prescribed medicines.[9] The advice was similar to that provided by David Macbride's *A Methodical Introduction to the Theory and Practice of Physic* (1772), which argued that hectic fevers were the result of an "agitation of the blood" and suggested they required "artificial management ... to be attempted more in the dietetic than the pharmaceutic way."[10] Like Anne's regimen, Macbride recommend "courses of goat's whey, asses' milk, and fresh butter-milk ... which are usually prescribed in hectic cases."[11] Although her treatment was consistent with the approach to hectic fevers generally, Anne's physician completely missed the seriousness of her illness, a fact William even acknowledged when he later wrote, "He did not apprehend that she was in a Decline or Consumption."[12]

Consumption's vague and nonspecific symptoms made diagnosis difficult and a cure even more elusive.[13] Early intervention was key. How was this to be accomplished, though, in a disease whose early symptoms (paleness, coughing, low-grade fever, and diarrhea) could easily be attributed to a number of other illnesses? Misdiagnosis was common and it was often not until the disease progressed to the stage of wasting, emaciation, and hemoptysis (spitting of blood) that the victim's fate became apparent, and by this point the disease was believed to be fatal. It is not surprising, then, that Anne's consumption was confused with a different, more tractable illness. Rather than blaming the physician for his oversight, William contextualized the mistake by acknowledging the doctor was not familiar with all the circumstances surrounding the beginning of the illness, which explained the misdiagnosis.

Anne and William returned home with medications, but before she could take them, on January 26 she suffered violent bouts of vomiting that lasted for several days, greatly weakening her.[14] Concerned, four days later, William again contacted the physician, who sent additional medications, but these made no difference. Just a few days later, on February 2, William dispatched another messenger. This time the physician sent an apothecary to Steeple Ashton, who, alarmed after examining the patient, advised an immediate return to Bath. Frantic, William bundled his ailing wife into a carriage the following morning (February 4) for the journey.

---

9 *Narrative*, folio 60–1.
10 David Macbride, *A Methodical Introduction to the Theory and Practice of Physic* (W. Strahan, 1772), 394.
11 Macbride, *A Methodical Introduction to the Theory and Practice of Physic*, 394.
12 *Narrative*, folio 61.
13 These "cures" were often dismissed by physicians as cases of misdiagnosis, or an instance when the treatment occurred before a confirmed consumption took hold.
14 *Narrative*, folio 61.

Already exhausted from the trip, Anne was forced to endure "an emetic Opera-tion" and her situation was reassessed.[15] After a careful examination and a more comprehensive understanding of the circumstances of Anne's case, the doctor "pronounc'd the young Lady dangerously ill." He then delivered devastating news to her worried husband that Anne's "Recovery was very doubtful."[16]

While Anne fought for her life, another drama was occurring outside the sick-room. On that same day (February 5), Anne's great aunts, Sophia and Dorothy Beach, arrived in Bath from their home in Kelston. According to Wainhouse, here they had a curious encounter with Anne's physician. The doctor, while on his way to examine another patient, ran into their servant and inquired if the family had heard the news? The servant replied that Sophia Beach had been to see him at his residence. The doctor assumed it was to learn of Anne's condition and stated he would return in ten minutes, instructing the aunts to come by then. Upon his return, he was surprised to find his home empty, and went in search of the women, eventually locating them socializing with an acquaintance.

After introductions and polite social niceties were observed, the physician waited and waited for the family to ask after their niece, anticipating questions that never came. Stunned by this lack of feeling and decorum, he returned home. On his way out, he was stopped by a relative of Sophia Beach (but not the woman herself), who had followed to ask after Anne. Seeing his opening, he immediately stated she was on her deathbed and chastised her for the family's behavior, stating "that it was shameful & uncharitable for none of her Relations to visit her in her Distress." The relative replied she was stuck in a "critical Situation" but "that she did not know what to do." Whatever she might have done or said seems to have fallen on deaf ears, as the Beach aunts returned to Kelston without visiting Anne or even sending a note to their expiring niece.[17]

This was not the last effort made by Anne's physician, who felt strongly that her family's behavior lacked Christian decency, and as the end rapidly approached he made one last attempt. The evening of Friday, February 8, 1771, he sat down to pen two notices. The first letter, sent to the lady visiting the Kelston contingent, stated "that his Patient had not, in his Judgement, many Hours to live." This went unanswered until a note of inquiry, sent not to the physician but to the apothecary, arrived too late on Sunday morning.[18] Knowing that Anne only had a few hours to live, the rather weak response two days later addressed to the apothecary does

---

15 *Narrative*, folio 62.
16 *Narrative*, folio 63.
17 *Narrative*, folio 65–6.
18 *Narrative*, folio 74.

not demonstrate much real concern for their niece's fate and tends more to the notion to preserving social niceties and personal reputation. The physician sent his other notice directly to Anne's father. This second letter was "a very handsome & friendly Epistle," in which the doctor was careful to assure William Beach that this was not a trick to affect a family reunion. Instead, he stated "that his Daughter, then under his Care, lay dangerously ill, that there was not the least Probability of her Recovery."[19] As we know, these overtures proved futile and none of her relatives made any attempt to see the dying woman, and it was the physician, rather than the family, who made efforts at reconciliation. Though abandoned by her family, Anne was still well regarded by her friends, many of whom visited to comfort the dying girl, who was described as bearing "her Sufferings with Christian Resignation. Her natural Goodness of Heart, and Sweetness of Temper, did not desert her."[20] Anne "gently breath'd forth her quiet Spirit, in her Sleep, on Sunday Morning, February the 10th 1771."[21]

Although Anne's suffering had finally ended, the battle over the meaning of, and blame for, her illness was just beginning. This was a fight for reputation, one that had begun when the couple's feelings for each other had first been revealed. Anne's illness was a contested site, as both William Wainhouse and the Beaches used ideas about the disease process of tuberculosis and the romance to lay the groundwork for character assassination.[22] Wainhouse carefully answered the charges against him and his wife before casting his own aspersions in an attempt to restore both of their reputations. The curate painted an extremely unflattering picture of Mrs. Beach, casting her as a jealous, bad-tempered shrew who listened at keyholes and berated her unsuspecting daughter, while Mr. Beach was characterized as her weak-willed accomplice. How is it possible that Anne's illness could be a battleground of blame? The answer lies in the nature and understanding of consumption during the eighteenth century.

William Wainhouse set out to absolve Anne of blame in her own illness, vehemently denying the charge that his wife had caught "Cold on the Night she attempted to go off with her Lover" and that after being discovered "very wet & dirty ... was taken Care of, kept in Bed ... to prevent ill Consequences." He exclaimed that "[a]ll this is false," and that "she took no fresh Cold then."[23]

---

19 *Narrative*, folio 68.

20 *Narrative*, folio 67.

21 *Narrative*, folio 73.

22 The disease was not called tuberculosis until the end of the nineteenth century. Instead, it was called by a variety of names, including consumption, phthisis, hectic fever, inflammation of the lungs, or even graveyard cough, and, in its non-pulmonary form, scrofula.

23 *Narrative*, folio 85, 88.

Furthermore, he asserted that her family did not permit her to rest and recover and that she was forced to wear the same wet and dirty clothes she had been wearing during her ill-fated escape attempt.[24] Instead, he offered an alternative timeline, stating that the night she was discovered her mother had scolded her, saying, "So, I suppose, you have <u>increas'd</u> your Cold, but it don't signify if you have." This, William claims, was "Proof, that the Daughter had before, & that the Mother knew she had, a Cold! ... She had one: it was known to the Family. Her Mother was perfectly acquainted with it."[25]

As further evidence of Mrs. Beach's culpability, during Anne's incarceration, her mother initially ordered that the door to her room be kept open that she might listen to Anne's conversations with her maid. However, once the illness progressed in severity, Mrs. Beach "sent to have the Door shut, giving as a Reason, that her Daughter <u>cough'd</u> so much, her Father cou'd not get any Sleep."[26] The doorway to the room above the porch is in the far left corner of a bedroom at the front of Keevil Manor, lending credence to this claim that Anne's coughing could have kept her father up at night. *A New Theory of Consumptions* provided a description of the progression of the disease and the ravages of the cough that became particularly troublesome at night.

> The unhappy patients ... appear with ghastly Looks, more like stalking Ghosts than living Bodies ... And besides the bodily Misery they necessarily feel by Day, which is commonly more exasperated by Night, through violent Coughing, and uneasy feverish Heat, Restlessness, and melting Sweats.[27]

Mrs. Beach refused to see her daughter and instead sent a missive through a servant "that, if she was ever so ill, 'she wou'd not come near her, nor send for any one, but her Apothecary' she wou'd not be at the Expence [sic] of a Physician."[28] Mrs. Beach refused to pay for a doctor and was only willing to send for an apothecary, though it is unclear if she actually did have Anne treated. Not only was her family aware of her illness, but William claims she had been ill since the February before their elopement attempt and that the family did not have her cold properly treated even before Anne's disobedience.[29] It was commonly believed that a

---

24 *Narrative*, folio 88.
25 *Narrative*, folio 86–7.
26 *Narrative*, folio 87.
27 Marten, *A New Theory of Consumptions*, 3.
28 *Narrative*, folio 31–2.
29 *Narrative*, folio 88.

consumption could originate in a neglected cold, though Anne's case would be complicated by the traumas of her incarceration and the physical privations associated with it.[30] These, William argued, broke her constitution and turned her cold to a consumption.

In 1769, William Buchan's popular *Domestic Medicine* listed the causes of consumption as "Want of exercise ... Violent passions or affections of the mind," including grief and disappointment. It also listed proximate causes, including temperature variations and infection, stating, "Consumptions are often caught by sleeping with the diseased," something that was to be "carefully avoided." Other important antecedents included cold, and Buchan argued that "[m]ore consumptive patients date their disorders from wet feet, damp beds, night air, wet cloaths, and such like, than from all other causes."[31] Buchan also lists, among the causes of pulmonary consumption, a number of the same things that were raised in the *Narrative* as playing a part in Anne's illness. The status of *Domestic Medicine* meant there would have been familiarity with the stated etiology of consumption among the inhabitants of Keevil, the target audience of the *Wainhouse Narrative*. Although determining *Domestic Medicine*'s actual readership of the work remains an elusive task, there is little doubt of its widespread popularity. It went through over 142 separate editions in the century after it was published and may have sold as many as 80,000 copies between 1769 and 1805.[32] Historian of medicine Charles Rosenberg argues that *Domestic Medicine* provides "concrete insights into ... medical thought and practice" and that there was a "broad diffusion of medical knowledge" among the populace in the eighteenth century.[33]

---

30 For instance, the *Practice of Physic* in 1765 stated, "The sign of an approaching Phthisis is a dry Cough, which may continue for some Months." Brookes, *General Practice of Physic*, Vol. I, 257.

31 William Buchan, *Domestic Medicine; or the Family Physician* (John Dunlap, 1772), 122–3.

32 Charles E. Rosenberg, "The Fielding H. Garrison Lecture. Medical Text and Social Context: Explaining William Buchan's *Domestic Medicine*," *Bulletin of the History of Medicine* 57, no. 1 (1983): 22–42, 22; John Britton, *The Auto-biography of John Britton* (London: 1850), 67. Buchan's initial 5,000-copy run of *Domestic Medicine*, which was dedicated to Sir John Pringle, the president of the Royal Society, quickly sold out. The work was unique, and Christopher Lawrence states it only had one clear antecedent: S.A. Tissot's *Avis au peuple sur sa santé*, which had been published eight years earlier. Buchan's work was intended to function "as a guide to preserving health," but it also could be used "to identify and prescribe for diseases." See also Christopher Lawrence, "Buchan, William (1729–1805)," in *Oxford Dictionary of National Biography*, online edition, eds. H.C.G. Matthew and Brian Harrison (Oxford University Press, 2004). For more information on William Buchan's *Domestic Medicine*, also see Mark Jackson, *The Oxford Handbook of the History of Medicine* (Oxford University Press, 2013); Lawrence I. Conrad et al., *The Western Medical Tradition: 800 BC to AD 1800*, 9th ed. (Cambridge University Press, 2009); Roy Porter, ed., *The Popularization of Medicine 1650–1850* (Routledge, 1992); Porter and Porter, *Patient's Progress*; and Porter, ed., *Patients and Practitioners*.

33 Charles E. Rosenberg, *Explaining Epidemics and Other Studies in the History of Medicine* (Cambridge University Press, 1992), 38. *Domestic Medicine* also articulated a specific role for the parish

William Wainhouse was certainly familiar with these ideologies of disease and clearly employed them in his account. Given contemporary understandings of tuberculosis, the Beaches' behavior as laid down in the *Narrative* could almost have been designed to produce the illness. It addresses all of the finer points of the consumptive etiology, speaking to a neglected cold, want of exercise, confinement with sick persons, temperature variations, and emotional battery. All of these circumstances were articulated as having a role in Anne Wainhouse's illness. Beyond locating the origin of her complaint, the *Narrative* uses eighteenth-century understandings of consumption to address three other major causes of her disease: physical privation, emotional trauma, and infection, which Wainhouse claimed was the original seed of the disorder and the consequence of the family's long-term abuse of their eldest daughter.

William charged that Anne's imprisonment after their botched elopement was not the first she had been subjected to, but that in 1763 her health had been damaged "by improper Confinement, long before <u>That</u> she suffer'd on the account of Love." Mrs. Beach purportedly forced Anne "to be shut up with, attend upon, & do the meanest, the most disagreeable Offices for, an old, infirm, diseas'd Female, who had nurs'd the Mother in her Infancy." She was "pent up with this sick Woman in her Chamber.... The Consequence was, she fell into a bad Disorder."[34] In the seventeenth century, Gideon Harvey's *Morbus Anglicus: Or the Anatomy of Consumptions* argued that "many having fallin [sic] into Consumptions only by smelling the breath or spittle of Consumptives."[35] Richard Morton likewise asserted in his *Phthisiologia: Or a Treatise of Consumptions* (1720) that "this disease is also propagated by infection. For this distemper ... does infect those that lie with the sick person with a certain taint."[36]

Although there is no direct evidence to corroborate this part of the story, there are intriguing glimpses that point to the validity of these claims. In 1763 and early 1764, at the same time Anne would have been taking care of her mother's old nurse, she was also treated for a significant bout of illness. In September, she was prescribed no fewer than 85 separate medicinal draughts,

---

clergy in the lay medical hierarchy, stating that "almost all rural clergymen knew 'something of medicine. Almost all of them bleed, and can order a purge.'" William Buchan quoted in Rosenberg, *Explaining Epidemics*, 38. Buchan's claims about the role of the clergy in the medical lives of eighteenth-century Britons provides further insight into the *Wainhouse Narrative*. Not only did William Wainhouse's claims draw heavily on lay understandings of disease, the medical claims made in the narrative may have gained an additional layer of legitimacy from his position as a clergyman.

34 *Narrative*, folio 90.

35 Gideon Harvey, *Morbus Anglicus: Or the Anatomy of Consumptions*, 2nd ed. (Thomas Johnson, 1674), 2.

36 Richard Morton, *Phthisiologia: Or a Treatise of Consumptions*, 2nd ed. (W. and J. Innys, 1720), 67.

and in December 1764 the family invested in a dozen bottles of hot-well water, thought to be particularly beneficial for inflammatory diseases like consumption.[37]

The timing of Anne's second incarceration may have also played a role in her disease progression. The attempted elopement occurred at the end of May, and her incarceration began on June 6. As Gideon Harvey argued, "The Spring is bad for Consumptives, so is the Fall,"[38] while *A New Theory of Consumptions* argued that those who were first afflicted in summer progressed through the stages of the disease more rapidly due to the "hot and acrid" nature of their blood. It also stated that "consumption of the Lungs is often introduced" when the victim, "being, to all outward appearance, in perfect health and strength, is, upon taking cold, through the inclemency of the season, or for want of due care" afflicted. The lack of attention, combined with the timing of the insult, was believed to "speedily hasten" the victim to their grave.[39]

During Anne's second incarceration – this time "for Love" – William charges that the Beaches visited upon her emotional cruelty and physical privation that "greatly injur'd & impair'd her Spirits & Constitution."[40] The uninsulated stone room above the porch where Anne spent part of her five-month incarceration was small, only measuring six and a half by seven feet, and could only be accessed by traveling through one of the second-floor front bedrooms. The front wall was dominated by six windows, and the room had two recessed trefoil windows on the side walls. Large windows and uninsulated walls were known hazards, as the 1761 *A Treatise of the Disease Called a Cold* made clear, arguing that "all currents of air, from staircases, from large openings of doors, or windows, beating on any part of the body, are dangerous."[41] The author, John Chandler, went on to lament that in England "nature's dictates" were often ignored and that "when the cold is

---

37 "Receipts for the medical care of Nancy [Ann] Beach," D2455/F2/4/2/6, Gloucestershire Archives, UK. "The Hot-well water is a faithful Medicatrix of last Cast, and that in the most deplorable Consumptive Cases, by restraining and temperating the Humours." *Johannis Subtermontani Thermologia Bristoliensis, Or, Underhill's Short Account of the Bristol Hot-Well Water, its Uses and Historical Cures* (W. Bonny, 1703), 32. "Of all the Disorders which seek relief from Bristol Water, there is none more common than the Phthisis Pulmonaria; none, in which more is expected from it; none, in which the Hopes of our Patients are oftener deceived." George Randolph, *Enquiry into the Medicinal Virtues of Bristol-Water: And the Indications of Cure Which it Answers* (James Fletcher, 1745).

38 Harvey, *Morbus Anglicus*, 2. This conviction continued well into the eighteenth century – for instance, in 1774 John Gregory stated of consumption, that the "disease is most fatal in spring and autumn." John Gregory, *Elements of the Practice of Physic* (W. Strahan, 1774), 164.

39 Marten, *A New Theory of Consumptions*, 8–9.

40 *Narrative*, folio 83.

41 John Chandler, *A Treatise of the Disease Called a Cold*, 2nd ed. (A. Millar, 1761), 86.

severe" it was crucial to provide "suitable ... fires and clothing, as the proper fence against mischiefs."[42]

Having a fire proved problematic in the room above the porch – there was only a small hearth less than a foot deep. It was recessed into the wall but lacked a chimney, meaning only a small brazier of coals could be used, but not an actual fire. Beyond the temperature, the lack of proper ventilation was also a key component in disease causation and thought to produce lung ailments. As Richard Morton argued, "a foggy and thick Air, and that which is filled with the Smoak of Coals, does extremely promote a Consumption."[43]

In this closed, inhospitable, "very small Bed-Chamber" Anne was "Shut up." Eventually, she and her maid prevailed upon her mother to allow her "two small Chambers."[44] Although an upgrade, the situation had not improved as much as it might at first seem. These rooms were also small, containing a bed and not much else, and restricted her free movement. More concerningly, in the summer the air in the room was "corrupt, stagnated, and suffocating," exacerbating her shortness of breath.[45] While incarcerated, Anne often had "No Air & Exercise abroad," though she was occasionally permitted to leave her prison, but only when her mother sent for her.[46] Often days would pass before Mrs. Beach would call her, and William lamented that her periods of incarceration were frequently "in the warmest Weather." When she was permitted to go "out into the open Air, she felt a Shortness of Breath; a Complaint, that oblig'd her to shorten her Walks, & that follow'd her to the Grave."[47] Excessive heat and lack of ventilation were not her only challenges, as Anne's improved accommodations came with "incidental Hardships" and a "Mode of Punishment [that] greatly injur'd & impair'd her Spirits & Constitution," punishments that were both physical and emotional.[48]

---

42 Chandler, *A Treatise of the Disease*, 120–1. John Chandler (1699/1700–1780) was an apothecary who was a partner in the London-based apothecary firm Smith and Newsom, located in Cheapside on King Street. He published a number of treatises, including a 1729 reply to Richard Holland's *Observations on the Small Pox* (1728) and became active in the Royal Society, giving a lecture in 1734 that became the basis for his *A Treatise on the Disease Called a Cold*. In 1735 he was made a fellow of the Royal Society, with the support of such notables as the president of the Royal College of Physicians, Henry Plumptre. See G.T. Bettany and T.A.B. Corley, "Chandler, John (1699/1700–1780), Apothecary," *Oxford Dictionary of National Biography*, September 23, 2004 (accessed April 17, 2020), https://www.oxforddnb.com/view/10.1093/ref:odnb/9780198614128.001.0001 /odnb-9780198614128-e-5104.

43 Morton, *Phthisiologia*, 66.

44 *Narrative*, folio 35, 83.

45 *Narrative*, folio 84–5.

46 *Narrative*, folio 83.

47 *Narrative*, folio 35.

48 *Narrative*, folio 83.

As the temperature dropped, Anne was not permitted a fire, even "in cold Weather" and sat huddled in bed "shivering with the Cold."[49] By October 25, 1770, the temperature had dropped to a point where the maid could not feel her fingers while staying in the room, and it was only after the woman complained to Mrs. Beach that Anne was allowed a source of heat.[50] Other charges against Mrs. Beach include that she sometimes spitefully refused to allow "any Breakfast to be carried to her."[51] Even more shockingly Wainhouse stated that Anne was even denied "a proper Convenience for the common Necessities of Nature!"[52]

Although these physical privations were harsh and believed to cause consumptions all on their own, Anne's mental sufferings were accorded an even greater share of responsibility in creating her illness. William pleaded with the reader to "consider, what must be the Anguish & Feelings of a Mind ruminating on the Desertion, the Hypocrisy, the Insults, the alarming Threatnings [sic] of mean & wicked Relations! ... Needs there the Skill of a Physician to pronounce, that these Afflictions hurt the Mind & Body? Undoubtedly they must."[53] Though the skill of a physician may not have been necessary, many certainly argued for a strong connection between the mind and body. For instance, doctor George Cheyne stated that the first stage of consumption was marked by its "great nervous Symptoms," particularly "in tender, delicat [sic], lovely young persons."[54] Robert Whytt likewise ranked consumption as a nervous disorder.[55]

Over the course of the eighteenth century, illness was increasingly linked to the workings of the nervous system; medical practitioners thus tried to determine the specifics of the mind-body connection, paying particular attention to the ability of emotions to cause disease.[56] Strong passions had long been counted among the causative agents of consumption. In the late seventeenth century, Harvey called it a disease of "deep lovers,"[57] while in 1720 Benjamin Marten laid out the disease's multifaceted etiology when he argued that causes of consumptions included the "Troublesome Passions of the mind, especially Fear, Grief, [and] Anger."[58] Peter

---

49 *Narrative*, folio 83–5.

50 *Narrative*, folio 83.

51 *Narrative*, folio 36.

52 He is referring to a chamber pot, for Anne to relieve herself. *Narrative*, folio 84.

53 *Narrative*, folio 84.

54 George Cheyne, *The Natural Method of Curing the Diseases of the Body and the Disorders of the Mind*, 4th ed. (Geo. Strahan, 1742), 186.

55 *The Works of Robert Whytt* (T. Becket and P.A. Dehondt, 1768), 630.

56 Clark Lawlor, *Consumption and Literature: The Making of the Romantic Disease* (Palgrave Macmillan, 2006), 52; Roy Porter, "Diseases of Civilization," in *Companion Encyclopedia of the History of Medicine*, ed. W.F. Bynum and Roy Porter, Vol. 1 (Routledge, 2001), 591.

57 Harvey, *Morbius Angelicus*, 2.

58 Marten, *A New Theory of Consumptions*, 43.

Shaw's *New Practice of Physic* in 1753 stated that "Consumptions from grief … emaciate fast."[59]

Wainhouse charges that the Beaches' neglect of their daughter was long-standing and posits a role for both parents. Mr. Beach is charged with permitting "the Mother's continued ill Treatment of the Daughter."[60] There were brief moments of kindness; for instance, when Anne "catch'd [sic] this Cold at <u>Bath</u> the February (1770).… Her Father, indeed, (who was <u>suppos'd</u> to love her) offer'd her some Liquorice [sic], & said, she might have a Linctus; for he did not want to have her ill."[61] But these instances of compassion were few and far between. Mr. Beach did more than turn a blind eye to his wife's behavior. Whenever he was given an opportunity to intervene, he chose not to, and even promised his wife not to see his daughter.[62] Far more damning however, was Wainhouse's characterization of Mrs. Beach, both as a mother and as a Christian. The accusations ranged from petty jealousy to mercenary tendencies, and from overbearing, unnatural behavior to outright cruelty.

In the face of Anne's refusal to give William up, and seeing the incarceration was not having the desired effect, Mrs. Beach called in reinforcements from her "little Band of Mercenaries."[63] Prominent among these was Sophia Beach (1705–1787), a fact that shocked Wainhouse, since she had been extremely close to his mother, Mary. The two even lived together in Bath from 1762 until Mary's death in 1767, and Sophia had "had often given the Clergyman very good Character, & own'd him as one of her best Friends."[64] Wainhouse expected this sort of behavior from Mrs. Beach, but not from Sophia, whose actions he characterized as "very inconsistent, & almost unaccountable," particularly as Anne's aunt had frequently observed "that <u>Mrs. Beach</u> us'd her Daughter very ill & very severely," even predicting Anne's rebellion.[65] Sophia Beach had purportedly stated that her family "shou'd not wonder, if she [Anne] shou'd be guilty of any low or improper Step, or Action, in the Way of Marriage, considering how badly she was treated by her Mother."[66]

Prompted by Anne's mother, Sophia Beach, whom Wainhouse labeled a Termagant,[67] was apparently set loose upon the prisoner:

---

59 Shaw, *A New Practice of Physic*, 109.
60 *Narrative*, folio 92.
61 *Narrative*, folio 88.
62 *Narrative*, folio 31.
63 *Narrative*, folio 24.
64 *Narrative*, folio 25.
65 *Narrative*, folio 26–7.
66 *Narrative*, folio 27.
67 *Narrative*, folio 50.

> She came open-mouth'd into the Room, & scolded most outrageously.... She made use of the roughest, the most low Language, the most ungenteel Arguments, the chief of which was, that she shou'd never have a Penny from her, or her Sister, if she persisted in her Resolution.[68]

Wainhouse once again charged that money was both the motive and the cudgel for the Beaches. When these threats left Anne unmoved, Sophia Beach changed tactics, "blasting the Clergyman's personal Character," railing on "all the past Faults against him & his she cou'd recollect, or invent."[69] She then turned her sights upon his entire family, including her deceased friend, Mary Wainhouse. During the tirade, Anne reminded her aunt "that both she & her Family us'd to be very fond of him," a comment that derailed the outburst and left her aunt speechless.[70] Though complicit in the treatment of Anne, it seems Sophia was worried about the effects of her incarceration, even though she told her niece "she deserv'd all she suffer'd." Concerned, Sophia mentioned to Mrs. Beach "that the Daughter look'd ill & melancholy." Mrs. Beach responded, "It was no Matter; it did 'not signify what she suffer'd.'"[71]

What did Anne endure at the hands of her mother? If William Wainhouse is to be believed, it was a serious ordeal marked by both physical and mental suffering. Anne was repeatedly reminded "that her Parents & Relations wou'd never give her any Thing, if she married <u>so wicked a Villain</u> as the Clergyman."[72] She was repeatedly harangued with the "sordid Superiority of Money!"[73] but remained resolved in her attachment, even in the face of her mothers' repeated "Menaces."[74] Stymied, Mrs. Beach turned to other tactics to secure her daughter's compliance, inflicting upon her speeches and sending spiteful messages. William characterized her actions as "exceed[ing] common Beleif [sic] & Practice."[75]

Anne's nervous symptoms would have been exacerbated by her mother's constant berating. Mrs. Beach was charged with telling her daughter that "[s]he wish'd she was dead ... she also wish'd she was a Spider, a Toad; for then she wou'd trample her under her Feet with Pleasure." She told her that, if she was determined to have the Clergyman, "she might go & be hang'd"; she did not care what "became of her" and that "if she wanted a Bit of Bread, it shou'd not be given

---

68 *Narrative*, folio 24.
69 *Narrative*, folio 25.
70 *Narrative*, folio 26.
71 *Narrative*, folio 89.
72 *Narrative*, folio 28.
73 *Narrative*, folio 25.
74 *Narrative*, folio 28.
75 *Narrative*, folio 29.

her."[76] Wainhouse characterized Mrs. Beach's behavior as the ravings of a lunatic and also as transgressions of propriety and common decency. Given Billy's condition, likening Mrs. Beach's angry tirades to "the Ravings of Insanity" would have cut deeply.[77] However, these very family circumstances ensured Mrs. Beach was careful in her public persona, as she limited her vitriol to the house and private communications.

Mrs. Beach was careful to present a positive social face during this time, mitigating her abuse in the lead up to the appearance of any visitors, to obscure her treatment of her daughter and secure her cooperation. However, this only lasted until they left, at which point she reverted to her anger.[78] She played the doting mother in company, discussing her concerns about Anne's health with visitors, telling them that out of her "Concern for her <u>dear</u> Daughter's Health, Anne walk'd out whenever she pleas'd, nay, every Day." William labeled this an "an insidious, wilful [sic] Falshood [sic]."[79]

There are no letters surviving from the time of the incarceration, however it is curious that none of the remaining letters (over the course of Anne's life), either to or from Mrs. Beach, ever mention the health of her daughter, nor do the letters from family members. All of these only inquire after Henny and William, but never Anne, even before her transgression. Anne's absence in earlier correspondence is suggestive of a lack of consideration for her health in comparison to that shown for her siblings and would make Mrs. Beach's attention to her well-being to visitors an aberration.

Interestingly, this seems to have been a consistent tactic employed by Mrs. Beach, as William argued her unkind treatment of Anne was of a long-standing nature. Even before her love affair with the clergyman, "the Mother was generally cross & unkind to her eldest Daughter in private, though openly, by fair Speech, deceitfully kind."[80] This hypocrisy had been noticed by relatives who observed that Anne was not permitted to go out much, and when they requested she be permitted to "spend some Time with them" Mrs. Beach replied, "Oh! – no! ... <u>Nanny</u> is all the <u>Comfort</u> I have got." However, in private, she would then tell other family members that she "was the Cause of all the <u>Quarelling</u> between her &

---

76 *Narrative*, folio 30.

77 *Narrative*, folio 30–1.

78 "Just before she expected, & when she had in her House, any particular Visitors, or Relations, she us'd the Daughter more gently, & made great Shew of Tenderness. She even sent to know what she wou'd have for Dinner. When the Relations & Visitors were safe out of Knowledge of the Mother's Behaviour, it was quite different." *Narrative*, folio 34.

79 *Narrative*, folio 35.

80 *Narrative*, folio 36.

<u>Mr. Beach</u>."[81] Here perhaps is a hint of the source of some of Mrs. Beach's anger with her elder daughter.

Whether or not the *Narrative*'s readership agreed with William's assertions about the cause of his wife's illness, her parents' treatment of her certainly countered the established parameters for treating consumptions. For instance, William Buchan asserted that "the patient's mind ought to be kept as easy and chearful as possible," because "consumptions are often occasioned by a melancholy cast of mind."[82] None of these directives were followed in Anne's case, and the perception of consumption as the physical manifestation of a psychological state was thoroughly exploited by William Wainhouse to cast blame upon the Beach family for the death of his wife.

In 1744 Bernard Lynch's *A Guide to Health Through the Various Stages of Life* not only argued "that Grief is a powerful cause to bring on a Consumption," but also illustrated the physiological mechanism by which the grief led to the production of tubercles.[83] The peddling of grief in medical treatises was bolstered by other non-medical works such as Benjamin Grosvenor's 1765 *The Mourner: Or, the Afflicted Relieved*, which stated that "[w]hen Sorrow is suffered to prey upon health ... it is as criminal as mischievous. A man may pine away his health and life.... It weares away the strength, and wastes the vital spirits."[84] Grosvenor used the language of tuberculosis for sorrow, stating "It wastes and consumes." Sorrow, like consumption, sometimes killed "outright, as effectually as if a man were shot through," but other times it was gradual, doing "its Business as surely as a slow Poison." In these cases, "the Food seldom nourished that is mingled with tears. When the Air doth not refresh, nor the Faculties of Nature perform their functions, then we say the Heart is broke."[85] He even states that "[i]n the Bills of Mortality we sometimes find this Article, Died of Grief. That Article would be much larger, and oftener inserted, if all who died of Grief were distinguished; but they are now put down under the word Consumption, or any other Disease, which Grief brought upon them."[86] This connection between consumption and

---

81 *Narrative*, folio 36–7.

82 Buchan, *Domestic Medicine*, 122–3.

83 He suggested that the constant action of the soul due to its "being continually emply'd in Affliction about the Object which causes it" stopped the free movement of "the animal Spirits" affecting "the Organs of Respiration," allowing the stagnation of blood in the lungs and leading to "sorrowful sighs," a mechanism by which the body tried to move the stagnated blood. Bernard Lynch, *A Guide to Health Through the Various Stages of Life* (London, 1744), 446.

84 Benjamin Grosvenor, *The Mourner: Or, the Afflicted Relieved*, 5th ed. (George Keith, 1765), 14.

85 Grosvenor, *The Mourner*, 14.

86 Grosvenor, *The Mourner*, 14–15.

sorrow or grief was well established and widely known, so William Wainhouse's assertions that Anne's grief and sorrow brought on her consumption would have been easily accepted. In the end, he implored the reader to "Drop thy Tear over the soft, oppress'd, expiring Virtue of the Daughter ... debas'd & brutaliz'd in the remorseless Parents! ... 'Malice has done her worst.'"[87]

---

87 *Narrative,* folio 73.

CHAPTER FIVE

Chasing Dr. Moysey: Mapping the Research Process

Oh! May gay health, that floats on Zephyr wing, With Moysey's art, and Bath's Salubrious spring.[1]

It is of course always fantastic when your internet search turns up a huge cache of information and your trip to the archive reveals a fantastic pile of personal letters, or even better a diary, but sadly that is rarely the case, and the events surrounding the courtship and marriage of William Wainhouse and Anne Beach was no exception. The Gloucestershire Archives had a vast collection of documents, ranging from personal letters to land deeds and music books to estate receipts, but very little of this material was directly related to Anne and William's story. Perhaps they just were not part of the collection that was saved, or perhaps they were destroyed by the family themselves to wipe away the memory of an event that caused them such discomfort, or maybe they still remain in someone's attic somewhere despite all of my attempts to dig them out (and I definitely crawled through some attics, dusty archives, and a bat-infested church on my hunt). So, what do you do when faced with a lack of direct information that relates to the story you are hoping to interpret? This is when you must be resourceful and think of other ways to create meaning and reconstruct the historical relationships from the scraps available. Do not assume that just because you do not have the exact direct evidence you were looking for that you still cannot make a meaningful argument or tell a story.

---

1 Christopher Anstey, *The Priest Dissected: A Poem* (S. Hazard, 1774), 28.

Chasing the Doctor

While trying to piece together Anne's care and searching the family receipts for anything medical, I found the document shown in Figure 8. I first stumbled across Dr. Moysey (alternate spelling Moisey/Moisy) in the receipts for the family in 1758, but he continued to show up repeatedly as a practitioner used regularly by the Beach family (along with the apothecary, Mr. Horton). I was struck by how frequently he was consulted and especially by how much he charged. One pound per visit was an extraordinarily high amount, as was the £3 he charged "for his directions for me to take home."[2]

Who was this Dr. Moysey, and could he perhaps have treated Anne during her illness? Were there case notes, or letters to the family? I was so excited – here, finally, I could perhaps catch a glimpse into Anne's illness from someone other than her husband. Was Dr. Moysey the mysterious physician that treated Anne in her final days and contacted her family? I hoped to find some indication of this but remained cautious not to leap to conclusions, as one should always let the primary sources tell the tale and not try to force it into a narrative where it does not belong or where there is no evidence.

Steps for Chasing Abel Moysey

Armed with a last name, "Moysey," and an occupation, "Dr." (knowing that he might have trained as one, or simply called himself one), I began my search. Like most people, my first step was a quick internet search, but "Dr. Moysey + Bath + 18th century" only yielded a few hits. It did, however, point intriguingly to a link with the painter Thomas Gainsborough (to be discussed later). Beyond a general search, one of my first steps with anyone who is British and who might be notable is to search the *Oxford Dictionary of National Biography*. Frustratingly, Dr. Moysey did not rank his own article when I searched the titles, but when the search parameters were changed from "article title" to "text" I struck gold.[3]

In an article about physician Rice Charleton (1722/3–1788), I found my first mention of Dr. Moysey. Now just because the last name was the same, I could not assume it was my "Dr. Moysey," but it was a good start. Charleton was a member of the Royal Society and had established a practice on Alfred Street in Bath before

---

2 "Beach Family Receipts (1758)," D2455/E3/2/4/5, Gloucestershire Archives, UK.

3 Dr. Moysey did not publish any medical treatises during his lifetime, which is often the way physicians are remembered for their contributions to the profession. Instead, he seemed to only be a practitioner, which makes it more difficult to uncover the specifics of his life.

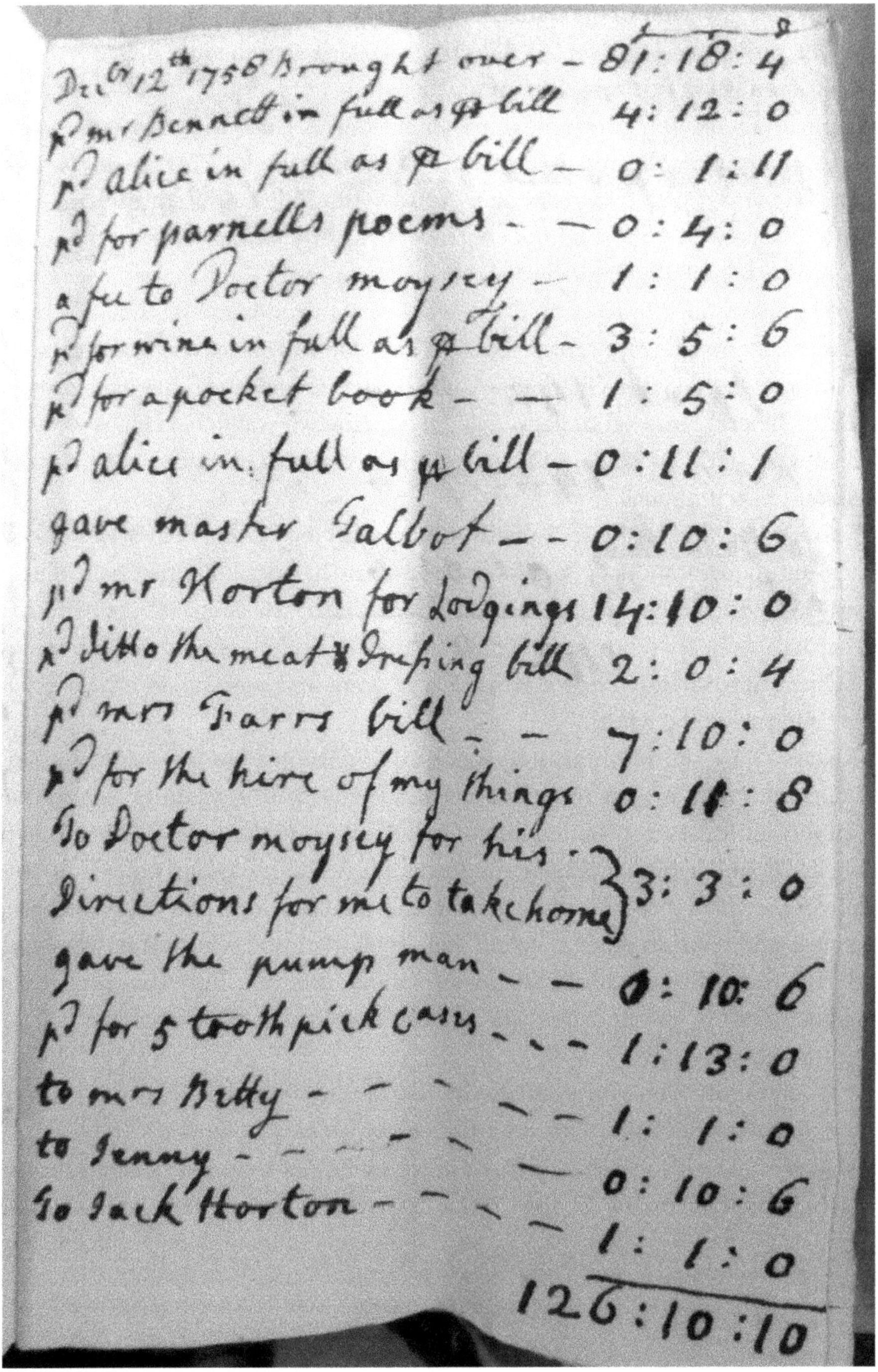

Decr 12th 1758 Brought over -	81:18:4
pd mr Bennett in full as p bill	4:12:0
pd alice in full as p bill -	0:1:11
pd for parnells poems - -	0:4:0
a fee to Doctor moysey -	1:1:0
pd for wine in full as p bill -	3:5:6
pd for a pocket book - -	1:5:0
pd alice in full as p bill -	0:11:1
gave master Talbot - -	0:10:6
pd mr Horton for Lodgings	14:10:0
pd ditto the meat & Dressing bill	2:0:4
pd mrs Tarrs bill - -	7:10:0
pd for the hire of my things	0:11:8
To Doctor moysey for his Directions for me to take home	3:3:0
gave the pump man - -	0:10:6
pd for 5 toothpick cases - - -	1:13:0
to mrs Betty - -	1:1:0
to Jenny - -	0:10:6
To Jack Horton - -	1:1:0
	126:10:10

FIGURE 8. Beach family receipt showing medical expenses. ("Beach Family Receipts (1758)," D2455/E3/2/4/5, Gloucestershire Archives, UK. Image courtesy of Gloucestershire Archives, UK.)

becoming the governor of the Bath General Hospital in 1752.[4] The location and the timing fit, indicating I was on the right track, so that was encouraging.

Charleton was a great proponent of the Bath waters, notably publishing a scientific analysis of their properties in 1750 entitled *A Chemical Analysis of Bath Waters*.[5] In 1754, he followed this with another work called *A Treatise on the Bath Waters*. However, just two years later he was embroiled in a controversy with Charles Lucas, who published the controversial *Essay on the Waters* (1756). This work asserted the Bath waters lacked "special properties" and was a direct attack on the economy of the town and the work of its prominent physicians. These men, and Bath itself, were economically reliant "on the use of the spa waters."[6] It is unsurprising, then, that Charleton banded together with the other physicians of the Bath General Hospital to denounce Lucas. His two staunchest allies were Dr. Abel Moysey and Dr. William Oliver, who joined their colleague "in boycotting consultations with Lucas."[7]

I now had a first name to go with my Dr. Moysey – Abel – as well as some details and acquaintances I could follow, as well as the possibility that he had been a physician at the Bath General Hospital. So what next? My adage is "work smarter, not harder," so I constantly search the sources. The scholars who are experts on the subject have already done a great deal of work and one should always try to avoid reinventing the wheel.

Always chase the footnotes (or endnotes)! Footnotes are important for several reasons. First, as with the materials and methods in a scientific paper, they are important for the reproducibility of results. Beyond the most obvious role of giving credit and avoiding plagiarism, footnotes reveal the broad knowledge and deep work (or lack thereof) of the author. It is quality control for acknowledging the voices and work of other scholars and archivists upon whose shoulders your work rests, as well as for identifying sources and archives. They also permit you to assess a work in an important way and can even reveal when a scholar has not taken the requisite care.

It is imperative that you evaluate the footnotes. Did the scholar use primary sources? Are the secondary sources current or older scholarship? These are all questions you should ask. It is important to remember that, like science, history requires interpretation of the data. Scientists do not present raw data but make

---

4 Anne Borsay, "Charleton, Rice (1722/3–1788), Physician," *Oxford Dictionary of National Biography*, September 23, 2004 (accessed April 28, 2020), https://www.oxforddnb.com/view/10.1093/ref:odnb/9780198614128.001.0001/odnb-9780198614128-e-5155.
5 Borsay, "Charleton, Rice (1722/3–1788), Physician."
6 John Jenkins, "Thomas Gainsborough's doctors," *Journal of Medical Biography* 13, no. 1 (2005), 59.
7 Borsay, "Charleton, Rice (1722/3–1788), Physician."

conclusions after running statistics and analyzing their experimental results. This is how one determines the significance of the results, and history is no different. Some historians even use the same kinds of statistical techniques used by scientists and social scientists. Additionally, it is important to remember that all history is an interpretation of the information.

Proper interpretation first requires sound data, and the footnotes can divulge not just the records and the interpretive structure but also when the criteria of sound research has not been met. For instance, national bestseller *The Ghost Map: The Story of London's Most Terrifying Epidemic – and How it Changed Science, Cities, and the Modern World* provides a glimpse into just how footnotes can expose process, as well as the obfuscation of the context of a source. The book provides the following description of London, which at first glance seems perfectly correct. "London, of course, had a long history of offending social critics, as in this cheery description from Scottish physician George Cheyne, written at the end of the eighteenth century:

> The infinite number of Fires, Sulphurous and Bituminous, the vast expense of Tallow and foetid Oil in Candles and lamps, under and above the Ground, the clouds of stinking Breathes and Perspirations, not to mention the ordure of so many diseas'd, both intelligent and unintelligent animals, the crouded Churches, Church Yards and Bury Places, with the putrifying Bodies, the Sinks, Butcher Houses, Stables, Dunghills, etc. and the necessary Stagnation, Fermentation, and mixture of Variety of all Kinds of Atoms, and more than sufficient to putrefy, poison and infect the Air for Twenty Miles around it, and which in Time must alter, weaken, and destroy the healthiest of Constitutions."[8]

The George Cheyne mentioned is the same physician you met in Chapter 4, and his works on the functioning of the nervous system were crucial in the understandings of disease in the eighteenth century – so he is a good source for describing the environment and how it "must alter, weaken, and destroy the healthiest of Constitutions."[9]

There is only one problem: George Cheyne died in 1743. Now, this could have been an honest mistake – we all get sloppy sometimes – so here is where the footnotes come in. When you look at the notes, it turns out Johnson did not even use

---

8 Steven Johnson, *The Ghost Map: The Story of London's Most Terrifying Epidemic – and How it Changed Science, Cities, and the Modern World* (Riverhead Books, 2006), 88.

9 Johnson, *The Ghost Map*, 88.

the original source for the quote. This is a big red flag, as he is already one degree of separation away from the original data. He instead used a secondary source, historian Roy Porter's *London: A Social History*. This leaves a few possibilities. The other scholar could have made a mistake, though the historian in question was a careful and well-respected one. Alternatively, Johnson was just sloppy in his writing, or even more concerning is the possibility that he did not have the data he wanted and altered the context to make the evidence fit his argument. The only way to tell is to chase the footnote. The following was Roy Porter's introduction to the very same quote: "Many doctors diagnosed London a hotbed of disease. In his influential *The English Malady* (1733), the Scottish physician George Cheyne credited the capital with being 'the greatest, most capacious, and close, and populous City of the Globe'; for those very reasons it was positively lethal."[10]

Now this may seem like a small thing, as the further away from a time period we live, the more compressed the time might seem. You may think, well it's the right century, so what is the big deal? However, this would be the same as saying that living in the London or New York City of today is that same as it would be living in the 1950s or '60s. My guess is that you would never make that claim, so saying something stated in 1733 applies to the 1790s is a comparable mistake. It is sloppy scholarship at best, and deceitful at worst, calling into question the validity of the work as a whole. Additionally, one should always try to work from the primary documents where possible, so Johnson should have read and used *The English Malady* (1733).

Anne Borsay, who wrote on Charleton Rice, is a well-respected scholar of medical humanities, and her article mentioned several sources, both secondary and primary (including manuscripts in archives).[11] So this is where I began to look for Abel Moysey, searching the listed sources for the elusive doctor and his world. I pored through the secondary sources for information on the people he interacted with, the medical community in Bath, and the society he lived in, all of which could offer insights even if Moysey was not directly mentioned. I also had a place to start with respect to archival sources, and my first stop for British archival and manuscript sources is usually the National Archives at Kew. They have a large online catalog that, although not comprehensive, is a very good place to start for both sources housed in London as well as those in other repositories around the United Kingdom and beyond. I also knew that a direct search of the local record

---

10 Roy Porter, *London: A Social History* (Harvard University Press, 1998), 162.

11 Anne Borsay, "Oliver, William (1695–1764), Physician and Philanthropist," *Oxford Dictionary of National Biography*, September 23, 2004 (accessed April 28, 2020), https://www.oxforddnb.com /view/10.1093/ref:odnb/9780198614128.001.0001/odnb-9780198614128-e-20736.

office mentioned in the article (the Bath & North East Somerset Record Office) was a must, as was a search of the other repositories in the area, and also those with holdings related to Anne and William's story.

A quick search of "Abel Moysey" with the dates limited from 1700 to 1799 in the National Archives catalog turned up a will for my elusive physician, as well as a number of other results that were most likely not him. There were two wills listed: one in the Record Office in Bath and one registered in the Prerogative Court of Canterbury and housed in the National Archives.[12] Wanting to be thorough and to ensure the wills matched, I obtained both. I physically went to the Bath & North East Somerset Record Office, and while there I looked not only for the will, but also for a list of subjects I thought might reveal Dr. Abel Moysey. I searched for the doctor, of course, but also for the hospital in Bath, the other doctors whose names I had identified, and other medical topics that might be relevant. It is sometimes very useful to cast a wide net and see what comes up after you look for the specifics. That is, after all, how I found Anne and William Wainhouse's story.

It is not always possible to travel to the archives, but fortunately, in this increasingly digital world, manuscript sources can be accessed in a variety of ways. Repositories of research evidence include databases (some paywalled, some not), online exhibitions – and do not forget the non-digital options, including the material resources in your own library's special collections or those available on microfilm and microfiche (which can often be accessed through interlibrary loan if your institution does not have them). It is always a good idea to talk to your librarian about options and strategies, as they are trained experts in locating sources. Fortunately, the wills housed in the National Archives are digitized on a number of platforms, including Ancestry.com (check your library's available databases, as most university and public libraries have subscriptions). I obtained a digital copy of that will – and then came the fun task of trying to decipher them both.

Now, you might look at these documents and think, "Well, only a professional historian could read those." But here is the thing: historians and literary scholars of the eighteenth century and later generally do not receive formal training in paleography (the practice of deciphering historic handwriting). So, you probably have the same amount of training (maybe more) as I did when I started. The first time I encountered a manuscript source, I had no idea what I was doing. I was sitting in the Wellcome Library in London, looking at a diary from the 1830s,

---

<ol start="12"><li>Until 1923 there were two ecclesiastical administrative provinces: York and Canterbury, with probate courts (prerogative or testamentary courts) where wills were registered. See Colin R. Chapman, Ecclesiastical Courts, Officials and Records: Sin, Sex and Probate, 2nd ed. (Lochin Publishing, 1997), 29–30.</li></ol>

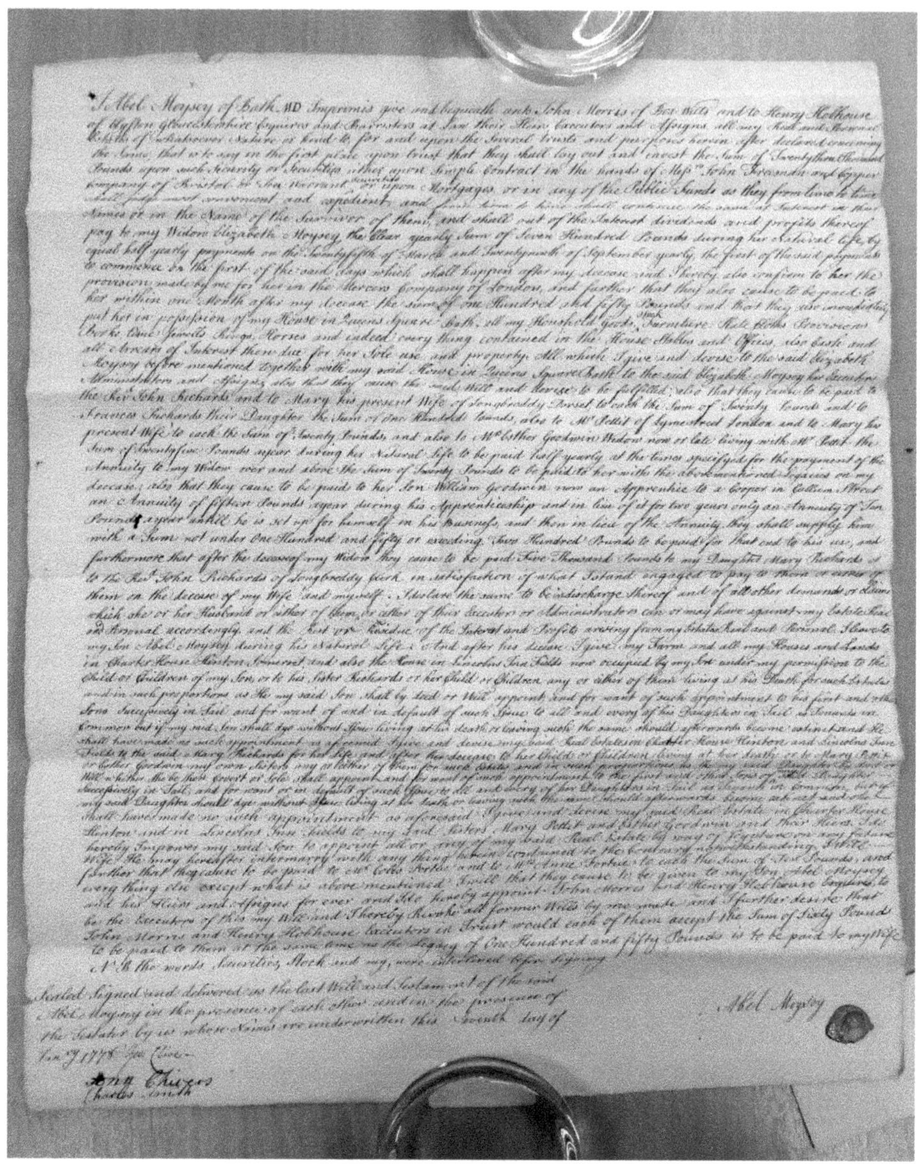

FIGURE 9. Will of Dr. Abel Moysey. ("Will of Abel Moysey, 7 January 1787," BC 3/2/1/10, Bath & North East Somerset Record Office, UK. Courtesy of Bath Record Office, Bath & North East Somerset Council. Image courtesy of Bath Record Office, Bath & North East Somerset Council.)

and I could only make out one in every five words. I seriously wanted to cry and thought, "Oh no! I will never be able to do this, why am I a historian?" First thing, do not be afraid to try; it really does get much easier with practice. I went from wanting to cry and not being able to decipher anything to being comfortable reading the atrocious and famously terrible handwriting of Princess Amelia, characterized by Flora Fraser, author of *Princesses: The Six Daughters of George III*, as "often difficult to read, sometimes illegible."[13] Fraser was not wrong, but the things I have managed to uncover because I was willing to challenge myself have been thrilling, with the scandal of Anne Wainhouse being just the tip of the iceberg.

Although wills might not seem very exciting, particularly when you are trying to find personal details about a person's life, they are a wonderful place to start. These documents allowed me to construct a family and friend network for Abel Moysey and revealed the names of other people who might have relevant letters or documents. The wills set me on a trajectory that proved far more interesting than I ever anticipated. It turns out Dr. Moysey, whom I thought was a simple Bath doctor with a local clientele, was connected in a variety of ways to a web of famous eighteenth-century personalities.[14]

I wondered, if he was so well-connected, why wasn't there a huge cache of personal letters and medical casebooks? The answer to this question is rarely satisfying, and in reality, the survival of historic documents is often down to luck or intentional preservation for a specific reason. In the case of Abel Moysey, there was also something more at work, as Hugh Belsey claims: "Dr. Moysey requested that his papers be destroyed after his death and this has unfortunately meant that little is known of him."[15] So, we have to deal not only with accidental survival, but also with intentional destruction (either by the individual, their family, friends, or even for other reasons, private or political). This practice, though incredibly frustrating for those of us trying to understand the past, was not uncommon, and literate individuals from different levels of society destroyed these personal items to create posthumous images, to keep family secrets safe, or simply out of privacy concerns. It is important to evaluate sources in light of these considerations,

---

13 Flora Fraser, *Princesses: The Six Daughters of George III* (Anchor Books, 2004), xi.

14 "Monday April 13, 1761 Dyed my Sister Hester Wansey ... January 6, She went to Bath, partly on Account of her own Health, & partly to see my Father (who went thither the 2d) But finding him Dead, She was greatly Shockt therby & sunk low: She continued at Bath, under the care of Dr. Moysey, being sometimes very low & weak, & at other times better till February 20, When she came home." "The Family Book of George Wansey of Warminster Clothier," 314/16, Wiltshire and Swindon History Centre, UK.

15 Hugh Belsey, *The Moysey Family: An Exhibition at Gainsborough's House, Sudbury, Suffolk 19th May to 8th July 1984* (Gainsborough's House Society, 1984), 1.

which can change our understanding or limit what is discoverable. This could certainly explain why I was having trouble finding letters from the elusive doctor, but the situation was not completely without hope.

Starting with the will, what could be discovered? First, it confirmed his profession, listing him as "Doctor of Physick Bath," and provided the names of his wife and children, allowing me more avenues for research. Abel Moysey married a woman named Elizabeth, and the couple had a son they named Abel and a daughter called Mary, who eventually married Reverend John Richards from Long Bredy, Dorset, and gave her parents a granddaughter named Francis Richards.[16] The will also named his sister and her husband, Mr. and Mrs. Mary Pettit, and indicated they lived on Lymestreet in London with Moysey's other sister, the widowed Mrs. Esther Goodwin, whose son, William Goodwin, was apprenticed to be a cooper (barrel maker). It also provided an indication of Moysey's financial status, mentioning, among other things, a "House in Queens Square Bath" (an affluent part of town a little more than 500 yards from Bath's New Assembly Rooms).[17] There were also substantial investments, including "the Sum of Twenty Three Thousand Pounds," with yearly interest payments "of seven hundred pounds."[18] I now had specific names and new places to investigate in my attempt to flesh out a picture of Dr. Abel Moysey of Bath.[19]

It turns out he was born in 1715, the first child of Abel Moysey (1690–1736) and his wife Mary Biddle, who married on February 24, 1714, at St. Mary Le Bow in the City of London and had their son baptized on December 4 the following year.[20]

---

16 "Will of Able Moysey, 7 January 1787," BC 3/2/1/10, Bath & North East Somerset Record Office, UK.

17 "Will of Able Moysey, 7 January 1787"; *The New Bath Guide; or Useful Pocket Companion*, new ed. (R. Crutwell, 1770), 48; *The Strangers' Assistant and Guide to Bath*, 86. A glimpse into the domestic life of Dr. Moysey is provided by a testimonial in 1756 for the character of a servant provided by Mrs. Elizabeth Moysey, who reported that she was "very good-natur'd, honest, and sober; not fond of gadding abroad, or scheming to bring Visitors home; can clean a Room; can wash small Things, and iron them up decently: and that she is not without some Knowledge in Cookery, which she believes was much improv'd whilst in her Service." This description provides some insight into the concerns of the Moyseys when they chose to bring a servant into their home, lists some of her duties, and implies she was not their only servant. "1756 Testimonial for a servant," Trevor Fawcett, *Voices of Eighteenth-Century Bath: An Anthology of Contemporary Texts Illustrating Events, Daily Life and Attitudes at Britain's Leading Georgian Spa* (Rutton, 1995), 380.

18 "Will of Able Moysey, 7 January 1787."

19 Just checking to see if you are chasing the footnotes. So, I was able to gain a wealth of material by simply using the records digitized in Ancestry.com. It was here I found the burial records for Dr. Moysey's father, his marriage record, Dr. Moysey's christening record, as well as Dr. Moysey's marriage record, and the records pertaining to the births of his children, and the wills, to name a few.

20 "Marriages," Reference Number: P69/MRY7/A/003/MS04998, *London, England, Church of England Baptisms, Marriages and Burials, 1538–1812* [database online], Provo, UT: Ancestry.com Operations, Inc., 2010; "Baptisms," Reference Number: P69/AND4/A/001/MS04107/003, *London, England, Church of England Baptisms, Marriages and Burials, 1538–1812* [database online], Provo,

Abel Moysey the younger attended the Merchant Taylors' School in London,[21] then at age sixteen, on June 30, 1732, he moved on to St. John's Oxford. While pursuing his Bachelor of Arts, his father, only forty-six years old, died suddenly in January 1736.[22] Despite this personal tragedy, Abel Moysey completed his Bachelor of Arts that year, then continued, gaining a Master of Arts in January of 1739 before moving on to undertake his medical training. He completed a Bachelor of Medicine on October 15, 1741, and then went on for the highest qualification, obtaining his Doctorate of Medicine from St. John's College, Oxford, on June 13, 1745.[23]

The newly qualified physician moved in 1741 to Sherborne in Dorset, and the following year, on June 22, 1742, he married Elizabeth Fortrie (1709–1789).[24] While in Sherborne, the couple had their first child in September 1743, naming him Abel, for his father and grandfather.[25] Hugh Belsey states that Moysey moved "to Bath in 1753, where he remained until his death in 1780," but Roger Rolls counters that "Abel Moysey moved to Bath in 1743."[26] This was a discrepancy of a decade and

UT: Ancestry.com Operations, Inc., 2010; Rev. Charles J. Robinson, *A Register of the Scholars Admitted into Merchant Taylors' School, from AD 1562 to 1874*, Vol. II (Farncombe & Co., 1883), 62. This work listed his date of birth as December 3, 1715.

21 The school was established by the Worshipful Company of Merchant Taylors in 1561. See Rev. Charles J. Robinson, *A Register of the Scholars*, 62; Harry Bristow Wilson, *The History of the Merchant-Taylor's School*, Volume I (F.C. & J. Rivington, 1812), 1–2.

22 "Will of Abel Moysey of Saint Andrew Undershaft London, City of London," PROB 11/681/126, National Archives, UK; "Will of Mr. Abel Moysey, of St. Andrew, Undershaft, London," Frederick William Weaver and Charles Herbert Mayo, eds., *Notes & Queries for Somerset and Dorset*, Volume V (J C. & A T. Sawtell, 1897), 82; "Burial of Abel Moysey, 14 January 1736," Reference Number: P69/AND4/A/001/MS04107/003, *London, England, Church of England Baptisms, Marriages and Burials, 1538–1812* [database online], Provo, UT: Ancestry.com Operations, Inc., 2010.

23 Foster, *Alumni Oxonienses*, 995; *A Catalogue of All Graduates in Divinity, Law, and Physick* (Clarendon Press, 1772), 246; Rev. Charles J. Robinson, *A Register of the Scholars*, Vol. II, 62. Robinson's *A Register of the Scholars* mentioned that Abel Moysey was a "F.R.S." This tidbit of information gave me another place to look, as F.R.S. stands for "fellow of the Royal Society." This was the only source where I found this mentioned, so it is possible it was incorrect. The only way to know was to search for corroboration. Unfortunately, he is not listed as one of the fellows of the Royal Society in that organization's records, and he was also not featured in *The Roll of the Royal College of Physicians of London* by William Munk. This source contains biographical information for prominent physicians, so I ran into a dead end on this front and was unable to substantiate this detail. As a consequence, I chose not to include it. If you cannot prove it, it is best to leave it out.

24 Belsey, *The Moysey Family*, 1. The secondary sources mentioning that Moysey lived in Sherborne (Rolls and Belsey) did not cite where that information came from, so I wanted to see if there were any other details. Fortunately, the christening records and subscription notices (these are often printed at the beginning of works, listing individuals who purchased copies of books, and they can list where the subscriber hailed from) provided another way of accessing that information. These records all confirmed that Moysey was a resident of Dorset.

25 "Christenings," Reference: PE/SH:RE1/; *Dorset, England, Church of England Baptisms, Marriages and Burials, 1538–1812* [database online], Provo, UT: Ancestry.com Operations, Inc., 2011.

26 Belsey, *The Moysey Family*, 1; Roger Rolls, *The Hospital of the Nation: The Story of Spa Medicine and the Mineral Water Hospital at Bath* (Bird Publications, 1988), 155.

could possibly be a typo, but neither work provided a footnote for where they sourced this information. So now what? I needed to reconcile the differences, but the Bath Rate Books do not exist before 1766, so I could not look for evidence of Moysey living in the city at the correct period.[27] I then moved to my other manuscript evidence, checking the Beach family receipts, hoping they may have consulted Moysey sometime in this decade, but the earliest mention was in November 1758, too late to be of use in this case.[28]

My next step was to consult leases and financial documents – perhaps they would show evidence of occupancy and help end the controversy? Unfortunately, all of the surviving Bath leases and mortgages post-date this problem, except for one very tantalizing glimpse.[29] On January 27, 1752, there was an exchange of land near the South Parade in Bath between a wine merchant, Edward Gillam, and Abel Moysey "doctor of physick," who was crucially listed as "of Bath."[30] This means, by 1752 at least, Moysey had acquired land in the city and was recognized as a resident. There were other glimpses of him in Bath that year – for instance, in February Julia Trevelyan wrote from Bath to her father of "Dr. Moisey … in this

---

27 Make a point of being as expansive as possible when you are collecting sources. Routinely, I have found that when I am too specific and think I only need one thing, I have to go back and do far more work than if I had just done it correctly the first time. This almost happened to me with the Bath Rate Books. I was tired and had to get through a lot of information in just a few hours, so I skipped steps. I went in looking for William Wainhouse's house in Duke Street and that of the apothecary, Mr. Horton, on Westgate Street. Not wanting to go through the entire book, I skipped to the relevant pages, but I thankfully realized this was a bad strategy and went back and photographed the whole book. If I had taken that shortcut, I never would have been able to trace Abel Moysey and would also have missed the other house belonging to Wainhouse in Bath. It is always better to over-collect your sources, because they can often be used for future projects. Additionally, as you delve deeper into your topic you may find (as I did) that you actually need them. For instance, the *Bath Rate Books* also provided other types of useful information, like neighborhood character, relative cost, and proximity to other important people in Bath society, all of which would have been missed if I had given in to my impulse to just grab the specific thing rather than the whole document. This was all valuable context that emerged from those boring columns of numbers, necessary for a detailed analysis and for telling Moysey's story. For all of these reasons, this sort of collection strategy will save you time-consuming extra work and possibly a costly trip back to an archive. And what will you do if returning to the archive is not an option? Financial constraints, a global pandemic, and changing access conditions may sometimes mean that necessary material is lost to you. Believe me, you will be kicking and cursing yourself later for shortcutting it.

28 "Beach Family Receipts, 4 November 1758," D2455/E3/2/4/5, Gloucestershire Archives, UK.

29 The various financial documents for Dr. Moysey in Bath: "Copy Mortgage [1 Sep 1767]," BC/6/2/9/3057/5; "Copy Surcharge [3 Dec 1767]," BC/6/2/9/3057/7; "Copy Surcharge [11 Aug 1768],"BC/6/2/9/3057/8; "Copy Assignment [24 Mar 1774]," BC/6/2/9/3057/11; "Assignment of Mortgage [24 June 1775]," 0810/4/3; "Mortgage [23 Oct 1776]," BC/6/2/9/3376/10/9; "Mortgage with Bond [1 Nov 1769]," BC/6/2/9/3376/10/6, Bath & North East Somerset Record Office, UK.

30 "Security for £1300 and interest, 27 Jan 1752," 0851/9/5, Bath & North East Somerset Record Office, UK.

neighborhood."[31] So now there was evidence that the Moyseys were living in the area before 1753 and I had an example of an alternate spelling of his name for my searches, but I still did not have a clear answer for how long they had been there.

Using christening records, I was able to get back first to 1751 and then to 1748. Abel and Elizabeth baptized a daughter named Frances on March 24, 1751, in the parish of Walcot (St. Swithin), located within the city limits of Bath. They had also christened their daughter Mary there on October 12, 1748.[32] A careful exploration of the Bath Rate Books reinforced these findings by revealing that all of the properties the family lived in were located in the Parish of Walcot.[33] Further evidence for Dr. Moysey being an established physician in Bath by 1748 was found in John Wood's *A Description of Bath*, which recorded him among the "Alphabetical List of the Governors [of the Hospital], as they stood the First of May 1748."[34] It is extremely unlikely that Moysey would have been made a governor of the Bath Hospital upon his arrival in the city. The hospital, established in 1738, was a significant charity that serviced patients from far outside of Bath who came to receive the waters for treatment. The hospital was staffed by three surgeons and the same

31 "Letter from Julia Trevelyan in Bath to her father John, Feb. 1752" DD/WO/56/4/58, Somerset Record Office, UK. Moysey was often also referred to as Moisey. It is always a good idea when searching for individuals in the eighteenth century to look for alternative spellings of the name, as it is not uncommon to have an individual denoted in a variety of ways. This is also important when searching online sources and databases. Be sure to use the kind of terms they would have during the period you are researching. For instance, looking for the term "tuberculosis" is unlikely to return much from the eighteenth century, but searching the common names during that period, like "consumption" and "phthisis," will pull up a number of records.

32 "Christenings," Reference Number: D\P\wal.sw/2/1/4; *Somerset, England, Church of England Baptisms, Marriages, and Burials, 1531–1812* [database online], Provo, UT: Ancestry.com Operations, Inc., 2016. "Christenings," Reference Number: D\P\wal.sw/2/1/5, *Somerset, England, Church of England Baptisms, Marriages, and Burials, 1531–1812* [database online], Provo, UT: Ancestry.com Operations, Inc., 2016; "Wainfleet – Walcott," in *A Topographical Dictionary of England*, ed. Samuel Lewis (S. Lewis, 1848), 432–6. The absence of Frances in Abel Moysey's will suggests she may have predeceased her father, or like in the case of Anne Wainhouse, been disinherited. Although a search of digitized sources failed to turn up a notification of her death, a 1915 book on Thomas Gainsborough, which reprinted a number of pieces of personal correspondence related to the artist, mentioned this: "Dr. Moysey, who should have had good reason to sympathise with Gainsborough at this crisis, as he had lost his own daughter in the preceding year, is the physician mentioned by the artist as 'Dr. Moisy' in his letter to Lord Royston. He was one of the prominent medical men of this time in Bath, and a person of importance in that city." See William T. Whitley, *Thomas Gainsborough* (Charles Scribner's Sons/Smith, Elder & Co., 1915), 80.

33 Bath Rate Books 1766–1772, BC/5/4/1/1-10, Bath & North East Somerset Record Office, UK. I only photographed up until 1772, because when I collected them I was looking for William Wainhouse and evidence for the two properties in Bath. This is where I am still kicking myself. Please do not make the same mistake, as this is what happens when you shortcut things! I did not know I would need to chase Dr. Moysey when I was at the Record Office, and having the Rate Books up until his death in 1780 would have been really useful.

34 Wood, *A Description of Bath*, 301–2.

number of physicians, while its governors were drawn from wealthy patrons.[35] Roger Rolls's *The Hospital of the Nation* also had an appendix that listed the physicians appointed to the Bath Hospital and their dates, and this had Moysey as associated with the establishment from 1747 until his death in 1780.[36]

Rolls's date was looking more plausible, but I still had the problem of five years. In the *Annals of Bath*'s (1838) discussion of the death of Dr. Moysey's son at the age of eighty-seven, another clue emerged. The author asserted, "Mr. Moysey came to Bath ten years of age, with his father, the well-known Dr. Moysey."[37] As he was born in September 1743, this would put him arriving in to Bath in 1753, which was Hugh Belsey's date! Well, now what? This cannot be correct given the evidence that the Moyseys were in Bath by 1748, and it is a good warning about accepting things at face value. Just because this source is closer to the date of the events in question, it is still a secondary source, and its proximity with respect to date does not necessarily make it a reliable one. Given that the evidence established Abel Moysey in Bath several years before 1753, I feel comfortable in assuming that date was a typo.

One of the most intriguing things to emerge from my searches of Dr. Moysey were some satirical treatments. Of course, these are caricatures of the man, but they indicate he had significant status in the city and speak to his reputation.[38] The 1763 caricature entitled *The Knights of Baythe* was published as a commentary on the city leadership's petition on the Peace of Paris that ended the Seven Years' War (1756–1763). Though political, this image was also a reaction to the personal quarrel between Ralph Allen and William Pitt. There were factions that felt the Peace was an abandonment of Britain's ally, Prussia, and it failed to exact the full advantage from the French defeat. Despite pockets of opposition, weary of war and its spiraling costs, there was wide support in Parliament and outside of London for the settlement. The member of Parliament (MP) for Bath was William Pitt, who was a major opponent of the treaty and took his city's support of it as a personal attack. He then turned his back on Ralph Allen, the man who helped him get elected.[39] *The Knights of Baythe* prominently features Allen at the center

---

35 Jenkins, "Thomas Gainsborough's Doctors," 59. Joining the governing body required a donation of £40 of more, or election by that entity. See Anne Borsay, "Visitors and Residents: The Dynamics of Charity in Eighteenth-century Bath," *Journal of Tourism History* 4, no. 2 (2012), 175.

36 Rolls, *The Hospital of the Nation*, 167.

37 Captain Rowland Mainwaring, *Annals of Bath from the Year 1800 to the Passing of the New Municipal Act* (Mary Meyler and Son, 1838), 381.

38 Do not forget that material culture objects and prints can also provide valuable insight that may be missing from the surviving written and other types of printed sources. As such, they should also be part of your research agenda.

39 Langford, *A Polite and Commercial People*, 350–1.

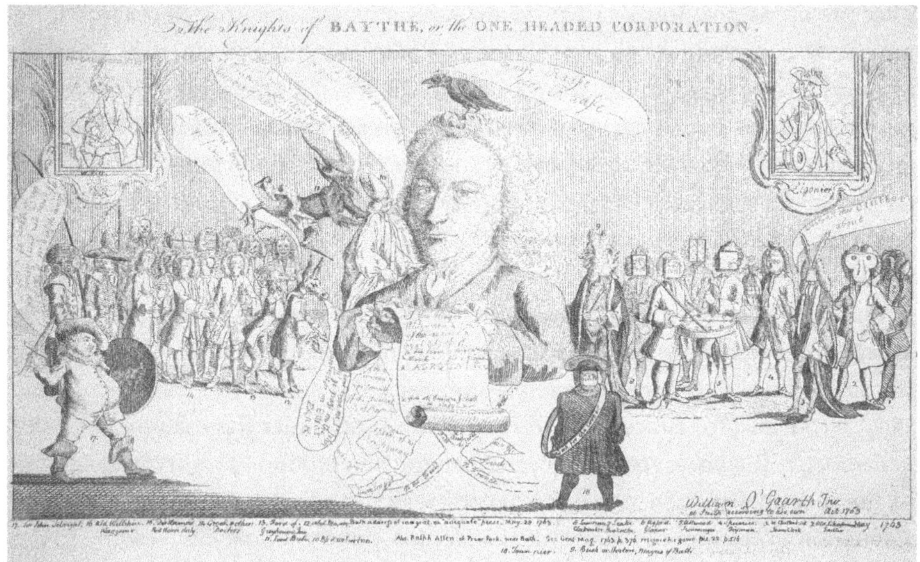

FIGURE 10. "The Knights of Baythe, or the One Headed Corporation." ("The Knights of Bay-the, or the One Headed Corporation," satirical print 1763, Museum number 1868,0808.4327, © The Trustees of the British Museum. Image courtesy of the British Museum.)

of the composition, reflecting his dominance in the city. Apart from Allen, the other members of the corporation are anthropomorphized either as animals or as symbols of their professions.[40]

Dr. Abel Moysey is positioned behind Ralph Allen's right arm, demonstrating his position as a man of standing, and he is grouped with others of the medical profession. Only one other man is identified – Dr. [Simon] Crook, who was not a doctor but an apothecary in Abbey-Green.[41] The other anonymous practitioners of the healing arts have medical jars as heads and are led at the front of the line by Moysey, who is represented as an Ass.[42]

So, why the Ass's head for Moysey, rather than some instrument of the med-ical profession? Though it could be a commentary on his personality, it is also

---

40 Langford, *A Polite and Commercial People*, 350–1; Trevor Fawcett, *Bath Administer'd Corporation Affairs at the 18th-Century Spa* (Ruton, 2001), 31–2.

41 *The Strangers' Assistant and Guide to Bath*, 61.

42 "An ass wearing a coat representing the physician Abel Moysey, saying, 'Pray dont drive me Sr John [Sebright] Il' go graze on the Common, or in Prior Park'; On the left, stands Sir John Sebright who had become MP for Bath on 28 April 1763, dressed as Falstaff and crying, 'Dam ye for a set of Poltroons, Il drive you from hence with this Dagger of Lath." "Catalog description," *The Knights of Baythe, or the One Headed Corporation,* Museum number Cc.3.44, 1763 © The Trustees of the British Museum, https://www.britishmuseum.org/collection/object/P_Cc-3-44.

reflective of his position as a physician. Ass's milk was a common remedy for a number of complaints – so much so that Philip Stanhope, the earl of Chester-field and later patient of Dr. Moysey, wrote in 1759, "I am rather better than I was; which I owe not to my physicians, but to an ass and a cow, who nourish me, between them, very plentifully and wholesomely; in the morning the ass is my nurse, at night the cow."[43] In 1766 he also sent the following advice to his son: "Guy Patin recommends to a patient to have no Doctor but a Horse; and no Apothecary but an Ass."[44]

Other, even less flattering representations of Dr. Moysey speak to his financial success and his possibly taking advantage of patients. Dr. Richard Warren, a prominent local figure, antiquarian, curate, and the author of a *History of Bath* (1801) wrote an 1807 satire entitled *Bath Characters* under the pseudonym Peter Paul Pallet.[45] The book grew in length from the first edition of eighty pages to 132 for the second and then 162 in the successive 1808 edition. It became a favorite occupation to attempt to determine the identities of the characters, leading to the development of numerous "keys."[46] There were manuscript explanations (some incomplete), like the one sent by William Siddons to Hester Lynch Piozzi in 1807, but there were also published keys, some of which identified Dr. Moysey as "Dr. Fleecem." However, not all the sources agree that he was the inspiration.[47] For instance, Hugh Belsey states that "Woodforde loc cit." believed "Moysey may have been characterised as Dr Fleecem," although he indicates that there were local sources in Bath that identified "Fleecem as either Drs. Frazer or Fothergill."[48]

It is also good to remember that the publication of *Bath Characters* occurred twenty-seven years after Moysey's death, which muddies the situation, as the

---

43 "Letter CCCXVII, 16 March 1759," Philip Dormer Stanhope Chesterfield, *Letters Written by the Late Right Honorable Philip Dormer Stanhope, Earl of Chesterfield, to His Son Philip Stanhope* (M. Eugenia Stanhope, 1775), 86–7.

44 "Letter CCCLXIX, 29 October 1766," Philip Dormer Stanhope Chesterfield, *Letters Written by the Late Right Honorable Philip Dormer Stanhope, Earl of Chesterfield, to His Son Philip Stanhope* (M. Eugenia Stanhope, 1775), 147–8.

45 Michael Hicks, "Warner, Richard (1763–1857), Antiquary," *Oxford Dictionary of National Biography*, September 23, 2004 (accessed May 27, 2020), https://www.oxforddnb.com/view/10.1093/ref:odnb/9780198614128.001.0001/odnb-9780198614128-e-28766.

46 Edward A. Bloom and Lillian D. Bloom, eds. *The Piozzi Letters: Correspondence of Hester Lynch Piozzi, 1784–1821* (formerly Mrs. Thrale), Vol. 4, 1805–1810 (University of Delaware Press, 1996), 180.

47 "Bath, 24 December 1807 (Ry. Eng. Ms. 574/26)," in Kalman A. Burnim, "The Letters of Sarah and William Siddons to Hester Lynch Piozzi in the John Rylands Library," *Bulletin of the John Rylands Library* 52, no. 1 (1969): 46–95, 91; Emanuel Green, *Bibliotheca Somersetensis: A Catalogue of Books, Pamphlets, Single Sheets, and Broadsides in Some Way Connected to the County of Somerset*, Vol. I (Barincott and Pearce, 1902), 555.

48 Belsey, *The Moysey Family*, 1.

more distance there is from an event the more skeptical one needs to be of the account or the relating of a story. Richard Warner introduces Dr. Fleecem as part of a conversation between an apothecary (Mixum) and a physician (Borecat).[49] Mixum instructs Borecat on the necessity of a fashionable Bath physician having London connections to recommend him patients, stating that "a good London connection" was "a thing as necessary for you as your diploma. – A London connection is half the battle for a Bath medical knight-errant."[50] This was a common practice and one alluded to by the earl of Chesterfield, who, after an attack of bilious fever, made his way to Bath on the advice of his London physicians, writing that "[t]he [medical] faculty hastened me to this place."[51]

Mixum warned Borecat that patients must remain in ignorance of such transactions "lest a rat should be smelt, and the gudgeon escape," holding up an incident involving Dr. Fleecem as instructive. In the story, the notable London physician Sir Timothy Humbug treated an older woman for "a chronic complaint … which had netted [him] … an annuity of £150 for several years." However, after so long without a cure "she began to wonder that she did not mend." Recognizing he might lose a patient, Humbug "advised her to try the Bath waters, and gave her a letter of introduction to his friend Dr. Fleecem." When the Bath physician met his new patient, she presented the sealed letter and after reading it he checked her pulse, asked her the appropriate questions, acquired his fee and then left. This is where the scheme fell apart because, on his way out, he dropped the letter without noticing and the contents were revealed to his curious patient:

Dear Doctor.
I send you herewith an old fat goose, whom I have long been in the habit of plucking: one wing I reserve for myself; the other is at the service of my friends.

yours truly,
Tim. Humbug.

---

49 Mixum was identified as apothecary Mr. Bowen and Dr. Borecat as Dr. Burkitt: "Key to Bath Characters, 1808," in Green, *Bibliotheca Somersetensis*, 555. William Bowen (1761–1815), an apothecary of the firm Spry & Bowen, located at the 1 Argyle buildings in Bath. Bowen treated a number of the members of Jane Austen's family. See Deirdre Le Faye, ed., *Jane Austen's Letters*, new ed. (Oxford University Press, 1995), 499. For more on Bowen, see Le Faye, *Jane Austen's Letters*, 96–7, 100, 123; David Selwyn, ed., *The Poetry of Jane Austen and the Austen Family* (University of Iowa Press/Jane Austen Society, 1997), 30. Dr. Burkitt (Birkit) was a physician practicing on Trim (Trym) Street. See *The New Bath Guide*, 78.

50 Peter Paul Pallet (Dr. Richard Warner), *Bath Characters, or Sketches from Life* (G. Wilkie and J. Robinson, 1807), 52.

51 "Bath, 5 December 1763," Philip Dormer Stanhope, earl of Chesterfield, *Miscellaneous Works of the Late Philip Dormer Stanhope, Early of Chesterfield*, 2nd ed., Vol. IV, ed. M. Maty (Edward and Charles Dilly, 1779), 304.

As you can imagine, this changed the dynamic, and the following morning Dr. Fleecem was in for a surprise. As he reached to check her pulse, the patient "thanked him for his kind intention to strip her of her remaining feathers; but observed, that though she might possibly be an old goose, she was not so far advanced in her dotage as to suffer such harpies as Sir Timothy and himself to prey longer on her unfortunate carcase [sic]."[52] This satirical commentary on the medical networks of practice reveals another possible level of connection between Dr. Moysey and those outside of the city of Bath.

Although there is some question over whether or not Fleecem was Moysey, and Sir Timothy Humbug remains an unidentified London practitioner, we do know from the archival evidence that Moysey was well connected. He apparently won the admiration of Dr. Richard Warren (1731–1797), the Cambridge-trained physician who served as doctor at both Middlesex Hospital and St. George's Hospital in London, before becoming the physician for the Prince of Wales in 1787. Warren was the preeminent fashionable physician of the period, earning an enormous annual income. It is believed that from 1788 onwards, he netted £9,000 per annum for his services and, upon his death, left his family an enormous fortune of approximately £150,000. Well respected for his "exceptional powers of mind and solidity of judgement," Warren was mostly contemptuous of the practitioners of the spa town of Bath, stating that "if a physician had common sense when he first settled there, he soon lost it all in looking out for Bile, and giving into the medical cant of the place." There was one exception, as Warren was reported to have said that "Bath had never produced a physician of talents except Dr. Moysey."[53] Given Warren's own achievements, this admiration may have in part been for Moysey's financial as well as medical acumen.

Like Warren, Moysey was a successful practitioner and one who was notoriously expensive, charging £1 per consultation. The Beach receipts give us a sense of the rhythm and financial scale of his practice. In the thirty-six days between November 7 and December 12, 1758, the Beach family paid Dr. Moysey twenty-one separate fees totaling twenty-four pounds and three shillings. This

---

52 Pallet, *Bath Characters*, 53–4.

53 D'A. Power and Catherine Bergin, "Warren, Richard (1731–1797), Physician," *Oxford Dictionary of National Biography*, September 23, 2004 (accessed May 22, 2020), https://www.oxforddnb. com/view/10.1093/ref:odnb/9780198614128.001.0001/odnb-9780198614128-e-28788; "News," *Oracle*, May 4, 1798, Seventeenth and Eighteenth Century Burney Newspapers Collection (accessed May 22, 2020), https://link-gale-com.libproxy.furman.edu/apps/doc/Z2001045106 /BBCN?u=furmanuniv&sid=BBCN&xid=2ce19dfe.

demonstrates not only his attention to his patents, but also the financial rewards he reaped as a benefit. Consulted again beginning March 7, 1759, and ending May 15, 1759, Moysey charged thirty-two separate fees totaling thirty-four pounds and thirteen shillings. In an approximately four-month period, the doctor made fifty-eight pounds and sixteen shillings from just one of his patients.[54] This practice of charging a pound or a guinea (one pound, one shilling) per visit continued well into the 1770s, when Rev. James Woodforde's father sought treatment. The pair traveled to the city on January 22, 1771, and "hoped the Bath waters would do the old man good."[55] The following day, Dr. Moysey prescribed "an opening draught … and to drink the Bath waters three times a day … and to drink it in the Pump Room, viz. to go there after it. My Father gave him a guinea for prescribing as usual."[56]

However, even his friends mocked his mercenary ways: Thomas Gainsborough wrote in 1763 that "Dr. Moisy [sic] has had a severe fit of the ague, and (as I am told) says he could make himself very easy with the loss of his money if he could get rid of the ague. But whether the loss of his money might not bring on a shaking fit that formed itself into an ague, I must leave."[57] The painter, however, also recommended the physician to his friend, musician William Jackson,[58] and intimated Moysey would not charge him:

> pray send me word whether there is any occasion for Dr. Moysey to come to you.… The Doctor shall come in a moment if there is the least occasion, and I know he will with pleasure without your hand touching your breeches pocket.[59]

This notion of Moysey and his fees is supported by another satire of the inhabitants of Bath published two years after his death. *Bath Anecdotes and Characters: By the Genius Loci* (1782) provides a more balanced view of the physician's skill and temperament. The work touted his skill as "one of those few men who have

---

54 "Beach Family Receipts, 1758–1759," D2455/E3/2/4/5, Gloucestershire Archives, UK.

55 "22 January 1771," Woodforde, *Diary of a Country Parson*, 103.

56 "22 January 1771," Woodforde, *Diary of a Country Parson*, 103.

57 "Thomas Gainsborough to Lord Royston, Bath, 21 July 1763," in Whitley, *Thomas Gainsborough*, 41.

58 William Jackson was the organist for Exeter Cathedral. See Hugh Belsey, "Gainsborough, Thomas (1727–1788), Painter and Phnrintmaker," *Oxford Dictionary of National Biography*, September 23, 2004 (accessed May 27, 2020), https://www.oxforddnb.com/view/10.1093/ref:odnb/9780198614128.001.0001/odnb-9780198614128-e-10282.

59 "Letter XI from Thomas Gainsborough to William Jackson, Tuesday Morning (no date)," as quoted in Appendix A of Whitley, *Thomas Gainsborough*, 388.

made physic their study," but the author also tackled the physician's mercenary reputation:

> Moysey is liable to the infirmities of human nature; for able as he is, he does not cease to be a man ... and he is often in the respect guided, as to interest. But it never was, nor ever will be known that he sacrificed his patient to his rapacity, or debased his prescription for want of a fee.... Dr. Moysey has been a fortunate man; but if he should die worth fourscore thousand pounds, he may be said to have earned them. He never indulges himself to detriment of his patient, but is always as studious and as much disposed to serve his patients as himself.[60]

This is a much kinder representation of the doctor than that of Fleecem, and the work also provides other clues about his skills. The author mentions an upstart surgeon who, inspired by "the rage of inoculation," made his way to "Bath, meaning, as he said, to succeed to the practice of Moysey and Delacour."[61] This asserts that these men were engaged in the practice of inoculation, a circumstance corroborated by the archival evidence. Further clues to Moysey's practice emerge in a letter from Julia Trevelyan in Bath to her father John when she begged him for funds to have her son Jack "Inoculated for the Small Pox." She wrote, "I am sorry to find it will be attended with so much expense in this neighborhood, but as Doctor Moisey is so good a Physician and been used to Inoculation, I cannot help beging [sic] your thorough consideration of it." Once again, there is a sign of the expense attended with consulting Dr. Moysey, but now there is another clue to the scope of his practice. We learn he was the preeminent smallpox inoculator in the neighborhood and, as he did for his other services, charged a premium. Julia was desperate to protect her son and promised her father that she would "half the expence [sic] as to Housekeeping" to defray the cost if he would assist in paying for the procedure.[62]

Although Abel Moysey destroyed his papers, and there is not a large collection of surviving personal letters, it doesn't mean that this part of the project is impossible or that we cannot get access to him. Remember that messages go both ways, and there are some letters from Moysey in the papers of others. In addition to being a physician of the Bath Hospital, providing inoculations, and servicing the

60 *Bath Anecdotes and Characters: By the Genius Loci* (Dodsley, 1782), 139–42.
61 *Bath Anecdotes and Characters*, 86–7.
62 "Julia Trevelyan in Bath to her father John Trevalyan, February 1752," DD/WO/56/4/58, Somerset Record Office, UK.

local gentry, it turns out that Dr. Moysey also had a number of prominent clients, ones that placed him firmly at the center of Georgian society. In 1761, reports from Bath indicate that he was appointed physician to the Duke of York (the brother of King George III). Newspaper accounts of local gossip provide yet another way to access the activities and reputation of individuals.[63] The "Country News" published in the London *General Evening Post* stated on November 12, 1761, that Moysey attended a ball "opened by his Royal Highness and Miss St. Quiatin [sic]. This day, Dr. Moysey kissed his Royal Highness' hand, on being appointed his physician."[64] These events were corroborated the following month by Lord Bath, who wrote in December to George Coleman that "his R.H. the Duke of York ... has, I hear, made Moysey his physician."[65]

Moysey was not just moving in court circles, but he was also corresponding with those high up in the government, particularly Thomas Pelham-Holles, Duke of Newcastle (1693–1768). A prominent Whig politician who had been at the center of politics for decades, Pelham-Holles left government for the final time at age seventy-three (in 1766), but kept his fingers entwined in politics despite his retirement.[66] In 1764, Abel Moysey corresponded with the duke about the health of his friend Henry Bilson Legge (1708–1764), whom he had assisted in obtaining the position of chancellor of the exchequer in 1754 (a position he held until 1757).[67]

---

63 Newspapers and printed letter collections provide other avenues of inquiry for your research, though it is important to remember these have often been heavily edited or published from a specific perspective that should be considered when assessing their content. However, many published letter collections may be the only accessible sources for these materials, as they reside in closed archives, family collections, or have been lost over time. If you can get to the originals you should always do so, but if not, these are still valuable sources. Just remember there are already layers of interpretation at work.

64 One of the daughters of Sir William St. Quintin, 4th baronet (c. 1700–1770); "Country News," *General Evening Post* (London), No. 4396, Tuesday December 15 to Thursday December 17, 1761.

65 "Lord Bath to George Coleman, December 18, 1761," Richard Brinsley Peake, *Memoirs of the Coleman Family*, Vol. 1 (Richard Bentley, 1841), 68.

66 Pelham-Holles had served as foreign minister under Robert Walpole from 1730 to 1739 and as defense minister during the War of Jenkins' Ear (1739–1748). He then served as foreign minister from 1748 to 1754, before a disastrous term as prime minster from 1754 to 1756 (which saw the outbreak of the French and Indian War that morphed into the Seven Years' War). Pelham-Holles continued to serve in government, but as the minister of finance from 1757 to 1762, before being ousted after a conflict with the new sovereign's favorite, the earl of Bute. By this point the seventy-year-old's influence was fading, though he returned to office in 1765 as lord privy seal. During this period, he was an outspoken supporter of the Stamp and Declaratory Acts, which had caused a great deal of resistance among the American colonists. See Reed Browning, "Holles, Thomas Pelham, Duke of Newcastle upon Tyne and First Duke of Newcastle under Lyme (1693–1768), Prime Minister," *Oxford Dictionary of National Biography*, September 23, 2004 (accessed May 27, 2020), https://www.oxforddnb .com/view/10.1093/ref:odnb/9780198614128.001.0001/odnb-9780198614128-e-21801.

67 Legge had begun his career as the secretary to Robert Walpole in 1736. A connection that served him well as his mentor helped him get elected to the House of commons in 1740 and again in 1741.

With the support of the duke, Legge returned to office until 1761 and thereafter remained in the House of Commons. In 1763 his health took a turn for the worse and, for five months, Legge experienced serious bouts of diarrhea and vomiting, which sent him to Bath and into the orbit of Dr. Abel Moysey.[68]

In Bath, he suffered greatly from bouts of "bilious vomiting which lasted all night with great violence & an increas'd Pulse," and his letters reveal his annoyance with his body's betrayal and even his frustration with his frustration. He complained, "Belonging to a human body & I am not at all sure that I should not recover sooner if I did not take it so mortal ill to be sick at present. I know this is very foolish but nobody is a fool on purpose or for any reason but because he can't help it." Legge did not like Bath and wrote on February 15, 1764, of his plans to travel to Hinton in Hampshire, feeling he had received "no particular benefit from this place." Despite planning to leave the city, he intended to continue following his physician's advice, writing, "[I] can carry the written counsel of Doctr Moysey along with me, I verily believe that change of air, exercise & the journey itself may be one of the most effectual remedies I can take."[69]

Three days later, Moysey wrote directly to the duke of Newcastle about his friend's health. His tone was appropriately ingratiating, beginning with "My ever honoured friend & patient Mr. Legge left this place to day," and followed with a report stating he was "much recovered from his last Relapse, which I must own, gives me inexpressible Concern, altho' his Spirits continue good & He is again much mended in all respects." Moysey also addressed Legge's determination to leave Bath and that Legge had promised to "return hither again almost immediately, if He should have any return of this Severe Illness." The doctor finished with a promise to update the duke with further accounts "of Mr. Legge & if any Material Circumstance should occur in it, shall take Leave to acquaint your grace with it."[70] Unfortunately, Legge's improvement was temporary and in March 1764 he wrote again to his friend, expressing regret: "I wish I will be able to come to you; but tho' I don't intend to dye I doubt I shall live to little purpose at least for

---

He then took the position as treasury secretary later that year, serving in that post until 1742. In 1745 he acquired a position in the Admiralty. In 1748 he was caught up between warring political factions, but received a new position as treasurer of the Navy in 1749. See P.J. Kulisheck, "Legge, Henry Bilson (1708–1764), Politician," *Oxford Dictionary of National Biography*, September 23, 2004 (accessed May 27, 2020), https://www.oxforddnb.com/view/10.1093/ref:odnb/9780198614128.001.0001/odnb-9780198614128-e-16356.

68 Kulisheck, "Legge, Henry Bilson."

69 "Henry Bilson Legge to the Duke of Newcastle, Bath, 15 February 1764," Newcastle Papers, Vol. 270, ADD/MS/ 32955, folio 501, British Library, UK.

70 "Abel Moysey to the Duke of Newcastle, Bath, 18 February 1764," Newcastle Papers, Vol. 270, ADD/ MS/ 32956, folio 45, British Library, UK.

some weeks to come; for I can neither recover Stomach nor brains which have a most marvellous connexion with that grosser organ of the human body."[71] With Bath not to his liking, his health continuing to fail, his body wasting, and the addition of new symptoms like jaundice, Legge decided to try a different spa town. He made his way to Tunbridge Wells at the end of July 1764 and finally succumbed to his illness on August 23, 1764.[72] On September 24, 1764, Philip Dormer Stanhope, fourth earl of Chesterfield (1694–1773) wrote of the impact of Legge's death and of Pelham-Holles's advanced age upon Britain's political situation.[73]

Stanhope was uniquely situated to comment, as he himself was a prominent political figure and yet another patient of Dr. Abel Moysey. Before his retirement, the gifted linguist had had a distinguished diplomatic career, but his declining health curtailed his political activities beginning in 1746. After officially leaving government in 1748, Stanhope made his way to Bath, beginning a long journey of declining health that lasted more than twenty-five years.[74] The first indication of Stanhope's relationship with Dr. Moysey comes in 1763 when he wrote from Bath that "I have found a *Monsieur Diafoirus* here, Dr. Moisey." This reference to Monsieur Diafoirus is a nod to Moliere's *Le Maladie Imaginare* and a character who uses medical terminology to obfuscate and take advantage of his patients without providing a cure. This is certainly in keeping with the Dr. Fleecem characterization; however, Stanhope goes on to state that Moysey "has really done me a great deal of good; and I am sure I wanted it a great deal, when I came here first. I have recovered some strength, and a little more will give me as much as I can make use of."[75] Other descriptions of Moysey illustrated both his condescension as well as his skill. For instance, James Woodforde said that he "seems high and mighty

---

71 "Henry Bilson Legge to the Duke of Newcastle, Hotel Foust, 5 March 1764," Newcastle Papers, Vol. 270, ADD/MS/ 32956, folio 214, British Library, UK.

72 Kulisheck, "Legge, Henry Bilson."

73 "Letter CCCXLVII, Blackheath, 14 September 1764," Philip Dormer Stanhope, Chesterfield, *Letters Written by the Late Right Honorable Philip Dormer Stanhope, Earl of Chesterfield, to His Son Philip Stanhope* (M. Eugenia Stanhope, 1775), 120.

74 In 1727 he was appointed to The Hague as ambassador before becoming lord steward in 1730, but fell from that position after opposing Sir Robert Walpole on the issue of the Excise Bill in 1732. He stayed in opposition politics for a decade, until Walpole's resignation. The outbreak of war with France brought Stanhope back into diplomatic service when he went back to The Hague in a successful attempt to woo the Dutch to ally with Britain against France. In 1745 he took up a post in Ireland, but on returning to England the following year he was plagued by illness and, wearied of political infighting, he eventually left the government in 1748. See John Cannon, "Stanhope, Philip Dormer, Fourth Earl of Chesterfield (1694–1773), Politician and Diplomatist," *Oxford Dictionary of National Biography*, September 23, 2004 (accessed May 27, 2020), https://www.oxforddnb.com /view/10.1093/ref:odnb/9780198614128.001.0001/odnb-9780198614128-e-26255.

75 "Letter CLIV, Bath, 24 December 1763," *Letters Written by the Late Right Honourable Philip Dormer Stanhope, Earl of Chesterfield*, Vol. IV (E. Lynch, 1774), 176.

but sensible."[76] However, Mrs. Hester Lynch Thrale simply saw him as a tedious conversationalist when she wrote in 1780 to Samuel Johnson: "Oh, here comes Dr. Moysey, to talk about Whig and Tory, and the reign of King Charles the Second; how that style of conversation does wear one out, especially from a professional man, and when one is wishing to bring forward a subject really interesting."[77]

Despite his early uncharitable characterization of Moysey, Stanhope obviously trusted him and made repeated trips to Bath for his various complaints, including rheumatism and deafness. He even asked the doctor's advice on his son's medical condition in 1766, but Moysey was unwilling to compromise his integrity and prescribe something without knowing the full situation of the patient:

> I have consulted Moisey, the great physician of this place, upon it; who says, that at this distance he dares not prescribe any thing, as there may be such different causes for your complaint, which must be well weighed by a physician upon the spot: that is, in short, that he knows nothing of the matter.[78]

The following year he wrote again of Moysey's treatments:

> A fortnight ago I had a little return of my fever, which Doctor Moisey called only a Febricula; for which he prescribed phlebotomy, and, of course, the saline draughts. The phlebotomy did me good, and the saline draughts did me no harm; which is all I ask of any medicine, or any medicus.[79]

Stanhope and Legge were among a number of notables who came to Bath for their health and who secured the services of Dr. Moysey; another was Sir Robert Clive (1725–1774), who made a name and a fortune in India.[80]

---

76 "22 January 1771," Woodforde, *Diary of a Country Parson*, 103.

77 "Letter CCXXXVI, Mrs. Thrale to Dr. Johnson May (1780)," *Letters to and from the Late Samuel Johnson*, Vol. II (A. Strahan & T. Cadell, 1788), 130.

78 "Letter CLXXXII, Bath, 15 November 1766," *Letters Written by the Late Right Honourable Philip Dormer Stanhope, Earl of Chesterfield*, Vol. IV (E. Lynch, 1774), 214.

79 "Letter to Doctor Monsey, Bath, 23 December 1767," *Letters Written by the Late Right Honourable Philip Dormer Stanhope, Earl of Chesterfield*, Vol. IV (E. Lynch, 1774), 302.

80 Like Dr. Moysey, Robert Clive attended the Merchant Taylors' School before eventually traveling to India as a clerk with the East India Company, arriving in 1744. Clive's situation would change with the outbreak of the War of Jenkins' Ear, which provided him the opportunity to join the military arm of the company, rising by 1749 to the rank of lieutenant and captain by 1751. Clive's time in India allowed him to amass a huge fortune and his fame was assured by his role on June 23, 1757, at the Battle of Plassey, and by his terms as governor in India. See H.V. Bowen, "Clive, Robert, First Baron Clive of Plassey (1725–1774), Army Officer in the East India Company and Administrator in India." *Oxford Dictionary of National Biography*, September 23, 2004 (accessed May 27, 2020), https://www.oxforddnb.com/view/10.1093/ref:odnb/9780198614128.001.0001/odnb-9780198614128-e-5697.

By 1750 the symptoms that would plague Clive throughout his life had begun to appear, and he suffered from bouts labeled as nervous in origin, often accompanied by pain and melancholy. These issues would lead him to spend the period between 1760 and 1764 focusing on his health, with frequent trips to Bath. Despite his attempts to mitigate his distress, by 1766 his physical and mental symptoms had returned, a circumstance Clive blamed on "the combined effects of the climate and hard work," which he felt "had 'destroyed' his constitution and reduced his body and mind to a 'state of imbecility.'"[81] He resorted to opium in an attempt to treat his symptoms, and recovered enough for one last trip to India in 1767, before returning to Britain permanently in July of that year.[82]

The Bath Rate Books show that in 1768, 1769, and 1771, Clive was ensconced in a house in King's Circus for his health.[83] This fashionable neighborhood, designed by the architect John Wood, had thirty substantial houses and was the residence of such notables as William Pitt (later earl of Chatham), the fourth duke of Bedford, and portrait painter Thomas Gainsborough.[84] Robert Clive consulted Abel Moysey during this period, who wrote on March 24, 1768, in rosy terms about "the fair prospect we now have of the reestablishment of your Lordship's Health." The doctor addressed the longevity of Clive's complaint and called for caution, writing, "Your Lordship has for Some Years gone thro' such a variety of painful and Dispiriting Illnesses that you cannot, I think be too careful or too attentive to every measure that may be judged Effectual or conducive to prevent a relapses." To this end, he recommended Clive repair to the milder weather of the continent for the winter, to protect his "tender Constitution from the pains & penalties of that Severe Season in this Climate." Moysey seemed confident this would allow him to decrease his dependency on "opium or [other] opening Medicines."[85]

On May 31, 1768, Dr. Moysey's discussion of symptoms provides a glimpse into his patient's sufferings:

> I am quite of your Lordship's opinion that, whilst the Stools remain green & fetid attended with frequent pricklings & uneasiness at the Stomach. There is an Acrimony in the Juices still to be attended to & a Disposition to breed morbid or redundant Bile yet to be attended to.[86]

---

81 "Clive to his directors," MS Eur G37/3, British Library, UK, quoted in Bowen, "Clive, Robert, first Baron Clive of Plassey (1725–1774).

82 Bowen, "Clive, Robert, first Baron Clive of Plassey (1725–1774).

83 Bath Rate Books BC/5/4/1/4 (81), BC/5/4/1/6 (80), BC/5/4/1/8 (84), Bath & North East Somerset Record Office, UK.

84 Whitley, *Thomas Gainsborough*, 48–9.

85 "Dr. Abel Moysey to Lord Robert Clive, Bath, 24 March 1768," MSS/ EUR/G37/52/1, British Library, UK.

86 "Dr. Abel Moysey to Lord Robert Clive, Bath, 31 May 1768," MSS/ EUR/G37/53/1, British Library, UK.

Moysey labeled the cramping and stinking green excrement that Clive suffered from as bilious (stemming from the excess of bile) and reiterated the benefits of traveling for health. He was understandably a proponent of the spa waters and was a noted authority, but his letters to Clive demonstrated not only his vast knowledge of the properties of Bath's waters, but also those of the specific waters at several European spas. He was also keenly aware of their limitations, as Lord Royston discovered while being treated for a stomach ailment in 1763. Though he found the waters disagreeable and unproductive, he reported that "Dr. Moisy [sic] says that out of 5 cases that appear to be the same the Bath waters will cure 4 & miss the 5th." When the waters proved ineffective, Moysey quickly resorted to other treatments. Royston wrote, "I cannot say that [the waters] have yet removed the complaints for wch I was advised to try them.... Dr. Moisy has offered me a draught by way of Bracer & I ride as others as often as the Weather permits, so that it will not be my fault if Bath does not set me up again."[87]

Moysey's advice to Robert Clive was not couched in obsequiousness, like his reporting to the Duke of Newcastle. Instead, his letters to this patient demonstrate his clear medical voice and mechanism for prescribing by mail:

I have taken the liberty of recommending a very reserved & cautious usage of it, at least at first. If it agrees, Correcting the Acrimony of the fluids, promoting proper discharges by Stool & Urine and bracing up the relaxed Fibres, the Point is gained by the entire reestablishment of your Health; but, if it should fail, I would then propose a tryal of Seltzer Water (from Seltz near Frankfurt upon the Mayn [sic]) the good effects of which I have very much experienced in Bilious Cases, where other Waters have hurt or failed.[88]

Moysey walked a fine line as a fashionable physician, mixing flattery with the acknowledgment of status in his dispensing of advice, as blunt wording would not suffice with patients of an elevated status. To Clive he wrote, "As to your return to England, if it is not impertinent to mention ... I should most humbly & earnestly intreat [sic] your Lordship not to expose your Health so soon again to the

---

87 "Lord Royston to the earl of Hardwicke, 5 May 1763, Hardwicke 35350, ff. 9–10. Hayes no. 7." Quoted in James Hamilton, *Gainsborough: A Portrait* (Weidenfeld & Nicolson, 2017), 174.
88 "Dr. Abel Moysey to Lord Robert Clive, Bath, 31 May 1768."

inclemency of the Winter Season here after having suffered so much by the last." He then played on the fear of a relapse to coax compliance:

> What the Consequences of a relapse may be, I shall not presume to say; what my apprehensions are, Your Lordship plainly see &, if I am justifyed in my opinion, I must presume to repeat my Solicitation for your Lordship's continuing the whole Winter in the South of France or near it; after which Sacrifice of your inclinations to your Health I persuade myself your Health may be thoroughly reestablished.

Moysey defines this return to health as Clive no longer requiring opium or laxatives, and he closed his letter with a reinforcement of the social connections between the two men, stating, "My Wife & Daughter beg dear to present their Compliments to Lady Clive & Mrs. Latham, and I am with very Sincere & just respect."[89]

Moysey did not just work with the political notables who traveled to Bath for their health; he was also closely connected with local celebrities, like painter Thomas Gainsborough (1727–1788), who memorialized the doctor and his family on canvas, painting the father, son and daughter.[90] Through the painter's circle of friends, as well as his own, Abel Moysey would have rubbed elbows with all manner of artists, musicians, actors, as well as physicians, apothecaries, and other prominent men about town. The first glimpse of Gainsborough and Moysey's relationship came in 1763, when the painter fell seriously ill from overwork and was even mistakenly reported in the *Bath Journal* as having died. On September 15, Gainsborough wrote to his friend, banker/attorney James Unwin, of the experience: "This is the first time I have been able to hold a pen since I wrote to you before I have had a most terrible attack of a Nervous fever so that for whole nights together I have thought it impossible that I could last til the Morning."[91] In this letter, Gainsborough gave credit for his recovery to Dr. Charleton and his sister's prescription "of six Glasses of good, old Port"; however, this proved a premature assertion as he relapsed with a "terrible fever," coming close enough to death to precipitate the false report of his demise.[92] Charleton had exhausted his

---

89 "Dr. Abel Moysey to Lord Robert Clive, Bath, 31 May 1768."

90 It seems these portraits were painted by the artist "in lieu of medical charges." Belsey, *The Moysey Family*, 1.

91 "Thomas Gainsborough to James Unwin, 15 September 1763," Museum number 1988.3, Holburne Museum, Bath, UK.

92 "Gainsborough to Unwin, 15 September 1763"; "Thomas Gainsborough to James Unwin, October 1763," quoted in James Hamilton, *Gainsborough: A Portrait*, 194.

FIGURE 11. Portrait of Dr. Abel Moysey by Thomas Gainsborough. ("Portrait of Dr Abel Moysey, by Thomas Gainsborough, on loan from a private collection since 1994," *The Holburne Museum of Art: Review 2004–2005*, page 32. © Holburne Museum / Bridgeman Images. Image courtesy of the Holburne Museum and Bridgeman Images.)

remedies and called in Dr. Moysey to assist. Within three days, the painter was "out of danger."[93]

Moysey and Gainsborough developed a close friendship that lasted until 1771, when they had a falling out over the physician's treatment and diagnosis of Gainsborough's daughter.[94] Devoted father of Mary (1750–1826) and her younger sister, Margaret (1751–1820), the painter was distraught when the elder daughter fell ill in autumn 1771. He sent for his friend Moysey, but was outraged by the pronouncement that his daughter's illness was mental and that nothing could be

---

93 "Gainsborough to Unwin, October 1763," 195.
94 Belsey, *The Moysey Family*, 1.

done.[95] Unwilling to accept this diagnosis, he sought assistance from Rice Charleton and another prominent physician, Ralph Schomberg (1714–1792), who had established a practice in Bath in 1761.[96] In 1771, John Palmer wrote the following account to actor David Garrick, stating, "Mr. Gainsborough has been so very indifferent, from his attention to and confinement with his daughter in her illness.... Miss Gainsborough is now as well as ever she was." Palmer then provided insight into Gainsborough's fury with his erstwhile friend, stating,

> He complains very much of Moysey's behaviour; who paid no attention to her, declaring that it was a family complaint and he did not suppose she would ever recover her senses again; so that Gainsborough was obliged to call in Schomberg and Charlton, who called it by its right name, a delirious fever, and soon cured her.

The artist not only cut off his former friend, but also "sent home after this the pictures of Moysey and his family, which he had painted gratis for him."[97] In the end Moysey, though supposedly unequal to the task of the "delirious fever," perhaps saw an inkling of what was to develop. He was proved right, as Mary and her sister Margaret would suffer from mental distress throughout their lives.[98]

Despite losing such a prominent client, Dr. Moysey's reputation remained strong. He continued to count among his patients elite members of society, religious figures, and the literati (including Henry Thrale and Bluestocking socialite and author Elizabeth Montagu, whom he treated at the end of his career).[99] Henry Thrale (1728–1781), whose family owned the Anchor Brewery (the third largest in London by 1778), served as MP for Southwark from 1765 to 1780. In 1763 he married Hester Lynch Salusbury (1741–1821), later Hester Lynch Piozzi, a writer and fashionable intellectual. Their marriage was not a happy one, as the bluff and gluttonous Thrale was a poor match for the vivacious, diminutive

---

95 Jenkins, "Thomas Gainsborough's doctors," 59.

96 W.P. Courtney and Edgar Samuel, "Schomberg, Ralph [formerly Raphael] (1714–1792), Physician and Writer." *Oxford Dictionary of National Biography*, September 23, 2004 (accessed June 16, 2020), https://www.oxforddnb.com/view/10.1093/ref:odnb/9780198614128.001.0001 /odnb-9780198614128-e-24827.

97 "John Palmer to David Garrick, Bath, Sunday Night, 1771," in Whitley, *Thomas Gainsborough*, 79.

98 "Palmer to Garrick, Bath, Sunday Night, 1771," 59.

99 "At Bath ... My kind friend, Miss Gideon ... it was grief to see her laboring under a complication of diseases, and one among these the dropsy, so that Dr. Moisey told me he apprehended there was great danger of her soon being called hence." "Letter from Mr. Venn to Miss Wheeler (Niece of Lady Huntington & Daughter of Lady Catherine Wheeler)," quoted in *The Life and Times of Selina Countess of Huntington*, Vol. I (William Edward Painter, 1839), 479.

intellectual. Thrale had a habit of overindulging in food, drink, and women, all of which caught up with him in the late 1770s when, plagued by venereal disease and melancholy, he began to suffer from seizures. Then between 1779 and 1780 he had multiple strokes.[100] His London physicians gave him a poor chance of survival, but he made his way to Bath to take the waters and there came under the care of Dr. Abel Moysey.[101] Initially, it seems Thrale's health scare had a positive effect and he was willing to adhere to the physician's orders. His wife "reported that, according to Dr. Moisey of Bath, Henry Thrale might be a well Man, if he continues that care of his Diet with which he [Dr. Moisey] boasts to have inspired him."[102] Samuel Johnson also provided a positive account: "We have been lately much alarmed at Mr. Thrale's. He has had a stroke, like that of apoplexy; but he has at last got so well as to be at Bath, out of the way of trouble and business, and is likely to be in a short time well."[103] All was not as it may have seemed however, and Hester Thrale was repeatedly frustrated in her attempts to moderate her husband's gluttony. She even called on their mutual friend Samuel Johnson for assistance, writing, "I wish though, that you would put in a word of your own to Mr. Thrale about eating less; for he will mind you more than us, and his too great spirits just at this moment fright me."[104] Hester was not hopeful about the long-term prognosis, fearing health was impossible "for a man whose mouth cannot be sewed up."[105] Despite

---

100 Peter Mathias, "Thrale, Henry (1728–1781), Brewer and Politician." *Oxford Dictionary of National Biography*, September 23, 2004 (accessed June 16, 2020), https://www.oxforddnb.com/view/10.1093/ref:odnb/9780198614128.001.0001/odnb-9780198614128-e-50467; Michael J. Franklin, "Piozzi [née Salusbury; Other Married Name Thrale], Hester Lynch (1741–1821), Writer," *Oxford Dictionary of National Biography*, September 23, 2004 (accessed June 16, 2020), https://www.oxforddnb.com/view/10.1093/ref:odnb/9780198614128.001.0001/odnb-9780198614128-e-22309.

101 Lee Morgan, *Dr. Johnson's "Own Dear Master": The Life of Henry Thrale* (University Press of America, 1998), 212; "Letter from Fanny Burney, South Parade, Bath, 13 April 1780," Fanny Burney, *The Early Journals and Letters of Fanny Burney*, Vol. IV, The Streaham Years: Part II, 1780–81, ed. Betty Rizzo (McGill-Queen's University Press, 2003), 62. "So dreadfully ill had Mr. Thrale been, that Dr. Heberden had quite given him up, & even left off visiting him; & Dr. Lawrence told us he had no hopes! – Sir Richard saw, as they did, the danger, but boldly, skillfully, ably undertook to master it, & his undertaking has nobly succeeded." "Letter from Fanny Burney," 62.

102 Samuel Johnson, *The Letters of Samuel Johnson*, Volume III, 1771–1781, Hyde Edition, ed. Bruce Redford (Princeton University Press, 2014), 261.

103 "Letter Samuel Johnson to Mrs. Porter, 8 April 1780," George Birkbeck Hill, ed., *Letters of Samuel Johnson, LL.D.*, Vol. II (Harper & Brothers/Clarendon Press, 1892), 135.

104 "Letter CCXXXVI, Mrs. Thrale to Dr. Johnson May (1780)," *Letters to and from the Late Samuel Johnson*, Vol. II (A. Strahan & T. Cadell, 1780), 130.

105 Lee Morgan, *Dr. Johnson's "Own Dear Master": The Life of Henry Thrale* (University Press of America, 1998), 216.

remonstrances from his wife, his daughter, and friend Fanny Burney, Thrale continued on as before.[106]

Dr. Moysey had been recommend to the Thrales by Elizabeth Montagu, who was in Bath at the same time as Hester and Henry.[107] Montagu and Hester Thrale were friendly rivals, but that did not stop her from recommending the physician in the wake of Henry's stroke. She even lectured Thrale and reported directly to Dr. Moysey whenever she saw him overindulging. For his part, Moysey did not mince words with his patient, stating plainly "that the lowliest apothecary's apprentice could see that he was 'knockt down like a Cok at Shrove tide' and that his behavior would lead him to a state no physician could amend."[108] This skepticism was shared by Samuel Johnson, but for a different reason – that of Henry Thrale's obstinate refusal to reform his ways. He wrote to Hester wondering what Dr. Moysey or any physician might do with a patient who refused to adhere to a regimen.[109] This proved prophetic as Henry Thrale never regained his health, dying in April 1781 at the age of fifty-two.[110]

At the end of his career, as he was wrestling with the obstinate Thrale, Moysey was also treating Elizabeth Montagu. She wrote in June 1779 that "[w]hen I left Bath, Dr. Moisey said I ought to return thither soon after Michalemas, as the

---

106 Morgan, *Dr. Johnson's "Own Dear Master,"* 216.

107 "It is happy, both for you and Mrs. Montagu, that the fates bring you both to Bath at the same time." "Letter from Samuel Johnson to Mrs. Thrale, April 6, 1780," Hill, *Letters of Samuel Johnson, LL.D.*, 132. Elizabeth Montagu [*née* Robinson] (1718–1800) was a literary hostess and author. A frequent visitor to the spa towns of Tunbridge Wells and Bath, Montagu established herself as a premier hostess whose gatherings were the closed approximation of the French literary salons in the country, drawing notables like Edmund Burke, Horace Walpole, Samuel Johnson, David Garrick, and Joshua Reynolds as well as Fanny Burney, Hannah More, and Hester Chapone. See Barbara Brandon Schnorrenberg, "Montagu [née Robinson], Elizabeth (1718–1800), Author and Literary Hostess," *Oxford Dictionary of National Biography*, September 23, 2004 (accessed June 16, 2020), https://www.oxforddnb.com/view/10.1093/ref:odnb/9780198614128.001.0001/odnb-9780198614128-e-19014.

108 Morgan, *Dr. Johnson's "Own Dear Master,"* 216. During Shrovetide it was common to play a number of violent games involving cocks. Beyond cockfighting, one popular iteration involved throwing sharpened stakes at a cockerel in an attempt to maim or kill the bird, with the winner getting the bird as a prize. Steve Roud, *The English Year: A Month-by-Month Guide to The Nations Customs and Festivals, from May Day to Mischief Night* (Penguin Books, 2008), 71–2.

109 "Nothing can keep him so safe as the method which has been so often mentioned…. If health and reason can be preserved by changing three or four meals a week, or if such a change will but encrease the chances of preserving them, the purchase is surely not made at a very high price…. I hope that to our anxiety for him, Mr. Thrale will add some anxiety for himself." "Letter Samuel Johnson to Mrs. Thrale, April 6, 1780," Hill, ed., *Letters of Samuel Johnson*, 133.

110 Mathias, "Thrale, Henry (1728–1781), Brewer and Politician"; Franklin, "Piozzi [née Salusbury; Other Married Name Thrale], Hester Lynch (1741–1821), Writer."

waters heated me the last fortnight of the six weeks I drank them this spring."[111] In August she reported:

> As Bath agreed so well with me, I stayed as long as Dr. Moisey thought it necessary…. I brought home such a stock of health that, I flatter myself, I shall not want any assistance from Tunbridge I found much more benefit from the Bath waters than I have from Tunbridge, for some years past.[112]

Yet in November 1780 she returned to the city again, only to find the landscape had shifted precipitously. She was forced to find another physician because Dr. Moysey had passed away.[113]

Although the majority of the source material speaks to Dr. Moysey's medical practice, there are glimpses of the wider impact of the man and his family. His son, Abel Moysey (1743–1831), became a lawyer and politician, serving as the MP for Bath from 1774 to 1790; his daughter, Mary, would unwittingly become embroiled in one of the century's biggest marriage scandals.

Born in 1744 in Bath, the young Mary caught the eye of notorious ladies' man, dubbed the "English Casanova," Augustus John Hervey, third earl of Bristol (1724–1779).[114] He had made a name for himself in the navy, distinguishing himself during the War of Jenkins' Ear. Charming, confident, and impetuous in 1744, at the age of twenty, Hervey fell for the beautiful and witty Elizabeth Chudleigh (c. 1720–1788). The pair recklessly entered into a clandestine marriage on August 4, 1744, one they would both come to regret.[115] The marriage remained a secret, which allowed Elizabeth to continue as a maid of honor to Augusta, Princess of Wales, while Hervey returned to sea. When he came home without warning in 1746, Hervey was enraged to learn his wife had not been faithful. The pair reconciled long enough to produce a child in 1747, but the infant died that same year.

---

111 "No. IX Mrs. Elizabeth Montagu to Mrs. Wm. Robinson, Sandleford, 13 June 1779," *The Ladies Companion and Monthly Magazine*, Vol. II, Second Series (Rogerson and Tuxford, 1852), 322–3.

112 "Mrs. Elizabeth Montagu to Mrs. Wm Robinson, Sandleford, 18 August 1779," *The Ladies Companion and Monthly Magazine*, Vol. IV, second series (Rogerson and Tuxford, 1853), 200–1.

113 "Dr. Moisey being dead, I applied to Dr. de la Cour, your friend, when I had my cold, to know if I might drink the waters." "Mrs. Elizabeth Montagu, Bath, 21 November 1780," in Dr. Doran, F.S.A., *A Lady of the Last Century: (Mrs. Elizabeth Montagu)* (Richard Bentley and Son, 1873), 262.

114 Catherine Ostler, *The Duchess Countess: The Woman who Scandalized a Nation* (Simon & Schuster, 2021), 63.

115 Ostler, *The Duchess Countess*, 68; Ruddock Mackay, "Hervey, Augustus John, Third Earl of Bristol (1724–1779), Naval Officer and Politician," *Oxford Dictionary of National Biography*, September 23, 2004 (accessed May 27, 2020), https://www.oxforddnb.com/view/10.1093/ref:odnb/9780198614128.001.0001/odnb-9780198614128-e-13109.

FIGURE 12. Mary Richards (née Moysey) (1744–1816). (Portrait by Jonathan Spilsbury, after Thomas Gainsborough mezzotint, 1768, NPG D39731 © National Portrait Gallery, London. Image courtesy of the National Portrait Gallery.)

By 1749 the relationship was irrevocably broken, and Hervey ended it.[116] Soon after the break, Elizabeth appeared at a masquerade ball in notorious fashion, nearly naked and dressed as Iphigenia.[117] Her costume was made of a flimsy gauze, and later descriptions mention foliage that barely covered her and provoked the Princess of Wales (Augusta) to fling her veil over her maid of honor. It garnered a different reaction from George II, who reportedly inquired if he might touch her bare bosom. Quick on her feet, Elizabeth "offered to put it on a still softer

116 T.A.B. Corley, "Chudleigh, Elizabeth [Married Names Elizabeth Hervey, Countess of Bristol; Elizabeth Pierrepont, Duchess of Kingston upon Hull] (c. 1720–1788), Courtier and Bigamist," *Oxford Dictionary of National Biography*. September 23, 2004 (accessed June 17, 2020). https://www.oxforddnb.com/view/10.1093/ref:odnb/9780198614128.001.0001/odnb-9780198614128-e-5380.

117 Moria Goff, John Goldfinch, Karen Limper-Herz, and Helen Peden, *Georgians Revealed: Life, Style and the Making of Modern Britain* (British Library, 2013), 102.

place and guided it to the royal forehead."[118] The amused king rewarded her with a watch and gave her mother a position at Windsor.[119] These events led to a proliferation of engravings both at the time of the event with "prints, rushed out to gratify the public's lubricious curiosity" and later to accompany the various memoirs published after her death.[120]

Elizabeth quickly moved onto greener pastures, taking up with Evelyn Pierrepont, second Duke of Kingston upon Hull (1712–1773). Hervey and Chudleigh lived separate lives, pretending as if their marriage had never occurred. As Matthew Kinservik has argued, "The informal separation left them in a sort of limbo, free to lead their own lives and pursue love affairs with others, but always conscious that they remained married, and always worried about the other's intentions."[121] This arrangement worked until 1768, when Hervey became determined to free himself. There is disagreement over the actual role played by Miss Moysey in precipitating this event, but contemporaneous gossip certainly cast her as the motivation for the ensuing actions.

Hervey had been plagued by ill health for years, with frequent attacks of what was labeled gout. Lady Hervey remarked on his situation in 1767, writing, "poor Augustus, who is gone to Bath with the gout in his stomach, where the best he can hope is to have it transferred to his limbs. He has never had tolerable health since he was at the Havana."[122] His ill health led him to spend a great deal of time in the city, and during these visits he unsurprisingly became acquainted with the family of one of that city's premier physicians, Dr. Abel Moysey. In 1767, he apparently fell for the charms of the young, beautiful, and virtuous twenty-four-year-old Mary Moysey. By August 1768, his attachment was fodder for the gossips, who postulated that his longing for the doctor's daughter had prompted his attempts to undo his marriage to Chudleigh, though it is likely his desire for a legitimate heir led him to pursue a divorce.[123]

Unsurprisingly, accounts of the events lack consistency and focused on the lurid details. Lady Mary Coke even corrected her own assertions about the divorce proceedings in her journal. The accounts provided by both Lady Mary

---

118 Corley, "Chudleigh, Elizabeth."
119 Corley, "Chudleigh, Elizabeth."
120 Corley, "Chudleigh, Elizabeth"; Goff, Goldfinch, Limper-Herz, and Peden, *Georgians Revealed*, 102.
121 Matthew J. Kinservik, *Sex, Scandal and Celebrity in Late Eighteenth-Century England* (Palgrave Macmillan, 2007), 88.
122 "Lady Hervey to Mr. Morris, 1767." Quoted in M.R.J. Holmes, *Augustus Hervey: A Naval Casanova* (Pentland Press, 1996), 211.
123 Ostler, *The Duchess Countess*, 178; Kinservik, *Sex, Scandal and Celebrity*, 87–8, 210.

FIGURE 13. Representations of Elizabeth Chudleigh's infamous masquerade appearance. *Top*: Miss Chudleigh in the dress of Iphigenia at the Masquerade Ball at Ranleigh, c. 1749. ("Miss-in the actual dress as she appear'd in ye character of Iphigenia, at ye Jubilee Ball or Masquerade at Ranelagh," Call number: 749.05.01.02, Production date: c. 1749 © Lewis Walpole Library. Image courtesy of the Lewis Walpole Library.) *Bottom*: Elizabeth Chudleigh, dressed as Iphigenia at the Venetian Ambassador's Masquerade, Ranelagh, London. (© Look and Learn / Peter Jackson Collection / Bridgeman Images. Image courtesy of Look and Learn / Peter Jackson Collection / Bridgeman Images.)

Coke and Horace Walpole contain mistakes, but they still offer insight into the public perception of the events. In August, Mary Coke identified the source of the gossip as "Mr. Walpole" and wrote that Hervey intended to pursue a divorce, but to do so he first needed to prove the marriage had occurred:

> Mr. Augustus Hervey ... is going to prove his marriage, as the first step towards suing for being unmarried, and has sent the Lady who goes by the Name of Miss Chudleigh a letter to signify his intention; to which she has return'd this answer: that if he proves the marriage, he will have sixteen thousand pounds to pay, as She owes that sum of money. As this answer is looked upon to be intended to stop the proceeding, everybody is much surprised, as it was the general opinion that if She was at liberty the Duke of Kingston wou'd marry her, which seems now to be doubtful.[124]

However on August 27 she corrected herself, writing that although Hervey intended "to sue for a Divorce" he had "told Ly Blandford that the answer which it was reported Miss Chudleigh had sent to his letter, was invention, for he had received none."[125] Lady Coke's confusion and the contradictory statements reflect the difficult nature of gossip, as she had not discussed the events with Hervey himself but simply reported the comments of others. Whether or not these assertions were true, they were certainly widely accepted, as was the supposed affection between Miss Moysey and Hervey. Horace Walpole mentions the intention to divorce on August 20 but on February 28 of the following year, he wrote a full account of the divorce affair in response to the upcoming marriage of Elizabeth Chudleigh to the Duke of Kingston.[126] He wrote to Horace Mann that "after a marriage of twenty years, Augustus Hervey, having fallen in love with a physician's daughter at Bath, has attacked his spouse, the maid of honour, the fair Chudleigh, and sought a divorce for adultery." Walpole also discussed Dr. Abel Moysey's response to the purported romance:

> The physician, who is little more in his senses than the other actors, and a little honester, will not give his daughter; nay, has offered her five thousand pounds not to marry Mr. Hervey, but Miss Rhubarb is as much above

---

124 "Journal Entry, 6 August 1768," *The Letters and Journals and Lady Mary Coke*, Vol. II (1767–1768) (Kingsmead Reprints, 1970), 330–1.
125 "Journal Entry, 27 August 1768," *The Letters and Journals and Lady Mary Coke*, Vol. II (1767–1768) (Kingsmead Reprints, 1970), 347.
126 "Augustus Hervey, thinking it bel air, is going to sue for a divorce from the Chudleigh." "Letter Horace Walpole August 20, 1768)," quoted in Holmes, *Augustus Hervey*, 234.

worldly decorum as the rest, and persists, though there is not more doubt of the marriage of Mr. Hervey and Miss Chudleigh, than that of your father and mother. It is a cruel case upon his family, who can never acquiesce in the legitimacy of his children, if any come from his bigamy.[127]

Despite Walpole's assertion that "[e]very word of this history is extremely true," and the widespread acceptance of the connection between the two, Hervey seems to have had second thoughts or had moved on by October 1768.[128] This was during the court proceedings, which may have played a role in his accounting to George Grenville, where he acknowledged the widespread gossip but denied his attachment to the unnamed woman, writing:

I find this town had made me a much more intrepid person than I really am, for they have already given me another person for a wife, and such a one as I am sure I should never have thought of; Very likely the report may have reached you, and I am sure you will treat it as it deserves, but it has been very industriously put about here.[129]

Whatever the truth of the connection, Hervey was outwitted by Chudleigh, who swore before the court in 1769 that she was unmarried. As all of the witnesses to the ceremony had since passed and Elizabeth had hidden the record, the court declared in her favor pronouncing "her a spinster and ordering Hervey not to assert otherwise."[130] Hervey did not receive his divorce and Miss Mary Moysey settled down in 1773 with a man more to her father's liking – Reverend John Richards of Long Bredy, Dorset.[131] As for Elizabeth Chudleigh, she managed to orchestrate a

127 "Horace Walpole to Horace Mann, 28 February 1769," W.S. Lewis, Warren Hunting Smith and George L. Lam with the assistance of Edwine M. Martz, eds., *Horace Walpole's Correspondence with Sir Horace Mann*, Vol. 23 (Yale University Press, 1967), 93–4.

128 "Horace Walpole to Horace Mann, Tuesday 28 February 1769, Arlington Street," Lewis et al., *Horace Walpole's Correspondence with Sir Horace Mann*, Vol. 23, 93–4; Belsey, *The Moysey Family*, 3.

129 "Mr. Augustus Hervey to Mr. Grenville, 31 October 1768," George Grenville, *The Grenville Papers: The Correspondence of Richard Grenville Earl Temple, K.G., and The Right Hon: George Grenville*, Vol. IV, ed. William James Smith (John Murray, 1853), 394.

130 Holmes, *Augustus Hervey*, 238.

131 "The Rev. John Richards, of Longbride, in Dorset, to Miss Moysey, daughter of Dr. Moysey, physician at Bath," *The Lady's Magazine; or Entertaining Companion for the Fair Sex*, Vol. IV (G. Robinson, 1773), 559; "Marriage, 12 October 1773 of John Richards, Clerk of the Parish of Long Bredy in the county of Dorset and Mary Moysey of this parish [Walcot St. Swithin, Somerset, England]," Reference Number: D\P\wal.sw/2/1/64; *Somerset, England, Marriage Registers, Bonds and Allegations, 1754–1914* [database online], Provo, UT: Ancestry.com Operations, Inc., 2016; Belsey, *The Moysey Family*, 3.

marriage to her lover Evelyn Pierrepont, the second Duke of Kingston, within a month of the ruling. Unfortunately for her, the duke died just four years later, precipitating a family fight over his estate, the outcome of which was that Elizabeth was tried for bigamy in 1776. She was found guilty by all 119 members of the House of Lords, then fled the country, never to return.[132] In the end, the mystery name scrawled on the receipts of the Beach family allowed me to construct a picture of an eighteenth-century social network, one that demonstrated that Abel Moysey was far from being an insignificant country doctor.

---

132 Holmes, *Augustus Hervey*, 239; Corley, "Chudleigh, Elizabeth."

Fortune-Hunting Rake or Loving Husband? Making Sense of the Accusations

The entirety of the *Wainhouse Narrative* is wrapped up in the question of reputation and legacy, a circumstance William acknowledged at the outset when he wrote:

> Reputation is a valuable Good. It survives our natural Decease. Anxiety for his own Reputation strongly prompted the present Writer to take up his Pen, but Sollicitude [sic] for the good Name of a dear, worthy, though injur'd and departed, young Lady, was a nobler & & [sic] more prevailing Motive.[1]

The legacy of Anne Beach and William Wainhouse continues, and this retelling of the story, rooted firmly in the evidence rather than personal conjecture and emotion, will anger some who have strong feelings on the subject. The couple's romance has taken on a mythology of its own and people still make judgments about the motives of the curate and the personal choices of the young woman.

One of the most frustrating aspects of this project included my attempts to either discount or prove William Wainhouse's status as fortune hunter. This continues to be a widely accepted notion, one that still holds strong in the involved villages and in what small literature there is on the subject. Given the status and considerable money and influence of the Beach family, and the fact that William eventually left the area, the feelings and local gossip that may have swirled in

---

1 *Narrative*, folio 3–4.

Keevil and Steeple Ashton are lost to us, and it is only the controlled narrative that remains. Today locals respond, when William is mentioned: "Oh yes, he didn't treat her well"; "No, he didn't have money so he could not have paid for both monuments, and he probably could barely afford her grave stone"; "Of course her parents erected the monument in the Beche Chapel, because it is their family chapel and he couldn't have afforded it."

These are the stories that permeate local attitudes toward William and Anne. They reinforce local histories of the Beach family written by a descendant in 1909, and it is her account that has dominated subsequent representations of this story.[2] Was he actually a fortune hunter? Or did his actions stem from his feelings for Anne? What is the actual evidence and what can it tell us?

The main and most egregious accusation was the charge of oath-breaking. William gave his word he would not make any private attempt on Anne's affections, and he definitely broke this promise, even admitting to doing so multiple times during the *Narrative* and in a personal letter to the Beach Family. In the first mention of the promise, he follows up with the statement: "Here was the Clergyman's great & capital Fault: the Breach of his Word, to his Shame & Sorrow he confesses, &, when liberally corrected for it, will kiss the Rod."[3] From the outset, Wainhouse did not try to hide this fault, but he did justify his actions as motivated by love.

Now this could be a convenient excuse, but his earlier attempts to find love and his own words from before he turned his sights on Anne reveal a man desperate to be "noos'd in Wedlock's Yoke."[4] Three years after giving his promise, in the spring of 1769, he broke his word when "he ventur'd on an offer to <u>Miss Beach</u>, private indeed, but honourable."[5] The breach of promise comes up twice more in the *Narrative*, first during the description of the elopement, when he stated:

> The Mother upbraided him with his former Promise & the Breach of it, which he acknowledg'd. He retorted on her a too great Regard for Money in the Affair of Matrimony, telling her, (what was his steadfast Belief) that he was sure she had no real Objection to him, but Inequality of Fortune.[6]

---

2 Hicks, *A Cotswold Family*, 297.
3 *Narrative*, folio 7–8.
4 "Wainhouse, Verses, 20 November 1767," D2455/F2/5/3/3.
5 *Narrative*, folio 12.
6 *Narrative*, folio 18–19.

He again addressed his misdeeds towards the end of the work, when he pleaded with the reader:

> The Writer will readily acknowledge any misconduct he has been guilty, or is convinc'd of. Willing he is to make due submission to just Censure, for his real Faults. His capital Offence to <u>Mrs. Beach</u>, he has confess'd, & is griev'd at the Transgression. He laments his having given his Enemies such Advantage over him. However, he hopes the Generous & Compassionate will forgive this one Offence, when they take into the Balance his Integrity & honourable Behaviour to the Daughter, especially in the Marriage Settlement. To this, indeed, he was bound by Love & Duty.[7]

Beyond the *Narrative*, William also directly addressed his breach of promise in a letter to Mr. and Mrs. Beach during Anne's incarceration, in which he characterizes his actions as a "Struggle between Love & Honour." He wrote, "my Conduct has been blameable & imprudent, I will not deny, but I conceive it not to be unpardonable, or irretrievable." He further stated, "Tis true, I clandestinely allur'd her to Marriage. Tho' the Means were wrong, the End, the Intention, was neither hurtful, dishonourable, nor criminal. Not only Obligations between common Acquaintance, but even sworn Friends of high Reputation & Integrity, have yielded to the Dictates of Love: And mine was of the virtuous Kind." To the charge of "Breach of Faith," he once again acknowledged the promise, writing, "Some few years ago I did indeed promise, on the Word & Honour of a Clergyman, not to make private Addresses to you Daughter. At that Time I had no Thoughts of so doing. I take Blame to myself for breaking my Word. The Promise was rash & foolish, but still it was obligatory."

He then offered this defense of his actions:

> Honour bade me address openly, but without Hope of succeeding. Love persuaded me to make an Offer privately with some Probability of Success. I yielded to Love, not that I deny the Obligation of Honour. I own I acted wrong; but am persuaded, that the Generality of People, even those now most censorious, wou'd have done the same in my Case.[8]

---

7 *Narrative,* folio 97–8.

8 "William Wainhouse to Mr. & Mrs. Beach, 27 September 1770," D2455/F2/5/1/22, Gloucestershire Archives, UK.

Imploring the Beaches, he detailed:

> Pray, good Parents, let me beseech you to think on these Things: no real Injury, or Disgrace, has been done or attempted against your Family. Your Daughter's Virtue is inviolate, the Honour of your House unsullied. I have been guilty of one Breach of my Word, & therefore am set down a Scoundrel. But, pray, be so good as to consider my general Character, the general Tenor & Course of my Life & Actions; then lay your Hands on your Hearts, & let your Consciences (if they can) pronounce me a Scoundrel, a Rascal. I am no Advocate for the Disobedience of Children, yet in Cases of Marriage, Obedience is often most difficult, sometimes entirely incompatible with their own Happiness.... Love is an involuntary Passion, not in our Power.[9]

Wainhouse certainly had an ax to grind with the Beach family, but as I began to sift through the documents and accusations, things were not lining up neatly. This was not a surprise, as they rarely do. William made no attempt to hide his fault with respect to the breach of promise but he does try to mitigate his behavior by explaining it as stemming from love. It is also curious that he seems to have been permitted free run of the house and access to Anne despite the family's suspicions. Was he actually a fortune hunter, and what evidence is there for this claim?

One of the major assertions was that William Wainhouse was a penniless curate, and on the face of it this seems plausible. By 1764, he had been appointed curate of Steeple Ashton, which lies next to Keevil, under the auspices of the vicar there, Robert Foulkes, whose £200 annual salary was controlled by Magdalene College, Cambridge.[10] Although Foulkes had a substantial living, curates were typically paid significantly less. Given this, the notion that William was simply out for an inheritance was certainly a possibility. However, it turns out the curate had far more resources then generally available to those of his station. In the *Narrative*, he mentions that in 1767, upon his mother's death, "he came into Possession of a considerable Increase of Income, a desirable Competency, his real & personal Estate (including a Curacy of forty-five Pounds) amounting to neat two hundred Pounds a Year."[11] It seems that Wainhouse was making as much per year as his employer

---

9 "William Wainhouse to Mr. & Mrs. Beach, 27 September 1770," D2455/F2/5/1/22, Gloucestershire Archives, UK.

10 "Steeple Ashton Bond of Foulkes to reside 1747," A/29/2/8, Magdalene College Archives, Pepys Library, Cambridge, UK.

11 *Narrative*, folio 8.

and had the ability to settle £2,000 on Anne upon their marriage. All of a sudden, the penniless curate idea seemed less plausible; however, these assertions were from William and so needed corroboration. The first mention of the properties comes in the will of his father, who left his wife a "house in Duke Street in the City of Bath" and there is evidence of a second house on Trym Street by 1766.[12]

Other indications of Wainhouse's financial situation came from his mother's marriage settlement in 1736. Mary brought substantial funds into her union, described as "a considerable fortune … far exceeding the sum of Eight hundred pounds" and then received a further £1,200 in Bank of England stock and a £40 per-year annuity.[13] These funds made their way into William's hands, as seen in his own marriage settlement to his second wife in 1772, which confirmed his ownership of at least £1,000 "of consolidated Bank Annuities … in the Books of the Company of the Bank of England."[14] It also revealed his possession of an additional property acquired in February 1770, "securing the sum of 2000L and Interest."[15] This date, before his marriage to Anne, meant he would have also had access to these funds to provide her portion upon their marriage. Other indicators of his financial security come from the details of the marriage itself, when the prospective groom had the ability to pay, with little notice, £100 to obtain a special license.[16] This was more than double his annual salary and was half the yearly salary of the vicar for whom he worked.

Although he certainly possessed funds, this does not necessarily negate the search for greater fortune. Wainhouse readily acknowledged to the Beaches that "[m]y Fortune is indeed unequal. But to make a good Match, a happy Union in Marriage, there is no Necessity of an equal Fortune on each side, but only a genteel Sufficiency, or rather, a decent comfortable Competency, made up by joining both Fortunes together." He went even further, stating that he himself had also taken a risk, hazarding "the Loss of Fortune with a Wife" and that with his income, he might have commanded a match with "a Lady of fortune," writing "that I have run a Venture as well as your Daughter, tho' not so great."[17]

There is plenty of evidence to suggest Wainhouse knew long before the marriage what Anne's financial prospects would be when he reiterated in September

---

12 "Will of Reverend Richard Wainhouse"; "Bath Rate Book 24 June–25 December 1766," folio 51, BC/5/4/1/1, Bath & North East Somerset Record Office, UK.

13 "Marriage Settlement of Mary Beach and Richard Wainhouse, 13 December 1736," 177/33, Wiltshire and Swindon History Centre, UK.

14 "Marriage Articles Between the Revd Wm. Wainhouse and Miss Sarah Madocks, 1772." DD/DP 21/4, Somerset Heritage Centre, UK.

15 "Marriage Articles Between the Revd Wm. Wainhouse and Miss Sarah Madocks, 1772."

16 "William Wainhouse 1770," D1/62, Wiltshire and Swindon History Centre, UK.

17 "Wainhouse to William and Ann Beach, 27 September 1770," D2455 Box 8/4.

1770 to Mr. and Mrs. Beach his promise to their daughter: "We are solemnly engag'd to each other. My Vow, made sometime since, of marrying your Daughter, & settling one hundred Pounds a Year on her, even if she has no Fortune, both Conscience & Inclination bind me to perform."[18] His actions could thus be interpreted in a variety of ways. One option was that he was hedging his bets that her family would not actually turn her off without a penny, or maybe they could be taken at face value and he knew going in that he would have no settlement. Another option is that it all could have just been a ploy to get Anne to agree to the marriage. The last seems less likely, given his familiarity with her parents' constant threats that Anne would have no money if she married him and the fact he was aware that the only legacy she was legally entitled to, £100 from her grandfather, was all she would come with.[19] He knew he would not have any money from her family before he married her and promised to take care of her if that proved the case, which he did, providing her a generous marriage settlement. As further evidence of his solvency, Wainhouse did not even try to recover the money he had settled on Anne until December 1790, close to nineteen years after her death.[20]

There is another accusation stating that William was still trying to get money when he wrote the Beaches a letter during Anne's incarceration, and again after she came to him. He did write her family, but this search for a settlement has another possible explanation, one intimately tied to reputation. Although Wainhouse professed that "[h]e had a real Love & Regard for her," he did acknowledge that the "Prospect of Fortune" was "very compatible with Love."[21] He certainly pushed for Anne to be given a marriage settlement proportionate to his own finances, claiming that this "was neither sordid, nor unreasonable." In this instance, given the societal expectations of marriage during this period, this was not outside the realm of what would have been considered acceptable. Wainhouse then confirmed he was not motivated by money, stating that "[w]hen the

---

18 "Wainhouse to William and Ann Beach, 27 September 1770," D2455 Box 8/4.

19 "I give to my Grandson William Wither Beach and to my granddaughter Ann Beach the sum of one hundred pounds a piece," "Will of Thomas Beach, Esq. of Keevil, Wilts, Probate date 22 March 1753," PROB 11; Piece: 800; *England & Wales, Prerogative Court of Canterbury Wills, 1384–1858* [database online], Provo, UT: Ancestry.com Operations, Inc., 2013; "The young Lady was illegally lock'd in for twelve Days after she was of Age, which was on Novr. the 1st. 1770. Her Mother came up to her Novr. the 10th, & told her, 'that her Father (then from Home) wou'd, before he left <u>Keevil</u>, pay her a Legacy of one hundred Pounds, left her by her Grand-Father, & give her her Liberty & Choice to go to Fittleton (a Country Residence of his) with them, or to come directly to the Clergyman.'" *Narrative*, folio 51.

20 "Administration of Anne Wainhouse formerly Beach (Wife of the Reverend William Wainhouse Clerk) deceased, Dated 8th December 1790." DD/DP/21/1, Somerset Record Office, UK.

21 *Narrative*, folio 99.

Prospect dis-appear'd, his Love did not vanish with it."[22] So William's actions can be interpreted as a money grab, but since he only asked for a small amount, there are other possible interpretations.

In throwing their daughter out without her coverture, the Beaches were making a serious implication about Anne's morals and sullying her reputation. In addition to forcing her to go to the home of an unmarried man, turning her out without her clothes was an important statement. Women generally brought clothing and household items into a marriage, and to come into one without such material goods said something about the character of the individual socially.[23] As Joanne Bailey [Begiato], has argued, "All women except the vagrant poor brought a portion to their union."[24] The deliberate discussion of Anne's clothing in the *Narrative* speaks to the importance of these items, particularly as Mrs. Beach stated that "if she cou'd not carry them herself, all at once, she shou'd leave them, and not have them afterward." This was an impossible task and Anne came to her new husband empty-handed, though "Fear of the Shame of the World" eventually prevailed upon Mr. Beach to deliver "the Obligation for the Clothes," so Anne had something to wear on her wedding day.[25]

The other evidence often proffered as an example of William's fortune-hunting ways was that he remarried within a year to another heiress. Now, this may seem like an unsurmountable event, but it is important to remember not to judge eighteenth-century circumstances by our own standards. Yes, he remarried quickly, but William seems to have been a romantic in love with the idea of love and a man desperate to be married. In his thirties and still a bachelor, he had for close to a decade been looking to settle down and secure a family, as demonstrated by his constant searching for a mate before Anne and his wooing of his second wife, Sarah Madocks, with poetry.[26] In the poem entitled "With a Smelling Bottle," the author gifts not only the bottle but "the love of the giver."[27] The choice of this item was significant, as Emily Friedman has argued that a smelling bottle often stood "as a signifier of the presence of overwhelming emotion."[28]

---

22 *Narrative*, folio 99–100.

23 Amy Louise Erikson, *Women and Property in Early Modern England* (Routledge, 1993), 95. There were also items that "were necessary for their future lives." See Bailey, *Unquiet Lives*, 102.

24 Bailey, *Unquiet Lives*, 85.

25 *Narrative*, folio 58.

26 "To Miss S.M.," later printed in *Poetical Essays, Latin and English; Intended for Instruction and Amusement. The Production of an Adventurous Muse, in the Moment of Contemplation, Leisure, Mirth and Fancy*, Rev. William Wainhouse, 1796, reprinted in *The British Critic, A New Review*, Vol. 8 (F. and C. Rivington, 1796), 304.

27 William Wainhouse, "To Miss S.M. (in the days of my Courtship) 'With a Smelling-Bottle,'" in *Poetical Essays: Intended for Instruction and Amusement* (R. Crutwell, 1796), 32.

28 Emily C. Friedman, *Reading Smell in Eighteenth-Century Fiction* (Bucknell University Press, 2016), 65.

Wainhouse's second marriage actually provides key insights into his personal reputation in Steeple Ashton and in Keevil after Anne's death. His new wife was the niece of his employer, vicar Robert Foulkes, a man who would have been intimately familiar with the curate's character and the events surrounding his marriage and the death of his first wife. Foulkes and his niece were from Wales and the match would not have happened without his assistance, as his niece still resided in Denbigh and not in Wiltshire.[29] If he was believed to be a fortune hunter, or a man of poor character, it seems unlikely that Foulkes would have supported the match. Additionally, Sarah Madocks was not an heiress and only brought £600 into the marriage, while William put £3,000 in trust for his new wife.[30] After his marriage on September 29, 1772, the couple settled in Steeple Ashton for the next three years, having two children (Frances Matilda and Mary Anne) during this period, both baptized at St. Mary's.[31] So, not only did he marry the relative of the vicar, but Wainhouse and his new family remained in the vicinity for several years after the death of Anne Beach. The Beaches were wealthy and important landowners, yet they were unable to run William Wainhouse out of the area and he remained the curate at Steeple Ashton for several years before moving on to a new living. If the Beaches' accusations against him were true, how was he permitted to stay in town? All of this points to a different reading of William and Anne's story.

One possibility is that Wainhouse had a wealthy and powerful patron who protected him, and he was the private chaplain to Lionel Tollemache, Fifth Earl of Dysart (1734–1799).[32] However, Wainhouse does not take up this position until September 9, 1789, making the Dysart connection irrelevant to his activities in Steeple Ashton and Keevil.[33] There also seems to have been a great deal of local support for the marriage between Anne Beach and William Wainhouse in 1770. Wainhouse described the ceremony in the following manner: "On Thursday Novr. the 22d 1770, the Clergyman was married at <u>Keevil</u> to the young Lady, in the Face of a large Congregation."[34] Although it is not possible to prove the size of the crowd, the pair were married at St. Leonard's Church, which lies just beyond the

---

29 Martin, *Magdalene College Cambridge and Steeple Ashton.*
30 "Marriage Articles Between the Revd Wm. Wainhouse and Miss Sarah Madocks, 1772," DD/DP 21/4, Somerset Heritage Centre, UK.
31 "Revd William Wainhouse, Ufton, Berks, His Book: (new bound in 1788)," DD/DP/21/4, Somerset Heritage Centre, UK.
32 *Poetical Essays*, Wainhouse, in *The British Critic*, 304.
33 "William Wainhouse (1761–1797)," Clergy of the Church of England database entry, https://theclergydatabase.org.uk/jsp/persons/CreatePersonFrames.jsp?PersonID=49840.
34 *Narrative*, folio 57.

front of Keevil Manor. This must have felt like a slap in the face to the Beaches, particularly if it was actually attended by a large number of the members of the congregation. Even more interestingly, the ceremony was performed by Mr. James Richardson, who was the nephew-in-law of Mr. and Mrs. Beach. So, not only was the congregation there, but the match itself was solemnized by a member of the Beaches' extended family. The fact that the Beaches' niece stood up for Anne, and her husband performed the ceremony, also lends credence to the idea of support for the pair – as does the fact that they resided in Keevil from the time of their marriage in November until Christmas Eve, when they moved into their new house in Steeple Ashton, just a few miles away. Even more telling is the fact that Wainhouse was permitted to remain in the area after Anne's death and his own remarriage, even though he had attempted to publish the *Narrative*. All of this seems unlikely if the inhabitants of Keevil or Steeple Ashton believed the Beaches' side of the tale.

So, what of the monuments to Anne in St. Mary the Virgin Church in Steeple Ashton? There are two: a tombstone marker on the floor of the south aisle and a more elaborate memorial in what was once known as the Beach Chapel (now the baptistery). Because of its location in what had historically been the family chapel, combined with the rhetoric that Wainhouse was penniless, it has often been asserted that the Beach family erected the monument. Since the claim of "penniless" has been disproven, meaning Wainhouse would have had the financial means, and there are no surviving documents related to the construction or installation of that memorial stone, we have to look at the material remains to gain some insight.

First, William Wainhouse was the curate in that church until 1775, so he would have had the access, proximity, and authority to have some sort of memorial put up. Although it was the Beach Chapel, by the mid-eighteenth century it had fallen into disuse by the family, who had begun using St. Leonard's in Keevil to bury their members by this generation and afterwards. Additional evidence is provided by the material composition of the monument, particularly the inscription and the cartouche. The inscription is a verbatim rendering of the opening page of William Wainhouse's *Narrative*, and given its accusatory nature it seems unlikely that Mr. and Mrs. Beach would choose that as the inscription on their daughter's monument. At the top of the monument is a shield that once housed two crests blended together. On one side, still clearly painted and visible, the Wainhouse standard; on the right remains only the impression of the second heraldic device that was once united with the other. The missing side is not simply a consequence of age and wear, but was carefully removed, and precisely matches the coat of arms for the Beach family.

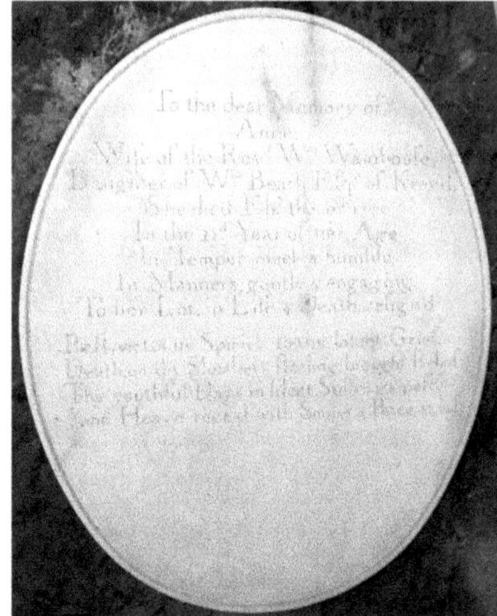
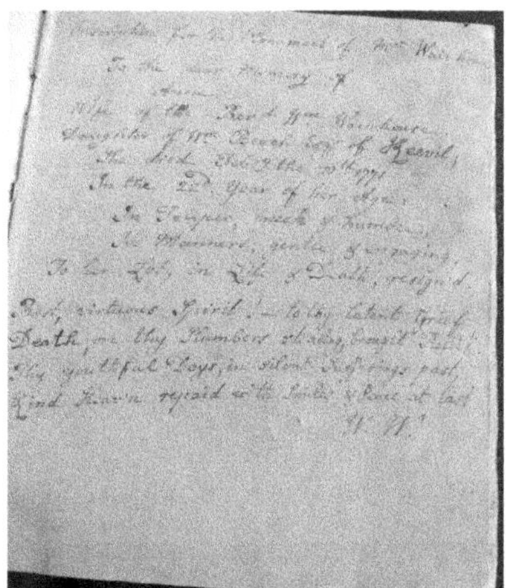

FIGURE 14. Anne Wainhouse monument and inscriptions. *Left*: Anne Wainhouse's memorial monument at St. Mary's in Steeple Ashton. (Author photograph.) *Top right*: Closeup of the circular tablet from Anne Wainhouse's memorial monument. (Author photograph.) *Bottom right*: The first page of the *Wainhouse Narrative*. (Image courtesy of the Gloucestershire Archives, UK.)

This curious circumstance suggests that it was removed by someone who wished to deny the family connection. This leaves two options: First, Wainhouse could have had it defaced out of anger with the Beaches once they put it up; second, perhaps a member of the Beach family had it removed after 1775, once Wainhouse left Steeple Ashton. We will never know for sure, but the second scenario seems more likely given that the inscription is suggestive of Wainhouse arranging the monument. The Beach family erasing their connection to Anne on the

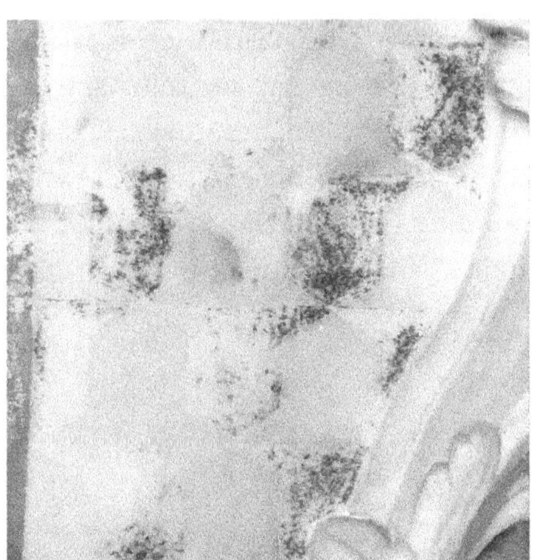

FIGURE 15. Cartouche and Beach crest closeups. *Top*: Closeup of the cartouche with family crest from Anne Wainhouse's stone wall memorial monument. *Bottom left*: Closeup of the family crest from a gravestone of Thomas Beach, a member of the Beach family, in the Beach Chapel of St. Mary's in Steeple Ashton. *Bottom right*: Closeup of the side of the cartouche with the paint removed from Anne Wainhouse's memorial, St. Mary's in Steeple Ashton. (Author photographs.)

monument is also in keeping with their removal of her from their family and from the archival records.

In the end, despite all of William Wainhouse's attempts to assert the rightness of his case and his wife's blameless reputation, the Beach family eventually took control of the narrative and the couple are dismissed as a cliché – a young girl led astray by a fortune-hunting curate. Diedre LeFaye, in her edited collection of *Jane Austen's Letters*, characterizes the events in the following manner: "The elder daughter, Anne, eloped with the fortunate-hunting curate of Keevil, Revd William Wainhouse, and died very soon after her marriage."[35]

Anne's story echoes in the writings of family members seeking to assert their own interpretation of these events, as well as in local lore that paints her as a pastiche and not as a real person who lived, experienced social pressures, losses, suffering, trauma, tragic illness, and death. One could certainly argue I am doing the same – putting my own interpretation on Anne. Stories have power, and they have afterlives. They resonate, not just reflecting the past, but also constructing it. Revisiting, reconstructing, and remembering is important not only for understanding embodied lived experience in the past, but also for understanding those same pressures in the present. The lives of the famous people you follow on social media have little to do with your personal lived experience, so why should the stories of only the rich, the powerful, and those present in the archives shape our understanding of life in the past? Anne Beach's personal agency was compromised by gender and social norms, ones that, once transgressed, led to a loss of control over her own life and even its legacy. In death her narrative was taken over, her personhood ignored, she was reduced to her marriage, and to what that meant socially. Her entire life was dismissed, and the afterlife of her story reflected the consequences of one single decision, that of whom she chose to marry. Anne Beach's life was more than the scandal surrounding her end, and I hope that in some small way I answered the plea in the windowpane, by remembering.

---

35 Henrietta Maria Hicks Beach, the youngest daughter of William and Anne Beach, who, along with her husband, inherited everything, were members of Jane Austen's circle. See Le Faye, *Jane Austen's Letters*, 495. For more on this connection, see Le Faye, *Jane Austen's Letters*; Joanna Martin, ed., *A Governess in the Age of Jane Austen: The Journals and Letters of Agnes Porter* (Hambledon Press, 1998).

BIBLIOGRAPHY

Archives

Bath & North East Somerset Record Office
British Library
Gloucestershire Archives, UK
Gray's Inn Archives, London, UK
Greater Manchester Record Office, UK
Hampshire Archives and Local Studies, UK
Holburne Museum, Bath, UK
Magdalene College Archives, Pepys Library, Cambridge, UK
Mansel-Talbot Family Papers, private collection
National Archives, UK
Parliamentary Archives, UK
Queens College Archives, Oxford, UK
Somerset Heritage Centre, UK
Vernon Family Papers, private collection
Wiltshire and Swindon History Centre, UK
Winchester College Archives, UK
Worshipful Company of Barbers Archives, UK

Select Primary Sources

Anstey, Christopher. *The Priest Dissected: A Poem*. S. Hazard, 1774.

The Bath and Bristol Guide: Or, Tradesmen's and Traveller's Pocket-Companion. Thomas Boddely, 1753.

Bath Anecdotes and Characters: By the Genius Loci. Dodsley, 1782.

Battie, William. *A Treatise on Madness*. J. Whiston & B. White, 1758.

Beach, William Wither. *Abradates and Panthea: A Tale Extracted from Xenophon*. B. Collins, 1761.

Boyse, S. *An Impartial History of the Late Rebellion in 1745 from Authentic Memoirs*. Edward & John Exshaw, 1748.

Brookes, Richard. *The General Practice of Physic*, Vols. I–II. 5th edition. J. Newberry, 1765.

Buchan, William. *Domestic Medicine; or the Family Physician*. John Dunlap, 1772.

Carter, Charles. *The London and Country Cook or Accomplished Housewife*. 3rd edition. Charles Hitch, 1749.

A Catalogue of All Graduates in Divinity, Law, and Physick. Clarendon Press, 1772.

Chandler, John. *A Treatise of the Disease Called a Cold.* 2nd edition. A. Millar, 1761.

Cheselden, William. *The Anatomy of the Human Body.* 4th edition. W. Bowyer, 1730.

Cheyne, George. *The Natural Method of Curing the Diseases of the Body and the Disorders of the Mind.* 4th edition. G. Strahan, 1742.

The Compleat Confectioner; or the Art of Candying and Preserving. 3rd edition. R. Montagu, 1742.

Cooke, William. *Poetical Essays on Several Occasions.* S. Smith, 1774.

Douglas, James. *The History of the Lateral Operation.* G. Strahan, 1726.

George Keysler, John. *Travels Through Germany, Bohemia, Hungary, Switzerland, Italy and Lorrain,* Vol. 2. 2nd edition. A. Linde, 1757.

Gregory, John. *Elements of the Practice of Physic.* W. Strahan, 1774.

Grosvenor, Benjamin. *The Mourner: Or, the Afflicted Relieved.* 5th edition. George Keith, 1765.

Harvey, Gideon. *Morbus Anglicus: Or the Anatomy of Consumptions.* 2nd edition. Thomas Johnson, 1674.

Hill, John. *The Family Herbal, or an Account of All Those English Plants, Which Are Remarkable for Their Virtues, and of the Drugs Which Are Produced by Vegetables of Other Countries, with Their Descriptions and Their Uses, as Proved by Experience.* C. Brightly & Co., 1812.

Holland, Richard. *Miscellaneous Reflections on the Smallpox.* W. Owen, 1755.

Holwell, J.Z. (John Zephaniah). *An Account of the Manner of Inoculating for the Small Pox in the East Indies. With Some Observations on the Practice and Mode of Treating that Disease in Those Parts. Inscribed to the Learned the President, and Members of the College of Physicians in London. By J.z. Holwell, F.R.S.* London, 1767. *Eighteenth Century Collections Online.* Gale.

James, R. *Pharmacopoeia Universalis, or A New Universal English Dispensatory.* J. Hodges, 1747.

Johannis Subtermontani Thermologia Bristoliensis, Or, Underhill's Short Account of the Bristol Hot-Well Water, its Uses and Historical Cures. W. Bonny, 1703.

Lynch, Bernard. *A Guide to Health Through the Various Stages of Life.* 1744.

Macbride, David. *A Methodical Introduction to the Theory and Practice of Physic.* W. Strahan, 1772.

Marten, Benjamin, *A New Theory of Consumptions: More Especially of a Phthisis or Consumption of the Lungs.* R. Knaplock, 1720.

Mead, Richard. *A Discourse on the Smallpox and Measles.* John Brindley, 1748.

Morton, Richard. *Phthisiologia: Or a Treatise of Consumptions.* 2nd edition. W. & J. Innys, 1720.

The New Bath Guide; or Useful Pocket Companion. New edition. R. Crutwell, 1770.

Pallet, Peter Paul (Dr. Richard Warner). *Bath Characters, or Sketches from Life.* G. Wilkie & J. Robinson, 1807.

Penrose, F. *A Dissertation on the Inflammatory, Gangrenous and Putrid Sore Throat, also on the Putrid Fever.* D. Prince, 1766.

Perry, Charles. *Essay on the Small Pox.* A. Long, 1747.

Pringle, John. *Observations on the Diseases of the Army*. 4th edition. A. Millar, 1764.

Quincy, John. *Pharmacopoeia Officinalis & Extemporanea, or a Complete English Dispensatory*. Thomas Longman, 1739.

Randolph, George. *Enquiry into the Medicinal Virtues of Bristol-Water: And the Indications of Cure Which it Answers*. James Fletcher, 1745.

Report, Together with the Minutes of Evidence, and an Appendix of Papers, from the Committee Appointed to Consider of Prevision being Made for the Better Regulation of Madhouses in England. Baldwin Craddock, 1815.

Robinson, Nicholas. *A New System of the Spleen, Vapours and Hypochondriack Melancholy*. A. Bettesworth, 1729.

Shaw, Peter. *A New Practice of Physic*. 7th edition. T. Longman, 1753.

Smith, W. *A Dissertation upon the Nerves*. W. Owen, 1768.

The Strangers' Assistant and Guide to Bath. R. Cruttwell, 1773.

Strother, Edward. *Materia Medica: Or a New Description on the Virtues and Effects of All Drugs, or Simple Medicines*, Vol. II. Charles Rivington, 1727.

Sutton, Daniel. *The Inoculator; or, Suttonian System of Inoculation*. T. Gillet, 1796.

Swan, John. *The Entire Works of Dr. Thomas Sydenham*. Edward Cave, 1742.

Thompson, Thomas. *An Enquiry into the Origin, Nature and Cure of the Small-Pox*. A. Millar, 1752.

A Treatise on the Nature, Properties and Medicinal Uses of the Waters of Pyrmont, Spa, and Seltzers. W. Owen, 1762.

Wainhouse, Richard. *Proposals for Printing by Subscription A SERMON Preach'd in the Abbey-Church, Bath November 5, 1755, 0557*. Bath & North East Somerset Record Office, UK.

———. *Two Sermons Preached in the Parish-Church of Keevil, Wiltshire (In September and October, 1745) on the Occasion of the Rebellion in Scotland*. J. Jolliffe, 1745.

Wainhouse, William. *Poetical Essays: Intended for Instruction and Amusement*. R. Cruttwell, 1796.

Whytt, Robert. *The Works of Robert Whytt*. T. Becket and P.A. Dehondt, 1768.

Willis, Thomas. *The Remaining Medical Works of that Famous and Renowned Physician Dr. Thomas Willis*, English by S.P. [Samuel Pordage]. T. Dring, C. Harper, J. Leigh, and S. Martyn, 1681.

Wood, Esq., John. *A Description of Bath*. 2nd edition. Bathoe, 1765.

Newspapers and Periodicals

The British Critic, A New Review
The Critical Review or Annals of Literature
Daily Journal (London)
Gazetteer and New Daily Advertiser
The General Evening Post (London)
The Gentleman's Magazine
Journals of the House of Commons

Journals of the House of Lords
The Ladies Companion and Monthly Magazine
The Lady's Magazine; or Entertaining Companion for the Fair Sex
London Chronicle
London Chronicle or Universal Evening Post
London Evening Post
The Monthly Review; or Literary Journal
Oracle
Public Advertiser
Salisbury Journal
The Universal Magazine of Knowledge and Pleasure

Select Secondary Sources

Andrews, Jonathan. "History of Medicine: Health, Medicine and Disease in the Eighteenth Century." *Journal for Eighteenth-Century Studies* 34, no. 4 (2011): 503–15.

———. "The Lot of the 'Incurably' Insane in Enlightenment England." *Eighteenth Century Life* 12, no. 1 (1988): 1–18.

Baggs, A.P., Elizabeth Crittall, Jane Freeman, and Janet H. Stevenson. "Parishes: Fittleton." In *A History of the County of Wiltshire: Volume 11, Downton Hundred; Elstub and Everleigh Hundred*, edited by D.A. Crowley. Victoria County History, 1980.

Bailey [Begiato], Joanne. *Unquiet Lives: Marriage and Marriage Breakdown in England, 1660–1800*. Cambridge University Press, 2003.

Barclay, Katie. *Love, Intimacy and Power: Marriage and Patriarchy in Scotland 1650–1850*. Manchester University Press, 2011.

Barczewiski, Stephanie, John Eglin, Stephen Heathorn, Michael Silvestri, and Michelle Tusan. *Britain Since 1688: A Nation in the World*. Routledge, 2015.

Bartlett, Peter, and David Wright, eds. *Outside the Walls of the Asylum. The History of Care in the Community, 1750–2000*. Athlone Press, 1999.

Bebbington, David W. *Evangelicalism in Modern Britain: A History from the 1730s to the 1980s*. Routledge, 1989.

Beier, Lucinda M. *Sufferers and Healers: The Experience of Illness in Seventeenth-Century England*. Routledge and Kegan Paul, 1987.

Belsey, Hugh. "Gainsborough, Thomas (1727–1788), Painter and Printmaker." *Oxford Dictionary of National Biography*, September 23, 2004; accessed May 27, 2020. https://www.oxforddnb.com/view/10.1093/ref:odnb/9780198614128.001.0001/odnb-9780198614128-e-10282.

———. *The Moysey Family: An Exhibition at Gainsborough's House, Sudbury, Suffolk 19th May to 8th July 1984*. Gainsborough's House Society, 1984.

Bettany, G.T., and T.A.B. Corley. "Chandler, John (1699/1700–1780), Apothecary." *Oxford Dictionary of National Biography*, September 23, 2004; accessed April 17, 2020. https://www.oxforddnb.com/view/10.1093/ref:odnb/9780198614128.001.0001/odnb-9780198614128-e-5104.

Bhattacharya, Sudip. *Unseen Enemy: The English, Disease, and Medicine in Colonial Bengal, 1617–1847*. Cambridge Scholars Publishing, 2014.

Black, Shirley Burgoyne. *An 18th Century Mad-Doctor: William Perfect of West Malling.* Darenth Valley Publications, 1995.

Blandy, John P., and John S.P. Lumley, eds. *The Royal College of Surgeons of England: 200 years of History at the Millennium.* Royal College of Surgeons of England and Blackwell Science, 2000.

Bloom, Edward A., and Lillian D. Bloom, eds. *The Piozzi Letters: Correspondence of Hester Lynch Piozzi, 1784–1821 (formerly Mrs. Thrale),* Vol. 4, 1805–1810. University of Delaware Press, 1996.

A Book of Keevil. Volume 3. The Keevil Society, 2001.

Borsay, Anne. "Charleton, Rice (1722/3–1788), Physician." *Oxford Dictionary of National Biography,* September 23, 2004; accessed April 28, 2020. https://www.oxforddnb.com /view/10.1093/ref:odnb/9780198614128.001.0001/odnb-9780198614128-e-5155.

———. *Medicine and Charity in Georgian Bath: A Social History of the General Infirmary c. 1739–1830.* Routledge, 2020.

———. "Oliver, William (1695–1764), Physician and Philanthropist." *Oxford Dictionary of National Biography,* September 23, 2004; accessed April 28, 2020. https://www .oxforddnb.com/view/10.1093/ref:odnb/9780198614128.001.0001/odnb-9780198614128 -e-20736.

———. "Visitors and Residents: The Dynamics of Charity in Eighteenth-century Bath," *Journal of Tourism History* 4, no. 2 (2012): 171–80.

Bowen, H.V. "Clive, Robert, First Baron Clive of Plassey (1725–1774), Army Officer in the East India Company and Administrator in India." *Oxford Dictionary of National Biography,* September 23, 2004; accessed May 27, 2020. https://www.oxforddnb.com /view/10.1093/ref:odnb/9780198614128.001.0001/odnb-9780198614128-e-5697.

Britton, John. *The Auto-biography of John Britton.* London, 1850.

Brockliss, L.W.B. *The University of Oxford: A History.* Oxford University Press, 2016.

Brooks, Christopher. "Apprenticeship, Social Mobility and the Middling Sort, 1550–1800." In *The Middling Sort of People: Culture, Society and Politics in England, 1550–1800,* edited by Jonathan Barry and Christopher Brooks. Macmillan, 1994.

Browning, Reed. "Holles, Thomas Pelham, Duke of Newcastle upon Tyne and First Duke of Newcastle under Lyme (1693–1768), Prime Minister." *Oxford Dictionary of National Biography,* September 23, 2004; accessed May 27, 2020. https://www.oxforddnb.com /view/10.1093/ref:odnb/9780198614128.001.0001/odnb-9780198614128-e-21801.

Brunton, Deborah Christian. "Pox Britannica: Smallpox Inoculation in Britain 1721–1830." PhD dissertation. University of Pennsylvania, 1990.

Burke, John. *A Genealogical and Heraldic Dictionary of the Landed Gentry of Great Britain and Ireland,* Vol. 1. Henry Colburn, 1847.

Burney, Fanny. *The Early Journals and Letters of Fanny Burney,* Vol. IV, The Streatham Years: Part II, 1780–1781, edited by Betty Rizzo. McGill-Queen's University Press, 2003.

Burnim, Kalman A. "The Letters of Sarah and William Siddons to Hester Lynch Piozzi in the John Rylands Library." *Bulletin of the John Rylands Library* 52, no. 1 (1969): 46–95.

Burton, Antoinette, ed. *Archive Stories: Facts, Fictions, and the Writing of History.* Duke University Press, 2005.

Bynum, W.F. "Nosology." In *Companion Encyclopedia of the History of Medicine*, Vol. 1, edited by W.F. Bynum and Roy Porter. Routledge, 2001.

Cannon, John. "Stanhope, Philip Dormer, Fourth Earl of Chesterfield (1694–1773), Politician and Diplomatist." *Oxford Dictionary of National Biography*, September 23, 2004; accessed May 27, 2020. https://www.oxforddnb.com/view/10.1093/ref:odnb/9780198614128.001.0001/odnb-9780198614128-e-26255.

Carpenter, Peter K. "The Georgian Idiot Hospital at Bath." *History of Psychiatry* 4 (1998): 471–89.

Carrell, Jennifer Lee. *The Speckled Monster: A Historical Tale of Battling Smallpox*. Plume, 2004.

Chamberland, Celeste. "From Apprentice to Master: Social Disciplining and Surgical Education in Early Modern London, 1570–1640," *History of Education Quarterly* 53, no. 1 (2013): 21–44.

Chapman, Colin R. *Ecclesiastical Courts, Officials and Records: Sin, Sex and Probate*. 2nd edition. Lochin Publishing, 1997.

Charon, Rita. *Narrative Medicine: Honoring the Stories of Illness*. Oxford University Press, 2008.

Chester, Joseph Lemuel. *The Parish Registers of St. Mary Aldermary London Containing Marriages, Baptisms and Burials from 1555 to 1754*. London, 1880.

Chesterfield, Philip Dormer Stanhope. *Letters Written by the Late Right Honourable Philip Dormer Stanhope, Earl of Chesterfield*, Vol. IV. E. Lynch, 1774.

——. *Letters Written by the Late Right Honorable Philip Dormer Stanhope, Earl of Chesterfield, to His Son Philip Stanhope*. M. Eugenia Stanhope, 1775.

——. *Miscellaneous Works of the Late Philip Dormer Stanhope, Earl of Chesterfield*. 2nd edition. Vol. IV, edited by M. Maty. Edward & Charles Dilly, 1779.

Chivers, Janet Mary. "'A Resonating Void': Strategies and Responses to Poverty, Bath, 1770–1835." PhD dissertation. Bath Spa University, School of Historical and Cultural Studies, 2006.

Coke, Mary. *The Letters and Journals and Lady Mary Coke*, Vol. II (1767–1768). Kingsmead Reprints, 1970.

Colvin, Howard. "The Church of St Mary Aldermary and Its Rebuilding after the Great Fire of London." *Architectural History* 24 (1981): 24–31.

Conrad, Lawrence I., et. al, *The Western Medical Tradition: 800 BC to AD 1800*. 9th edition. Cambridge University Press, 2009.

Cook, Harold. J. *The Decline of the Old Medical Regime in Stuart London*. Cornell University Press, 1986.

——. *Trials of an Ordinary Doctor: Joannes Groenevelt in Seventeenth-Century London*. Johns Hopkins University Press, 1994.

Cope, Zachary. *The Royal College of Surgeons of England: A History*. Anthony Blond, 1959.

——. "William Cheselden and the Separation of the Barbers from the Surgeons." *Annals of the Royal College of Surgeons of England* 12, no. 1 (1953): 1–13.

Corley, T.A.B. "Chudleigh, Elizabeth [Married Names Elizabeth Hervey, Countess of Bristol; Elizabeth Pierrepont, Duchess of Kingston upon Hull] (c. 1720–1788), Courtier and

Bigamist." *Oxford Dictionary of National Biography*, September 23, 2004; accessed June 17, 2020. https://www.oxforddnb.com/view/10.1093/ref:odnb/9780198614128.001.0001 /odnb-9780198614128-e-5380.

———. "James, Robert (bap. 1703, d. 1776), Physician and Inventor of James's Fever Powder." *Oxford Dictionary of National Biography*. 2004; accessed March 23, 2019. http://www.oxforddnb.com/view/10.1093/ref:odnb/9780198614128.001.0001/odnb -9780198614128-e-14618.

Courtney, W.P., and Edgar Samuel. "Schomberg, Ralph [formerly Raphael] (1714–1792), Physician and Writer." *Oxford Dictionary of National Biography*, September 23, 2004; accessed June 16, 2020. https://www.oxforddnb.com/view/10.1093 /ref:odnb/9780198614128.001.0001/odnb-9780198614128-e-24827.

Crawford, Katherine. *European Sexualities, 1400–1800*. Cambridge University Press, 2007.

Cressy, David. *Birth, Marriage and Death: Ritual, Religion and the Life-Cycle in Tudor and Stuart England*. Oxford University Press, 1999.

Dabhoiwala, Faramerz. "The Construction of Honor, Reputation and Status in Late Seventeenth- and Early Eighteenth-Century England." *Transactions of the Royal Historical Society* 6 (1996): 201–13.

Dalrymple, William. *The Anarchy: The East India Company, Corporate Violence, and the Pillage of an Empire*. Bloomsbury, 2019.

Day, Carolyn A. *Consumptive Chic: A History of Beauty, Fashion and Disease*. Bloomsbury, 2017.

Dickson, Leigh Wetherall, and Allan Ingram, eds. *Depression and Melancholy, 1600–1800*. Pickering & Chatto, 2012.

Digby, Anne. *Making a Medical Living: Doctors and Patients in the Market for Medicine, 1720–1914*. Cambridge University Press, 1994.

Doran, Dr. *A Lady of the Last Century: (Mrs. Elizabeth Montagu)*. Richard Bentley and Son, 1873.

Erikson, Amy Louise. *Women and Property in Early Modern England*. Routledge, 1993.

Fawcett, Trevor. *Bath Administer'd Corporation Affairs at the 18th-Century Spa*. Rutton, 2001.

———. *Voices of Eighteenth-Century Bath: An Anthology of Contemporary Texts Illustrating Events, Daily Life and Attitudes at Britain's Leading Georgian Spa*. Rutton, 1995.

Fenn, Elizabeth A. *Pox Americana: The Great Smallpox Epidemic of 1775–82*. Hill & Wang, 2001.

Fissell, Mary E. *Patients, Power and the Poor in Eighteenth-Century Bristol*. Cambridge University Press, 1991.

"Fittleton and Hackleston: Notes of Manorial Descent." *Wiltshire Archaeological and Natural History Magazine*, Vol. XI. H.F. & E. Bull, 1869.

Fletcher, Anthony. *Gender, Sex and Subordination in England 1500–1800*. Yale University Press, 1995.

Foster, Joseph. *Alumni Oxonienses: The Members of the University of Oxford, 1715–1886, Volumes III and IV*. Parker, 1888.

———. *The Register of Admissions to Gray's Inn 1521–1889*. Privately Printed, 1889.

Franklin, Michael J. "Piozzi [née Salusbury; Other Married Name Thrale], Hester Lynch (1741–1821), writer." *Oxford Dictionary of National Biography*, September 23, 2004; accessed June 16, 2020. https://www.oxforddnb.com/view/10.1093/ref:odnb/9780198614128.001.0001/odnb-9780198614128-e-22309.

Fraser, Flora. *Princesses: The Six Daughters of George III*. Anchor Books, 2004.

French, Henry, and Mark Rothery. *Man's Estate: Landed Gentry Masculinities, 1660–1900*. Oxford University Press, 2012.

Friedman, Emily C. *Reading Smell in Eighteenth-Century Fiction*. Bucknell University Press, 2016.

Fuentes, Marissa J. *Dispossessed Lives: Enslaved Women, Violence, and the Archive*. University of Pennsylvania Press, 2016.

Gillis, John R. *For Better, For Worse: British Marriages, 1600 to the Present*. Oxford University Press, 1985.

Glover, Katherine. *Elite Women and Polite Society in Eighteenth-Century Scotland*. Boydell Press, 2011.

Glynn, Ian, and Jenifer Glynn. *The Life and Death of Smallpox*. Cambridge University Press, 2004.

Goff, Moira, John Goldfinch, Karen Limper-Herz, and Helen Peden, *Georgians Revealed: Life, Style and the Making of Modern Britain*. British Library, 2013.

Gomme, Andor, and Alison Maguire, *Design and Plan in the Country House: From Castle Donjons to Palladian Boxes*. Paul Mellon Centre for Studies in British Art. Yale University Press, 2008.

Green, Emanuel. *Bibliotheca Somersetensis: A Catalogue of Books, Pamphlets, Single Sheets, and Broadsides in Some Way Connected to the County of Somerset*, Vol. I. Barincott & Pearce, 1902.

Grenville, George. *The Grenville Papers: The Correspondence of Richard Grenville Earl Temple, K.G., and The Right Hon: George Grenville*, Vol. IV, edited by William James Smith. John Murray, 1853.

Guerrini, Anita. "Mead, Richard (1673–1754), Physician and Collector of Books and Art." *Oxford Dictionary of National Biography*. 2008; accessed February 27, 2019. http://www.oxforddnb.com/view/10.1093/ref:odnb/9780198614128.001.0001/odnb-9780198614128-e-18467.

Gygax, Franziska, and Miriam A. Locher. *Narrative Matters in Medical Contexts across Disciplines*. John Benjamins, 2015.

Hamilton, James. *Gainsborough: A Portrait*. Weidenfeld & Nicolson, 2017.

Harvey, Karen. *The Little Republic: Masculinity and Domestic Authority in Eighteenth-Century Britain*. Oxford University Press, 2012.

Haydon, Colin. *Anti-Catholicism in Eighteenth-Century England, c. 1714–80: A Political and Social Study*. Manchester University Press, 1993.

Heyck, Thomas William. *The Peoples of the British Isles: A New History, From 1688–1870*. Lyceum, 2002.

Hicks, Michael. "Warner, Richard (1763–1857), Antiquary." *Oxford Dictionary of National Biography*, September 23, 2004; accessed May 25, 2020. https://www.oxforddnb.com/view/10.1093/ref:odnb/9780198614128.001.0001/odnb-9780198614128-e-28766.

Hicks, Mrs. William. *A Cotswold Family: Hicks and Hicks Beach.* William Heinemann, 1909.

A History of the County of Wiltshire: Volume 8, Warminster, Westbury and Whorwellsdown Hundreds. London, 1965.

Hobart, Ann. *Household Medicine in Seventeenth-Century England.* Bloomsbury, 2016.

Holgate, Clifford Wyndham, ed. *Winchester Long Rolls, 1653–1721.* P. & G. Wells, 1899.

Holloway, Sally. *The Game of Love in Georgian England: Courtship, Emotions, and Material Culture.* Oxford University Press, 2019.

Holmes, Geoffrey. *Augustan England: Professions, State and Society, 1680–1730.* George Allen & Unwin, 1982.

Holmes, M.R.J. *Augustus Hervey: A Naval Casanova.* Pentland Press, 1996.

Hopkins, Donald R. *The Greatest Killer: Smallpox in History, with a New Introduction.* University of Chicago Press, 2002.

——. *Princes and Peasants: Smallpox in History.* University of Chicago Press, 1983.

Hoppit, Julian. *A Land of Liberty? England 1689–1727.* Oxford University Press, 2000, reprint 2010.

Houlbrooke, Ralph. *Death, Religion, and the Family in England, 1480–1750.* Clarendon Press, 2000.

——, ed. *Death, Ritual, and Bereavement.* Routledge, 1989.

Houston, R.A. "Clergy and the Care of the Insane in Eighteenth-Century Britain." *Church History* 73, no. 1 (2004): 114–38.

Hoyle, R.W. "The Listers of Gisburn: The Fashioning of a Gentry Family in the Early Eighteenth Century." *Northern History* 56, no. 1–2 (2019): 46–77.

Hunt, Margaret. *The Middling Sort: Commerce, Gender, and the Family in England, 1680–1780.* University of California Press, 1996.

Hunter, Richard, and Ida Macalpine. *Three Hundred Years of Psychiatry, 1535–1860.* Oxford University Press, 1963.

Ingram, Allan. *The Madhouse of Language: Writing and Reading Madness in the Eighteenth Century.* Routledge, 1991.

——, ed. *Patterns of Madness in the Eighteenth Century: A Reader.* Liverpool University Press, 1998.

Jackson, Mark. *The Oxford Handbook of the History of Medicine.* Oxford University Press, 2013.

Jacob, W.M. *The Clerical Profession in the Long Eighteenth Century, 1680–1840.* Oxford University Press, 2007.

Jenkins, John. "Thomas Gainsborough's Doctors." *Journal of Medical Biography* 13, no, 1 (2005): 59.

Jenner, Mark S.R., and Patrick Wallis, eds. *Medicine and the Market in England and its Colonies, c. 1450–c. 1850.* Palgrave Macmillan, 2007.

Johnson, Samuel. *Letters of Samuel Johnson, LL.D.,* Vol. II, edited by George Birkbeck Hill. Clarendon Press, 1892.

——. *Letters of Samuel Johnson,* Vol. III, 1771–1781, The Hyde Edition, edited by Bruce Redford. Princeton University Press, 2014.

——. *Letters to and from the Late Samuel Johnson,* Vol. II. A. Strahan & T. Cadell, 1788.

Johnson, Steven. *The Ghost Map: The Story of London's Most Terrifying Epidemic – and How it Changed Science, Cities, and the Modern World.* Riverhead Books, 2006.

Jones, Kathleen. *Lunacy, Law, and Conscience 1744–1845.* Routledge, 1999.

Jordanova, Ludmilla. "The Social Construction of Medical Knowledge." *Social History of Medicine* 8, no. 3 (1995): 361–81.

Kinservik, Matthew J. *Sex, Scandal and Celebrity in Late Eighteenth-Century England.* Palgrave Macmillan, 2007.

Kirkup, John. 2006 "Cheselden, William (1688–1752), Surgeon and Anatomist." *Oxford Dictionary of National Biography.* 2006; accessed November 12, 2018. http://www.oxforddnb .com/view/10.1093/ref:odnb/9780198614128.001.0001/odnb-9780198614128-e-5226.

Koplow, David. *Smallpox: The Fight to Eradicate a Global Scourge.* University of California Press, 2003.

Kotar, S.L. and J.E. Gessler, *Smallpox: A History.* McFarland & Company, Inc., 2013.

Kulisheck, P.J. "Legge, Henry Bilson (1708–1764), Politician." *Oxford Dictionary of National Biography,* September 23, 2004; accessed May 27, 2020. https://www.oxforddnb.com /view/10.1093/ref:odnb/9780198614128.001.0001/odnb-9780198614128-e-16356.

Lane, Joan. "The Role of Apprenticeship in Eighteenth-Century Medical Education in England." In *William Hunter and the Eighteenth-Century Medical World,* edited by W.F. Bynum and Roy Porter. Cambridge University Press, 1985.

Langford, Paul. *A Polite and Commercial People: England 1727–1783.* Oxford University Press, 1989.

Lawlor, Clark. *Consumption and Literature: The Making of the Romantic Disease.* Palgrave Macmillan, 2006.

———. *From Melancholia to Prozac: A History of Depression.* Oxford University Press, 2012.

———. "It is a Path I Have Prayed to Follow." In *Romanticism and Pleasure,* edited by Thomas H. Schmid and Michelle Faubert. Palgrave Macmillan, 2010.

Lawrence, Christopher. "Buchan, William (1729–1805)." *Oxford Dictionary of National Biography,* edited by H.C.G. Matthew and Brian Harrison, October 4, 2012; accessed March 31, 2016. http://www.oxforddnb.com/view/article/3828.

Lawrence, Susan C. *Charitable Knowledge: Hospital Pupils and Practitioners in Eighteenth-Century London.* Cambridge University Press, 1996.

Leach, Arthur F. *A History of Winchester College.* Charles Scribner's Sons, 1899.

Le Faye, Deirdre, ed. *Jane Austen's Letters.* New edition. Oxford University Press, 1995.

Lemmings, David. "Marriage and the Law in the Eighteenth Century: Hardwicke's Marriage Act of 1753." *Historical Journal* 39, no. 2 (1996): 339–60.

Leneman, Leah, and Rosalind Mitchison. "Clandestine Marriage in the Scottish Cities 1660–1780." *Journal of Social History* 26, no. 4 (1993): 845–61.

Leong, Elaine. "Collecting Knowledge for the Family: Recipes, Gender and Practical Knowledge in the Early Modern Household." *Centaurus* 55, no. 2 (2013): 81–103.

Lewis, Judith Schneid. *In the Family Way: Childbearing in the British Aristocracy, 1760–1860.* Rutgers University Press, 1986.

Lewis, Samuel, ed. *A Topographical Dictionary of England.* S. Lewis, 1848.

Lewis, W.S., Warren Hunting Smith, and George L. Lam, with the assistance of Edwine M. Martz, eds. *Horace Walpole's Correspondence with Sir Horace Mann,* Vol. 23. Yale University Press, 1967.

The Life and Times of Selina Countess of Huntington, Vol I. William Edward Painter, 1839.

Macalpine, Ida, and Richard Hunter. *George III and the Mad Business*. Allen Lane, 1969.

MacDonald, Michael. *Mystical Bedlam: Madness, Anxiety and Healing in Seventeenth-Century England*. Cambridge University Press, 1981.

Mackay, Ruddock. "Hervey, Augustus John, Third Earl of Bristol (1724–1779), Naval Officer and Politician." *Oxford Dictionary of National Biography*, September 23, 2004; accessed May 27, 2020. https://www.oxforddnb.com/view/10.1093/ref:odnb/9780198614128.001.0001/odnb-9780198614128-e-13109.

MacKenzie, Charlotte. *Psychiatry for the Rich: A History of Ticehurst Private Asylum 1792–1917*. Routledge, 1992.

Mainwaring, Captain Rowland. *Annals of Bath from the Year 1800 to the Passing of the New Municipal Act*. Mary Meyler and Son, 1838.

Mann, J. de L. "Clothiers and Weavers in Wiltshire during the Eighteenth Century." In *Studies in the Industrial Revolution*, edited by L.S. Presnall. Oxford University Press, 1960.

Manning, Victor and Marjory. "Anne Beach – A Keevil Tragedy." In *A Book of Keevil*, Vol. 2. The Keevil Society, 1998.

Marschner, Joanna, David Bindman, and Lisa Ford, eds. *Enlightened Princesses: Caroline, Augusta, and the Shaping of the Modern World*. Yale Center for British Art, 2017.

Martin, Ged. *Magdalene College Cambridge and Steeple Ashton, An Exploratory Essay*. Copy of record for the Magdalene College Archives, 2016.

Martin, Joanna, ed. *A Governess in the Age of Jane Austen: The Journals and Letters of Agnes Porter*. Hambledon Press, 1998.

———, ed. *The Penrice Letters 1768–1795*. West Glamorgan County Archive Service; South Wales Record Society, 1993.

Mathias, Peter. "Thrale, Henry (1728–1781), Brewer and Politician." *Oxford Dictionary of National Biography*, September 23, 2004; accessed June 16, 2020. https://www.oxforddnb.com/view/10.1093/ref:odnb/9780198614128.001.0001/odnb-9780198614128-e-50467.

Meli, Nico Bertoloni. "Visual Representations of Disease: The *Philosophical Transactions* and William Cheselden's *Osteographia*," *Huntington Library Quarterly* 78, no. 2 (2015): 157–86.

Michaleas, Spyros N., Gregory Tsoucalas, Halil Tekiner, and Marianna Karamanou. "William Cheselden (1688–1752): 18th-Century Pioneer of Lateral Lithotomy and Iridectomy." *Surgical Innovation* 27, no. 5 (2020): 543–8.

Milner, Rev. Dr. *Winchester College, with Additional Notes*. D.E. Gilmour, 1826.

Morgan, Lee. *Dr. Johnson's "Own Dear Master": The Life of Henry Thrale*. University Press of America, 1998.

Mounsey, Christopher. *Christopher Smart: Clown of God*. Bucknell University Press, 2001.

———. *Sight Correction: Vision and Blindness in Eighteenth-Century Britain*. University of Virginia Press, 2019.

Munk, William. *The Roll of the Royal College of Physicians of London*. Royal College of Physicians of London, 1878.

Neher, Allister. "The Truth about Our Bones: William Cheselden's *Osteographia*." Medical History 54, no. 4 (2010): 517–28.

Newton, Gill. "Clandestine Marriage in Early Modern London: When, Where and Why?" *Continuity and Change* 29, no. 2 (2014): 151–80.

Nutton, Vivian. "Humoralism." In *Companion Encyclopedia of the History of Medicine*, Vol. 1, edited by W.F. Bynum and Roy Porter. Routledge, 1993.

O'Hara, Diana. *Courtship and Constraint: Rethinking the Making of Marriage in Tudor England*. Manchester University Press, 2000.

Olsen, Kristen. *Daily Life in 18th-Century England*. Greenwood Press, 1999.

Ostler, Catherine. *The Duchess Countess: The Woman who Scandalized a Nation*. Simon & Schuster, 2021.

Parry-Jones, William Ll. *The Trade in Lunacy: A Study of Private Madhouses in England in the Eighteenth and Nineteenth Centuries*. Routledge and Kegan Paul, 1972.

Payne, Lynda. *With Words and Knives: Learning Medical Dispassion in Early Modern England*. Routledge, 2016.

Peake, Richard Brinsley. *Memoirs of the Coleman Family*, Vol. 1. Richard Bentley, 1841.

Pelling, Margaret. *Medical Conflicts in Early Modern London: Patronage, Physicians and Irregular Practitioners 1550–1640*. Oxford University Press, 2003.

Pevsner, Nickolaus. *The Buildings of England: Wiltshire*. Penguin Books, 1974.

Pointon, Marcia. *Hanging the Head: Portraiture and Social Formation in Eighteenth-Century England*. Paul Mellon Centre for Studies in British Art. Yale University Press, 1993.

Pollock, Linda A. "Honor, Gender, and Reconciliation in Elite Culture, 1570–1700." *Journal of British Studies* 46, no. 1 (2007): 3–29.

———. "Review Article: 'An Action Like a Stratagem': Courtship and Marriage from the Middle Ages to the Twentieth Century." *Historical Journal* 30, no. 2 (1987): 483–98.

Porter, Dorothy, and Roy Porter. *Patient's Progress: Doctors and Doctoring in Eighteenth-Century England*. Stanford University Press, 1989.

Porter, Roy. *Blood and Guts: A Short History of Medicine*. W.W. Norton, 2002.

———. "Diseases of Civilization." In *Companion Encyclopedia of the History of Medicine*, Vol. 1, edited by W.F. Bynum and Roy Porter. Routledge, 2001.

———. *English Society in the Eighteenth Century*. Revised edition. Penguin, 1990.

———. *London: A Social History*. Harvard University Press, 1998.

———. *Madmen: A Social History of Madhouses, Mad-Doctors and Lunatics*. Tempus, 2004.

———. *Mind-Forg'd Manacles: A History of Madness in England from the Restoration to the Regency*. Athlone Press, 1987.

———, ed. *Patients and Practitioners: Lay Perceptions of Medicine in Pre-Industrial Society*. Cambridge University Press, 1985.

———. "The Patient's View: Doing Medical History from Below." *Theory and Society* 14, no. 2 (1985): 175–98.

———, ed. *The Popularization of Medicine 1650–1850*. Routledge, 1992.

Powell, Margaret K., and Joseph R. Roach. "Big Hair." *Eighteenth-Century Studies* 38, no. 1 (2004): 79–99.

Power, D'A., and Catherine Bergin. "Warren, Richard (1731–1797), Physician." *Oxford Dictionary of National Biography*, September 23, 2004; accessed May 22, 2020. https://www.oxforddnb.com/view/10.1093/ref:odnb/9780198614128.001.0001/odnb-9780198614128-e-28788.

Prior, D.L. "Holwell, John Zephaniah (1711–1798), East India Company Servant." *Oxford Dictionary of National Biography.* November 6, 2018. http://www.oxforddnb.com /view/10.1093/ref:odnb/9780198614128.001.0001/odnb-9780198614128-e-13622.

Probert, Rebecca. "The Impact of the Marriage Act of 1753: Was It Really 'A Most Cruel Law for the Fair Sex'?," *Eighteenth-Century Studies* 38, no. 2 (2005): 247–62.

Probert, Rebecca, and Liam D'Arcy Brown. "The Impact of the Clandestine Marriages Act: Three Case Studies in Conformity." *Continuity and Change* 23, no. 2 (2008): 309–30.

Reid, Stuart. *Cumberland's Culloden Army, 1745–46.* Bloomsbury, 2012.

Richardson, Rev. A.T. *Annals of Keevil and Bulkington.* Add MS. 42048. British Library, UK.

Riding, Jacqueline. *A New History of the '45 Rebellion.* Bloomsbury, 2016.

Robinson, Rev. Charles J. *A Register of the Scholars Admitted into Merchant Taylors' School, from A.D. 1562 to 1874*, Vol. II. Farncombe, 1883.

Rolls, Roger. *The Hospital of the Nation: The Story of Spa Medicine and the Mineral Water Hospital at Bath.* Bird Publications, 1988.

Rosenberg, Charles E. *Explaining Epidemics and Other Studies in the History of Medicine.* Cambridge University Press, 1992.

———. "The Fielding H. Garrison Lecture. Medical Text and Social Context: Explaining William Buchan's *Domestic Medicine.*" *Bulletin of the History of Medicine* 57, no. 1 (1983): 22–42.

Roud, Steve. *The English Year: A Month-by-Month Guide to the Nation's Customs and Festivals, from May Day to Mischief Night.* Penguin Books, 2008.

Rousseau, George S. "Nerves, Spirits, and Fibres: Towards Defining the Origins of Sensibility." *Studies in the Eighteenth Century*, edited by R.F. Brissenden and J.C. Eade. University of Toronto Press, 1976.

Saint Thomas's Hospital Reports, Vol. 28. J.A. Churchill, 1901.

Schnorrenberg, Barbara Brandon. "Montagu [née Robinson], Elizabeth (1718–1800), Author and Literary Hostess." *Oxford Dictionary of National Biography*, September 23, 2004; accessed June 16, 2020. https://www.oxforddnb.com/view/10.1093 /ref:odnb/9780198614128.001.0001/odnb-9780198614128-e-19014.

Schweizer, Karl W. "Newspapers, Politics and Public Opinion in the Later Hanoverian Era." *Parliamentary History* 25, no. 1 (2006): 32–48.

Scott, Robert Forsyth, ed. *Admissions to the College of St. John the Evangelist in the University of Cambridge*, Part III, July 1715–November 1767. Printed for the College at the University Press, sold by Deighton Bell, 1903.

Scott, Susan, and Christopher J. Duncan. *Human Demography and Disease.* Cambridge University Press, 1998.

Scull, Andrew. *The Most Solitary of Afflictions: Madness and Society in Britain 1700–1900.* Yale University Press, 1993.

———. *Undertaker of the Mind: John Monro and Mad-Doctoring in Eighteenth-Century England.* University of California Press, 2001.

Selwyn, David, ed. *The Poetry of Jane Austen and the Austen Family.* University of Iowa Press/Jane Austen Society, 1997.

Shuttleton, David E. *Smallpox and the Literary Imagination 1660–1820.* Cambridge University Press, 2007.

Smail, John. *Merchants, Markets and Manufacture: The English Wool Textile Industry.* Springer, 1999.

Smith, Leonard. *Lunatic Hospitals in Georgian England, 1750–1830.* Routledge, 2007.

Smollet, Tobias. *The Critical Review or Annals of Literature,* Vol. 19. A. Hamilton, 1765.

South, Mary L. *The Inoculation Book: 1774–1783.* Southampton Records Series 47. 4word, 2014.

Stone, Lawrence. *The Family, Sex and Marriage in England 1500–1800.* Weidenfeld & Nicolson, 1977.

——. *Road to Divorce: A History of the Making and Breaking of Marriage in England 1530–1987.* Oxford University Press, 1995.

——. *Uncertain Unions: Marriage in England 1660–1753.* Oxford University Press, 1992.

Suzuki, Akihito. "The Household and the Care of Lunatics in Eighteenth-Century London." In *The Locus of Care: Families, Communities, Institutions, and the Provision of Welfare since Antiquity,* edited by Peregrine Horden and Richard Smith. Routledge, 1998.

Tadmor, Naomi. *Family and Friends in Eighteenth-Century England: Household, Kinship and Patronage.* Cambridge University Press, 2004.

Tague, Ingrid H. "Love, Honor, and Obedience: Fashionable Women and the Discourse of Marriage in the Early Eighteenth Century." *Journal of British Studies* 40, no. 1 (2001): 76–106.

——. *Women of Quality: Accepting and Contesting Ideals of Femininity in England, 1690–1760.* Boydell Press, 2002.

Taylor, David. *Crime, Policing and Punishment in England, 1750–1914.* Macmillan, 1998.

Tighe, M.F. *Silver Threads: A Study of the Textile Industries of Mere.* Mere, 1997.

Vickery, Amanda. *Behind Closed Doors: At Home in Georgian England.* Yale University Press, 2009.

——. *The Gentleman's Daughter: Women's Lives in Georgian England.* Yale University Press, 1998.

Wallis, Patrick, and Cliff Webb, "The Education and Training of Gentry Sons in Early Modern England." *Social History* 36, no. 1 (2011): 36–53.

Ward, Joseph P. *Metropolitan Communities: Trade Guilds, Identity, and Change in Early Modern London.* Stanford University Press, 1997.

Ward, Reginald W. *Early Evangelicalism: A Global Intellectual History 1670–1789.* Cambridge University Press, 2006.

Weaver, Frederick William, and Charles Herbert Mayo, eds. *Notes & Queries for Somerset and Dorset,* Vol. V. J.C. & A.T. Sawtell, 1897.

Webster, Charles, and Margaret Pelling, "Medical Practitioners." In *Health, Medicine and Mortality in the Sixteenth Century,* edited by Charles Webster. Cambridge University Press 1979.

Weightman, Gavin. *The Great Inoculator: The Untold Story of Daniel Sutton and his Medical Revolution.* Yale University Press, 2020.

Whitaker, Jeffery. *The Diaries of Jeffery Whitaker Schoolmaster of Bratton, 1739–1741,* edited by Marjorie Reeves and Jean Morrison. Wiltshire Record Society, 1989.

Whitley, William T. *Thomas Gainsborough.* Charles Scribner's Sons/Smith, Elder & Co., 1915.

Whittet, T.D. "Apothecaries and their Lodgers: Their Part in the Development of the Sciences and Medicine." *Journal of the Royal Society of Medicine Supplement* 76, no. 2 (1983): iii–32.

Wild, Wayne. *Medicine-by-Post: The Changing Voice of Illness in Eighteenth-Century Consultation Letter and Literature*. Rodopi, 2006.

Williams, Gareth. *Angel of Death: The Story of Smallpox*. Palgrave Macmillan, 2010.

Williams, J. Anthony. "Catholicism and Jacobitism: Some Wiltshire Evidence," *The Dublin Review* 485. Tablet, 1960.

———. *Catholic Recusancy in Wiltshire 1660–1791*. Catholic Record Society, 1968.

"William Wainhouse (1761–1797)," Clergy of the Church of England database entry. https://theclergydatabase.org.uk/jsp/persons/CreatePersonFrames.jsp?PersonID=49840.

Wilson, Harry Bristow. *The History of the Merchant-Taylor's School*, Vol. I. F.C. & J. Rivington, 1812.

Wilson, Philip K. "Acquiring Surgical Know-How: Occupational and Lay Instruction in Early Eighteenth-Century London." In *The Popularization of Medicine 1650–1850*, edited by Roy Porter. Routledge, 1992.

Woodforde, James. *The Diary of a Country Parson: The Reverend James Woodforde, 1758–1781*, edited by John Beresford. Oxford University Press, 1924.

Woodward, B.B. *A History and Description of Winchester*. J. Wells, 186?.

Young, Sidney. *Annals of the Barber-Surgeons of London*. East & Blades, 1890.

INDEX